South Island ~ T

- Great T...
- Heaphy Tr...
- Old Ghost Road 184
- Ghost Road Roundabout 190
- Pioneer Heritage Trail 194
- Big River 198
- West Coast Wilderness Trail 202
- Touring the Wild West 208
- Queenstown Trails 256
- Around the Mountains 262
- ...otte ... 146
- Picton to Nelson 150
- Rainbow 166
- St James Cycle Trail 172
- Hurunui Heartland Ride 218
- Little River Rail Trail 224
- Christchurch to the Alps 228
- Alps 2 Ocean Cycle Trail 234
- Otago Central Rail Trail 242
- Roxburgh Gorge Trail 246
- Clutha Gold Trail 250
- Catlins Coastal Route 272

CHRISTCHURCH

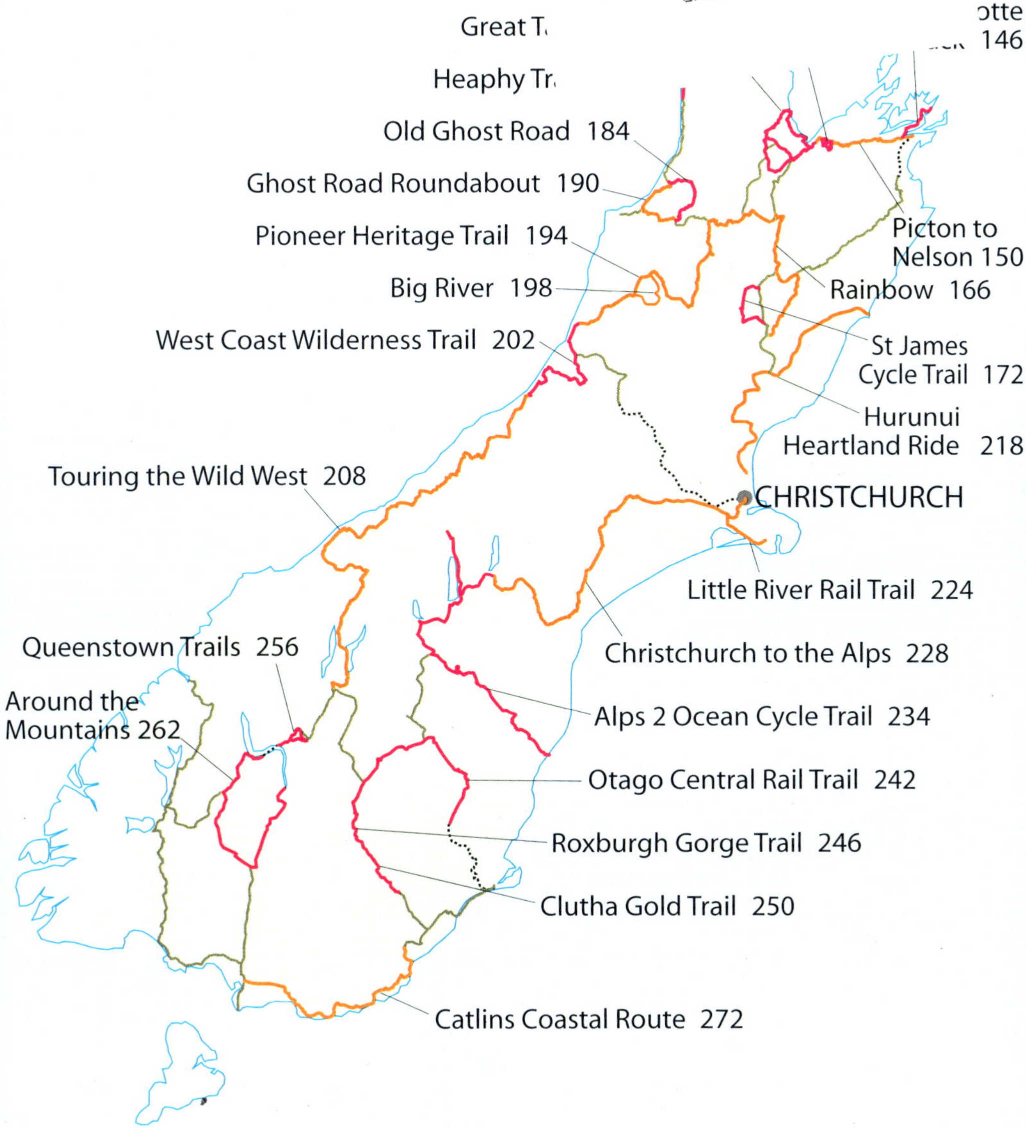

"***Classic New Zealand Cycle Trails*** has been written by the best in the business when it comes to New Zealand cycling guidebooks...."

- Simon Bloomburg, *The Nelson Mail*

Other guide books from the Kennett Brothers:

- Tour Aotearoa Official Guide
- Classic New Zealand Mountain Bike Rides
- Classic New Zealand Road Rides
- Short Easy Bikes Rides

Cycling history books from the Kennett Brothers:

- Phil O'Shea: Wizard on Wheels
- Harry Watson: The Mile Eater
- Bill Pratney: Never Say Die
- Warwick Dalton: The Lone Eagle
- Tino Tabak: Dreams and Demons
- Louise Sutherland: Spinning the Globe
- The Muddy Olympians: New Zealand's Olympic Mountain Bikers
- Tour Aotearoa: New Zealand's 3000 km bikepacking odyssey

Classic New Zealand Cycle Trails

A guide to 48 fantastic holidays

Fourth Edition

Every effort was made to ensure that the information in this book was accurate at the time of publication. The Kennett Brothers accept no responsibility or liability for any accident or injury associated with the book's use. If you note any errors, please contact us, and we'll post updates on www.kennett.nz

Maps in this book are intended as general guides only. For more detail, consult locally produced trail maps or Land Information New Zealand's Topomap series.

All rights reserved. No part of this book may be reproduced by any means electronic, mechanical, electrostatic photocopying or otherwise or stored in a retrieval system without the prior permission of the Kennett Brothers.

Published by
KENNETT BROTHERS
PO Box 11 310, Wellington
Phone +64 4 499 6376
info@kennett.co.nz
www.kennett.co.nz

1st edition copyright © 2012 Kennett Brothers Limited
2nd edition copyright © 2013 Kennett Brothers Limited
3rd edition copyright © 2015 Kennett Brothers Limited
4th edition copyright © 2018 Kennett Brothers Limited

ISBN 978-0-9941454-2-0

Front cover photo   Lake Wakatipu, credit Around the Mountains Cycle Trail
Back cover photo   Tauranga, credit Jonathan Kennett
All other photo credits are listed on page 286.

Writing	Jonathan Kennett
Editing	Bronwen Wall
Main Maps	Paul Kennett, David Laing and Bronwen Wall
Connector Maps	Adele Jackson
Elevation Charts	Paul Kennett and David Laing
Design	Paul Kennett
Printing	PrintLink in Petone, New Zealand

Contents

Introduction 6

Far North Cycleway 20
Twin Coast Cycle Trail, Pou Herenga Tai 24
Kauri Coast Cycleway 28
Kaipara Missing Link 32
Bike Waiheke 38
Auckland's Great Escape 42
Raglan to Waitomo Caves 48
Hauraki Rail Trail 52
Te Awa River Ride 58
Waikato River Trail 62
Te Ara Ahi, Thermal by Bike 68
The Motu Trails 72
Rere Falls Trail 76
Te Urewera Rainforest 82
Great Lake Trail 86
The Timber Trail 90
Forgotten World Highway 98
Mountains to Sea 102
The Three Rivers 108
Gorges to Sea Cycleway 114
Manawatu Cycleway 120
Gentle Annie 126
Hawke's Bay Trails 130
Route 52 136
Remutaka Cycle Trail 142

Queen Charlotte Track 146
Picton to Nelson 150
Dun Mountain Trail 154
Great Taste Trail 158
The Rainbow 166
St James Cycle Trail 172
Heaphy Track 178
Old Ghost Road 184
Ghost Road Roundabout 190
Pioneer Heritage Trail 194
Big River to Waiuta 198
West Coast Wilderness Trail 202
Touring the Wild West 208
Hurunui Heartland Ride 218
Little River Rail Trail 224
Christchurch to the Alps 228
Alps 2 Ocean Cycle Trail 234
Otago Central Rail Trail 242
Roxburgh Gorge Trail 246
Clutha Gold Trail 250
Queenstown Trails 256
Around the Mountains 262
Catlins Coastal Route 272

Tour Aotearoa: Cape Reinga to Bluff 276

Index 293

Introduction

One of the best ways to explore New Zealand is by bike. You will see more, hear more and meet more people when you're out on your bike. And you'll get in shape while you're at it!

New Zealand has a wide range of trails and roads. Some roads are busy and unsafe, some tracks are rough and hard going, but many are just perfect for a fabulous cycling holiday. For this book, we travelled the country, riding and talking with local cyclists, and drew on our combined 90 years of cycling experience to bring you the best rides available. Choose a trail, hop on your bike and enjoy the adventure.

Setting the scene

This is your complete guide to the New Zealand Cycle Trail network, plus a selection of our other favourite cycling holidays. New Zealand is a mountainous country and some of the trails are rough and steep. We recommend visiting cycle tourists travel much lighter than normal.

The New Zealand Cycle Trail network comprises 22 Great Rides, including the popular Otago Central Rail Trail and the dramatic Timber Trail. Most of the trails have been built over the last few years and showcase the best off-road cycling New Zealand has to offer. The Great Rides are connected by the best cycle paths and scenic back roads in the country.

The majority of the New Zealand Cycle Trail was complete when this book went to print in 2018. The trails are well signposted, local businesses are gearing up to cater for cyclists, and you will meet other riders during your trip. We have clearly identified the trails that were not yet complete at the time of writing or are not part of the New Zealand Cycle Trail brand. For more detail, see how the cycle trail network is growing by following their progress at the official New Zealand Cycle Trail website: **www.nzcycletrail.com**

A box of chocolates

The cycle trails are like a big box of chocolates. Everyone has their personal favourites, so it's worthwhile taking your time to choose carefully from the wide selection available. Will your favourites be smooth and easy, like Caramello, or rough and wild, like Rocky Road? Is coffee and culture essential, or do you just want to get away from it all? The variety is huge, and the choice is yours. Perhaps you'd like a taste of everything?

Fantastic riding on the award-winning Fox Glacier Trail, West Coast.

Three general categories of ride

This book contains all the best holiday rides in the country, regardless of whether they are officially part of the New Zealand Cycle Trail yet or not. If we really loved a ride, then it's in this book so that you can ride it and love it too.

Great Rides	Mostly new off-road cycle trails. Since 2010, over $100 million has been invested in them. They include rail trails and cycle paths and are designed for cyclists to enjoy.
Heartland Rides	Mostly quiet backcountry road rides, through scenic landscapes with small towns along the way. Heartland Rides pull together the best existing infrastructure in the country, as well as some bits of new cycle path/track that avoid busy roads and go to cool places.
Connector Rides	These are the safest and most enjoyable ways of linking Great Rides, Heartland Rides and key towns and cities. Often they are very good rides in their own right.

Trail components
All the trails are unique and are made up of a variety of the following components:

Off road path/track: separate from roads and traffic. This type of trail includes rail trails, bike tracks and urban concrete paths. All cycle paths/tracks are shared with walkers.

Cycle lane: painted on the side of the road and for cycles only.

Road with shoulder: sealed public road with space on the side for cyclists.

Busy road without shoulder: lots of traffic and no room to cycle safely. We avoid these roads in favour of more pleasant options, even if that means riding a few extra kilometres.

Quiet road: any public road with fewer than 1000 vehicles per day. It can be sealed or gravel. Gravel roads are the quietest and often have more sheep than vehicles.

Trail grades

The rides in this book are rated from 1 to 5 based on difficulty and traffic volumes. Choose carefully to ensure you have a great ride.

Grade 1 Very Easy

Flat, smooth and wide trails suitable for the whole family. The surface is concrete or smooth gravel. Any on-road sections will have little or no traffic, travelling at 50 kph or less.

Bike type Any bike is fine to ride on these trails, even a cruiser or an old Raleigh Twenty.

Grade 2 Easy

Some gentle climbs and narrow sections but still mostly wide enough to ride side by side. The surface is generally smooth gravel, and any on-road sections will still have very little traffic.

Bike type Any multi-geared bike with medium or wide tyres is recommended, for example, a comfort bike, hybrid or mountain bike.

Grade 3 Intermediate

Off-road sections of trail may be a bit rough and/or narrow, and there will be some good-sized hills.

On-road sections of trail will mostly follow quiet country roads, with less than 1000 vehicles a day on average. An adult should accompany any young rider.

Bike type For off-road intermediate trails, a mountain bike is recommended. For on-road trails, any multi-geared bike is fine, unless there are long sections of gravel road, in which case the bike should have medium to wide tyres.

Grade 4 Advanced

Off-road advanced trails have steep climbs with lots of obstacles, and there may be a few short walking sections.

On-road advanced trails will include long hills, with some gravel sections likely. The roads will be open to 100 kph traffic, with up to 1000 vehicles per day (possibly more, but only if there is a good road shoulder).

Bike type A mountain bike is essential for off-road advanced trails, and it should have less than 10 kg of gear loaded on it. For on-road trails, any multi-geared bike is just fine, although you will want medium to wide tyres if there are gravel sections.

Grade 5 Expert

Hardly anything in this book is Grade 5. These trails either require excellent mountain biking skills or fearless road riding skills. You must be fit and very experienced to ride Grade 5 trails safely.

Bike type A quality mountain bike with full suspension is ideal for off-road expert trails.

Trail grade examples

Grade 1 (Very Easy): Hawke's Bay Coastal Path, Otago Central Rail Trail, Hauraki Rail Trail, New Plymouth Coastal Path, Little River Rail Trail

Grade 2 (Easy): Clutha Gold Trail, Roxburgh Gorge Trail, West Coast Wilderness Trail, the off-road sections of the Alps 2 Ocean Cycle Trail

Grade 3 (Intermediate): Motu Road, The Timber Trail, Dun Mountain Trail, most of the Queen Charlotte Track

Grade 4 (Advanced): The Old Ghost Road, St James Cycle Trail, Forgotten World Highway, Heaphy Track

Grade 5 (Expert): Apart from a few kilometres on the Queen Charlotte Track and the Old Ghost Road, there are no Grade 5 trails in this book.

Trail experience

There are three ways the trails are commonly experienced:

Independent Self-organised from go to whoa. You arrange transport, food and accommodation. This is the most inexpensive and flexible option.

Supported This is the hassle-free option. Ask a reliable friend or tour operator to organise the trip for you. They arrange shuttles, book accommodation, possibly arrange your food, and can also supply bikes.

Guided A guiding company will arrange everything, plus join you on the ride so that you don't have to worry about getting lost, mechanical problems or even what you're going to eat.

Bike rentals and tours

Dozens of companies offer bike rentals and tours. We have listed local companies under the **Support Services** section for each ride.

If you decide to do a supported or guided trip, we recommend you choose a business from the Cycle Tour Operators of New Zealand (CTONZ, www.ctonz.co.nz). They know the country better than anyone and have excellent safety standards.

For a nationwide trip, try Natural High. They are based in Auckland and Christchurch and have depots in major cities around the country, so you can hire a bike in one city, do a big trip and drop off the bike in another city. As well as most types of bikes, Natural High also provides all the extras, including panniers, helmets, repair kits, lights, safety reflective clothing, etc. Hire options include short-terms rentals or a buy back option.

Fly to Auckland or Christchurch and start riding. For more information, check out www.natural-high.co.nz

Best time to ride

The best time for a cycling holiday in New Zealand is between mid February and mid April. The weather is usually settled, most holidaymakers are back at work or school and daylight hours are still reasonably long. But New Zealand can experience bouts of good and bad weather any time of year, so for short trips, try to be flexible with your plans and wait for a good forecast.

Some trails have specific open seasons (Heaphy Track, Queen Charlotte Track, Rainbow and Molesworth trails), and these are noted in the **Fact File** for each ride.

> *To me the bicycle is the closest you can get to total freedom. You are governed by no one ... You are totally free.*
>
> Louise Sutherland
> Kiwi cycle tourer extraordinaire (1926–1994)

Terms and symbols we've used

To differentiate between vertical and horizontal; **'m'** refers to vertical height, and **'metres'** refers to horizontal distance. Heights shown on elevation charts are metres above sea level.

The Department of Conservation is referred to as DOC.

All maps in this book are aligned to true north.

Fat tyres refers to any tyre wider than 45mm (i.e., mountain bike tyres). Skinny tyre refers to any tyre less than 25mm wide (i.e., road racing tyres).

Key to maps

- Main ride
- Other rides
- City
- Location of interest
- River/stream
- Lake/sea
- Sealed road
- Rail trail/gravel rd
- Single track
- Information
- Toilets
- Shelter
- Camping
- Hut
- Accommodation
- Cafe/Food
- Parking
- Viewpoint
- Bike Shop
- Airport
- Train

Good maps and free maps

It is important, for your safety and satisfaction, that you use the maps we have listed in the **Fact File**. While some of the recommended maps are give-aways, most will cost around $10. Many free travel maps at information centres aren't detailed enough to help with your cycling holidays.

Ride times

Each ride is divided into convenient stages, usually based on the location of food and accommodation along the trail. They generally range from 20 km to 50 km long. The stage times shown are based on people averaging 5 kph to 10 kph on gravel roads/tracks and 10 kph to 20 kph on sealed roads/tracks. On steep uphills, you may go a bit slower, and on downhills, you will go a lot faster. On top of the stage times, you need to allow extra time, especially between stages, for all the good holiday diversions like picnics, cafes, hot pools, side walks and just chilling out with mates.

It pays to rest early and often. And don't forget that riding on unsealed paths/roads generally takes twice as much energy as riding on sealed paths/roads.

Tour Aotearoa

The one enduring cycling holiday concept, which is shared by almost every nation on the planet, is to ride from one end of a country to the other. In New Zealand, that trip is 3000 km long and stretches from Cape Reinga to Bluff.

For those who have 1–2 months available, we have listed the best way to complete the **Tour Aotearoa** at the back of this book (see page 276).

Types of bikes

Cruiser: upright riding position, heavy frame, riser handlebars, wide saddle, single speed or just a few gears. These are only suitable for Grade 1 trails.

Comfort: upright riding position, flat handlebars, suspension forks and seat post, medium to wide tyres and a range of gears. These are reasonably inexpensive bikes but sometimes a bit heavy.

Touring/trekking/hybrid: medium-weight frame, flat or dropped handlebars, medium tyres, a good range of gears. These are highly versatile bicycles.

Road: lightweight frame, sporty riding position, drop handlebars, narrow tyres, a moderate range of gears. These are fast on the road but not suitable off road.

Cyclocross: medium-weight frame, sporty riding position, drop handlebars, medium tyres, multi gears. Versatile and fast but not as comfortable as a touring bike over long distances.

Mountain bike: strong frame, flat handlebars, front suspension forks, and possibly rear suspension, wide tyres with knobby tread and a good range of gears. These are very versatile bikes.

Downhill/freeride: heavy, bomb-proof bikes with wide tyres, loads of suspension and a moderate range of gears. These are not good for riding on trails with uphill sections.

The best place to get a bike is from a bike shop or a bike hire company. You will get professional advice to help you choose the right size bike and have it adjusted to suit you. You will also get back-up service if you need it. Buying a bike over the internet can be risky.

Accommodation

In this book, we only list accommodation providers in remote areas, where there is little or no choice and it is important you know about them. In towns where there are plenty of options, we have not listed all the possibilities but have left you to choose your preference. To find out about accommodation, follow the regional website addresses in the **Support Services** section or pick up a free accommodation guide at any i-SITE, airport or ferry terminal. Jasons Guides publish up-to-date booklets, one for each type of accommodation – holiday parks, backpackers, bed and breakfasts, and motels.

General costs for different types of accommodation are:

Camping: From nothing to $20 per person

Backpackers dormitory room: $15 to $30 per person

Backpackers twin room: $40 to $90

Standard motel/hotel twin room: $80 to $180

Luxury hotel twin room: $180 to $400

Five-star hotel room with a chocolate on your pillow: $400 to $3000+.

Gearing up

What to take on a cycling holiday has been a source of vigorous debate since the 1870s, when penny farthings started touring the world. Since then, two extremes have developed – the minimalist lightweights and the extravagant heavyweights: those who pack little more than their credit cards through to those who won't stop packing until the kitchen sink is strapped to the top of their fully loaded trailer. There is a 'middle way' growing in popularity - bikepacking with lots of light gear, but not many luxuries.

This typical bikepacking set-up is ideal for New Zealand's varied trails.

Don't worry, we won't try to convince you towards one extreme or the other, at least not directly. Instead, we have created two gear lists, one for each camp. However, we have noticed that age, experience and disposable income usually move people from the heavyweight camp to the lightweight camp.

Our 'Lightweight versus Heavyweight' gear lists are provided on page 19.

Environmental Care Code
Protect plants and animals
Treat New Zealand's forests and animals with care and respect. They are unique and often rare. Clean your bike between rides to avoid transporting weeds and dydimo.

Remove rubbish
It seriously irritates landowners and other trail users to have rubbish left on trails. Take all your rubbish with you and use recycling facilities where available.

Toilets
Plan your day to use the public toilets (or cafe toilets) marked on our maps. If you get caught short in the wilderness, make sure you do your business well out of sight and away from farms, tracks and waterways.

Keep streams and lakes clean
When cleaning and washing, do it well away from streams and lakes. Soaps and detergents are pollutants.

Take care with stoves and fires
Fires destroy forests and homes. Never leave a fire unattended and make sure it is completely extinguished before leaving it.

Share with care
The trails in this book are open to the public, including walkers and often motorised vehicles. Share these trails with care.

Respect our cultural heritage
Many places in New Zealand have a spiritual and historical significance. Treat these places with consideration and respect.

The future
New Zealand has an amazing variety of cycle trails and more are being built all the time. Some trailbuilders seek to replicate the success of the Otago Central Rail Trail and cater for families and retiring baby boomers. Those who come from a mountain biking background want to create multi-day adventures in New Zealand's spectacular back country. Others are looking for ways to recreate the cycle touring experiences that were so popular in the 1970s and 80s.

Largely because of the New Zealand Cycle Trail project, the current boom in trail construction has transformed cycling in this small country. Some of the trails that have been opened are not completely finished. Work to improve and extend them is ongoing, and at the same time, the businesses supporting the trail riders steadily grow and improve. Within a few years, there will be several thousand kilometres of trails to explore nationwide – enough for a lifetime of fun and fitness on your cycling holidays.

Stopping to regroup on a Christmas tour around East Cape.

Trains, planes, buses and boats

Using public transport has several advantages for cycling holidays. It makes it easy to do cycling trips from one point to another, and you can relax on the way to and from your holiday. Here are some tips to get you going.

On international flights, you will commonly be charged US$200 each way for bike carriage alone, so you may like to consider hiring a bike, or buying one in New Zealand and selling it when leaving. A good option is to fly into Auckland, travel down the country and fly out of Christchurch or Queenstown.

The long-distance train services that operate in New Zealand are scenic and make an excellent way to start a trip in style. For example, the Taieri Gorge train from Dunedin to the start of the Otago Central Rail Trail is absolutely brilliant.

Buses service most of the country, but taking more than two bikes on a bus can be a hassle. Some buses (Waiheke Island and Christchurch) now have bike racks. You can't book your bike on a bus, and the drivers reserve the right to refuse to carry it if they don't have enough space. We've never been refused, but every now and again, you hear stories of others who have.

Ferries are much better set up to carry bikes, and it is never a hassle. In fact, it is often a joy to relax on a ferry and recharge your batteries.

In all major cities, you can hire shuttle taxi vans with trailers that can take bikes. They're not cheap, but are convenient as you can leave when and from wherever you want.

Contact details

KiwiRail Scenic Journeys (train)	www.kiwirailscenic.co.nz
Interislander (ferry)	www.interislander.co.nz
Bluebridge (ferry)	www.bluebridge.co.nz
Air New Zealand	www.airnewzealand.co.nz
InterCity Coachlines	www.intercity.co.nz
Auckland commuter trains	www.maxx.co.nz
Wellington commuter trains	www.tranzmetro.co.nz
Christchurch buses (most now have bike racks)	www.metroinfo.org.nz

Smaller operators are mentioned in the relevant ride notes.

Fees for unbagged bikes

Some ferries and trains, and most buses, charge $10–15 for an unbagged bike. Wellington and Auckland commuter trains no longer charge for bikes, but space can be limited; some peak-hour trains have no room for bikes.

Intercity buses require bikes to be broken down (take off the wheels and pedals, turn the handlebars and cover the chain). If this is only one of two luggage items then it's free. Otherwise it'll cost $10 per bus connection.

The Interislander ferry charges $15 per bike, and Bluebridge Cook Strait ferry charges $10 per bike. You'll be required to walk your bike on and off these ferries.

Air New Zealand does not charge for bikes but does charge for your second bag or item ($15 for a bag up to 23 kg). They expect you to pack your bike well or at least wrap the chain and cogs in newspaper, remove the pedals and turn the handlebars. They sell bike boxes for $25 or you can often pick one up from a bike shop for nothing. Budget airlines will charge an arm and a leg!

The cost of car travel

The AA estimates that (taking into account fuel, tyres, maintenance, etc) an average-sized, fully loaded car costs around $1 per km to run. Landcare Research estimates that an average-sized fossil-fuel car will emit 1 tonne of CO_2 for every 4,000 km driven – larger cars emit much more.

To save petrol, pack your bikes inside your car and share your trip with others. Also check out the public transport options or cycle to and from the ride!

Gear list

Lightweight day trip

Helmet
Shoes and socks
Cycle shorts
Thermal top
Cycling top (or T-shirt)
Cycle gloves
Windbreaker
Sun glasses
Sun block
Wallet (with ID and eftpos card)
Cell phone
Map and/or GPS
1 inner tube
Pump
Multi-tool/Allen keys
Tyre lever
1 drink bottle (or bladder)

Total weight = 3 kg

Heavyweight day trip

add some or all of the following:

Rain coat
Cable lock
Handkerchief
Survival blanket
GPS
PLB (Emergency locator beacon)
Pocket knife or Leatherman
Chain breaker
Tyre boot
Notebook and pen
Oil (small bottle)
Chapstick
Front and rear lights
Camera
First aid kit
Insect Repellent

Total weight = 5–7 kg

Lightweight multi-day trip

minimal, no camping:

All of the above (both columns) plus:
Underwear
Warm socks
Polypro/wool inner layer top
Warm outer layer top
Trousers
Thin hat or balaclava
Over trousers
Toothbrush and paste
Toilet paper and soap
A second spare tube
Cell phone charger
Sleeping bag
Frame bag and/or under-the-seat bag

Total weight = 7–10 kg

Heavyweight multi-day trip

add the following:

Sleeping bag liner, sleeping mat, pillow, tent, sandals/jandals, dress clothes, casual clothes, thermal gloves, spare batteries, small towel, shampoo, billy and cooker, cup and plate (or bowl), knife and spoon, washing detergent, tea towel, dry bag/plastic bags, laptop or iPod, etc, camera tripod, coffee percolator, trowel, extra fuel for stove, book or two, deodorant/perfume, make up, repair kit (tape, needle and thread, etc), spare tyre, crank tool, freewheel tool, spoke tool, overmitts, hair brush, musical instrument, pets and children, and a trailer to carry it all in.

Total weight = 15–30 kg

HEARTLAND RIDE

Far North Cycleway
Cape Reinga to Hokianga Harbour
Distance 168 km   Time 2 days   Grade 3- (Intermediate)

A trip to Cape Reinga is a rite of passage for any Kiwi and a journey that shouldn't be rushed. The Far North is culturally, historically and ecologically unique, and the bicycle is the best way to explore it.

From the iconic lighthouse at Cape Reinga, there are expansive views where the Tasman Sea meets the Pacific Ocean. According to Maori, this is where spirits depart for the underworld.

The ride heads south for an hour on the only road before jumping onto the misnamed Ninety Mile Beach (it is only 55 miles) for a flat blat down the coast. During dawn or dusk, this is a stunning landscape, but on a mid-summer's afternoon, there is no escaping the heat.

The beach ends at Ahipara, an ideal destination for the night, while from Ahipara, a sealed road weaves through sleepy countryside to the historic Hokianga Harbour.

ITINERARY

Stage 1: Ninety Mile Beach: Cape Reinga to Ahipara
103 km, 5–8 hours

From Cape Reinga, cycle down Highway 1 for 15.6 km before turning southwest at Te Paki, to continue down Kauaeparaoa Stream (also called Te Paki Stream) to the northern end of Ninety Mile Beach, which is another 7 km. From there, it is 80 pancake-flat kilometres south to Ahipara, which lies 14 km southwest of Kaitaia. Ahipara and Waipapakauri are the only places beside the beach that have shops.

During low tide only! During 3 hours either side of low tide the beach surface is as hard as concrete – easy but boring. The only sluggish bits will be where streams flow across the beach. Ride with an entertaining bunch of friends! Practise cycling no hands or with your eyes closed – or both!

Stage 2: Ahipara to Rawene
65 km, 4–7 hours

From Ahipara, take Foreshore Road east and then Roma Road out into the country. Turn right when you hit a T-intersection at Kaitaia-Awaroa Road. At Herekino (14 km), turn left to stay on this road. About 35 km from Ahipara, you will reach Broadwood, which has a general store (closed on Sundays).

Smooth riding along Ninety Mile Beach.

From Broadwood, cycle 3.2 km before turning right onto Paponga Road. When you are 16.5 km from Broadwood turn left onto Rahautapu Road which leads to Kohukohu, 25 km from Broadwood.

Kohukohu is a lovely place, with good cafes, accommodation and a general store. The next 4 km to the Rawene ferry terminal skirts the coastline, with ethereal views across a serene harbour.

The ferry runs hourly during the day and costs a couple of dollars for the 2-km trip to Rawene; another lovely coastal town, about twice the size of Kohukohu. Both of these towns have galleries, cafes and lots of heritage. It's well worth spending some time there.

FACT FILE

How to get there Cape Reinga is 113 km from Kaitaia via Highway 1 (fully sealed but hillier than you might expect). To shuttle up to Cape Reinga, contact Johanna Maaka on: ☎ 09 409 8152 or 027 4252 8785

Riding surface 50% solid sand (during low tide only), 50% sealed road

History Reinga is Maori for 'underworld' and relates to the belief that the spirits of the dead leave Aotearoa from the Cape to begin the journey to their spiritual homeland, Hawaiiki-A-Nui.

Special considerations Kaitaia is the nearest main town, with banks, accommodation, and supermarkets. Waitiki Landing is the northernmost shop in the country – make sure you are stocked up when you leave it. Food isn't sold or allowed to be eaten at Cape Reinga to respect the spiritual importance of the site. Eating at the car park is fine.

During **low tide** Ninety Mile Beach is used daily by half-a-dozen tourist buses and a few private vehicles. It has claimed several motorised vehicles that tried to navigate it too close to high tide, but no bicycles to date. The tide times are printed every day in the local newspaper, *The Northland Age* and are available by calling the Kaitaia i-SITE ☎ 09 408 9450. Bikes should be thoroughly cleaned of salt and sand at the bottom of Ninety Mile Beach (Ahipara).

Special features The quaint Cape Reinga lighthouse was built in 1941.

Important contacts Kaitaia i-Site for tide times and conditions: ☎ 09 408 9450

Maps Kiwimap *Far North Rural Road Map*

SUPPORT SERVICES

Cape Reinga Interpretation centre with informative displays, drinking water and toilets. No other facilities. Note: no eating at the Cape.

Waitiki Landing Restaurant/bar, store, petrol station, holiday park: ☎ 09 409 7508

Hukatere Utea Park (100 m off beach) camping and cabins. Payment by koha (e.g., $40 cash): ☎ 021 804 002. Hukatere Lodge: ☎ 021 884 145, www.hukatere.com

Waipapakauri Food and accommodation: Ninety Mile Beach Holiday Park: ☎ 0800 367 719, www.ninetymilebeach.co.nz

Ahipara Food, petrol, accommodation: Ahipara Holiday Park: ☎ 0800 888 988, www.ahiparaholidaypark.co.nz, Baylinks Lodge Motel: ☎ 0508 265 100, www.baylinks.co.nz

Kaitaia (14 km off the trail) Major town with banks and everything else: www.northlandnz.com

Broadwood General store (closed Sundays). Farmstay: ☎ 09 809 5055

Kohukohu General store, cafes, accommodation: Lavender Cottage: ☎ 09 405 5843/(mob) 021 176 6698, Night Sky Lodge: ☎ 09 405 5841, www.nightskylodge.co.nz, also see: www.kohukohu.co.nz. Tree House Backpackers Lodge (2 km off route): ☎ 09 405 5855, www.treehouse.co.nz

Hokianga ferry service The ferry crosses the Hokianga Harbour to Rawene every 45 minutes: www.hokiangatourism.org.nz for timetable and fares

Rawene Cafe, shops, accommodation: Rawene Holiday Park: ☎ 09 405 7720 www.raweneholidaypark.co.nz, The Masonic Hotel: ☎ 09 405 7822

GREAT RIDE

Twin Coast Cycle Trail
Pou Herenga Tai
The heart of Northland
Distance 84 km Time 2 days Grade 2–3 (Easy–Intermediate)

From Bay of Islands to Hokianga Harbour, the Twin Coast Cycle Trail is a fantastic opportunity for riders to explore the tranquility and history of heartland Far North.

The trail connects four completely distinct stages leading from Opua to the Hokianga Harbour. Two stages follow an old railway line, one uses a mix of rail trail and country roads and another a mix of fantastic new trail and country roads. Each stage can be completed independently and in either direction.

Discover the yin and the yang of Northland in one holiday: from the bustling hum of the Bay of Islands to the laid-back Hokianga. Both coasts exude their own stunning beauty, and cycling is the perfect way to fully appreciate all they have to offer.

ITINERARY

Stage 1: Opua to Kawakawa
11 km, 2–3 hours, Grade 2 (Easy)

This is one of the most stunning sections of the trail. Meet up at the cafe beside the Opua marina and get a feel for the Bay of Islands before heading inland. The trail is built on top of the railway tracks, which one day may be uncovered and used again by trains from the local vintage railway club.

The trail skirts around the coast for 7 km before crossing the longest curved railway bridge in the southern hemisphere and leading to Taumarere Station. From there the trail continues for 4 km into Kawakawa.

The bustling small town of Kawakawa is great for lovers of art, coffee, and toilets. Yes, toilets! The public loos were designed by the famous Friedensreich Hundertwasser and are now a major tourist attraction.

Stage 2: Kawakawa to Kaikohe
35 km, 3–5 hours, Grade 3 (Intermediate)

From Kawakawa Railway Station, nip around to the end of Station Road (beside the Caltex) and follow the rail trail for 5 km to Pembroke Road where you can divert to the Moerewa shops 300 metres away. The trail continues, partly on

Cruise your way through the verdant heart of Northland.

old railway formation and partly beside country roads. After climbing Jacobs Ladder, cross Mangakahia Road and follow the rail trail as it curves around the hillside all the way to Kaikohe 7 km away.

To head into the town centre for a coffee, veer right onto Station Road East when you reach the waste station.

Kaikohe – the hub of Northland – is a good base for the night, with the Mid North Motor Inn offering a warm welcome. The town has an interesting museum, a fantastic coffee house and the Ngawha Springs hot pools (6 km out of town).

Stage 3: Kaikohe to Okaihau
14 km, 1.5–2.5 hours, Grade 2 (Easy)

This section is easy rail trail and heads through a curved tunnel before skirting around Lake Omapere and ending at the small town of Okaihau.

From the shops in the centre of Kaikohe, head west on the main road. When you are 500 metres past the Mid North Motor Inn, you will see the trail signposted on your right. Squeeze across a narrow cattlestop and follow the smooth gravel path all the way to Okaihau. At the main street, there is a good cafe on your left.

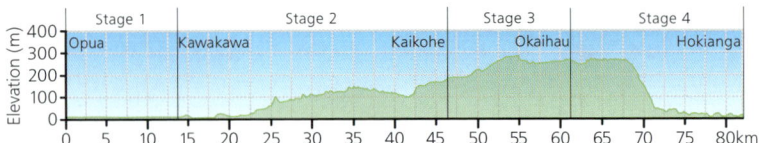

Stage 4: Okaihau to Hokianga Harbour
24 km, 2–3 hours, Grade 3 (Intermediate)

From the shops in Okaihau, head southwest through the town on Settlers Way. This becomes Horeke Road and the cycle trail runs beside it. After a few kilometres, keep your eyes peeled for signposts directing you left, through a farm, and down beside Utakura River. It eventually pops back out onto Horeke Road, and leads to a long boardwalk ending at Horeke, one of the oldest towns in New Zealand.

From Horeke settlement, you can ride (on the road) for another 2 km to Mangungu Mission House, which is on a small hill with great views. From Horeke, catch a boat to Rawene or arrange a shuttle with Top Trail (see page 27).

FACT FILE

Access/how to get there Most cyclists start from Opua, in the Bay of Islands. See Support Services for a shuttle to any parts of the trail.

Riding surface Mostly smooth rail trail with a few short bits of gravel road.

History Construction of the main trunk line reached Okaihau in 1923. It was planned to continue to Kaitaia, but the great depression put paid to that idea. The trains ran from Auckland to Okaihau until 1987, when the line was closed.

Horeke was the first settlement on the Hokianga and is the second oldest town in the country. The tavern has been serving beer since 1823.

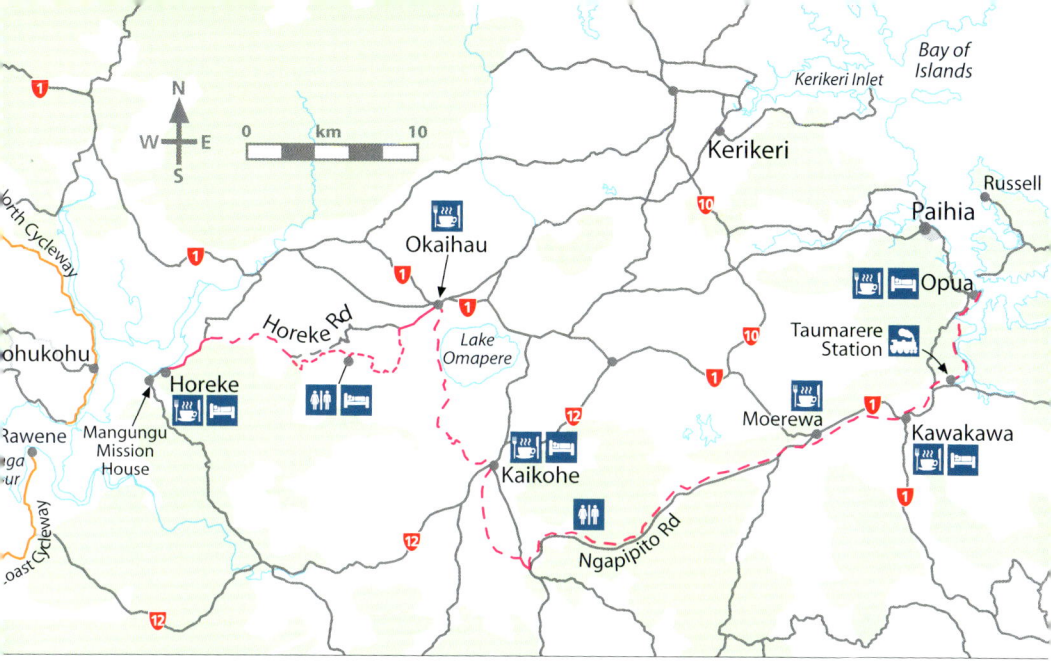

Special considerations Beautiful as Lake Omapere looks, it's heavily polluted by dairy farming: don't be tempted to dive in.

Special features Kawakawa is the home of the renowned Hundertwasser public toilets and Bay of Islands Vintage Railway – both well worth a visit.

Trail website www.twincoastcycletrail.kiwi.nz

SUPPORT SERVICES

Transport and bike hire Top Trail just out of Kaikohe for transport, bike hire and guided tours: ☎ 0800 867 872, www.toptrail.co.nz. Paihia Mountain Bikes: ☎ 021 187 8192, www.paihiamountainbikes.co.nz. Hokianga Express Charters for boat across Hokianga Harbour: ☎ 021 405 872, email hkexpress@xtra.co.nz

Opua Plenty of shops and accommodation: Opua Motel: ☎ 09 402 7632, www.opuamotel.co.nz, Pine Lodge Bay of Islands: ☎ 09 402 7808, www.pinelodgebayofislands.co.nz, Pukeko's Nest: ☎ 09 403 7951, www.pukekosnest.co.nz

Kawakawa Plenty of shops, accommodation and the Hundertwasser toilets: Try Centrepoint Motel: ☎ 09 404 1175, www.kawakawamotel.co.nz

Kaikohe Plenty of accommodation and shops: www.kaikohe.co.nz, Mid North Motor Inn: ☎ 09 405 3160, www.midnorthmotorinn.co.nz

Okaihau Two dairies, a takeaway shop, a pub and even a hardware store

Horeke Food and accommodation: Horeke Tavern: ☎ 09 401 9133, www.horeketavern.co.nz, Riverhead Guest House: ☎ 09 401 9610 or 021 814 562, www.riverhead-guesthouse-horeke.co.nz

HEARTLAND RIDE

Kauri Coast Cycleway
Hokianga Harbour to Dargaville
Distance 110 km   Time 1–2 days   Grade 3 (Intermediate)

Its remote west coast is one of the Far North's better-kept secrets. Outside holiday season, it presents a sparsely populated, dramatic landscape that is a dream come true for cyclists.

From the historic settlement of Rawene on the Hokianga Harbour to the sparkling sand-duned harbour entrance, past the giant lords of the Waipoua Kauri Forest and across the rural farmscape of Dargaville to the tip of Kaipara Harbour, this tour serves up a fantastic variety of natural and cultural heritage.

ITINERARY

Stage 1: Rawene to Tane Mahuta
47 km, 3–4 hours

From Rawene, take Parnell Road up the hill, past the hospital and on to Highway 12. Turn right to follow the highway all the way to Omapere, at the entrance to the Hokianga Harbour. There are a couple of 10-minute hills to grind over in this 23-km stretch, but the coastal views are worth it. Before long you'll reach the extended harbour-side holiday towns of Opononi and Omapere. Both have dozens of places to eat and stay (the Opononi Beach Holiday Park is fairly basic), with the Copthorne Hotel being the pick of the bunch.

From Omapere, the highway deals a sharp 110-metre climb. Half way up, it's worth taking a 1-km diversion to a fantastic lookout over the Hokianga Harbour.

Just 12 km further on is Waimamaku, a blip of a settlement, and the last opportunity for a coffee break before heading up into the misty rainforest of Waipoua.

Beyond the cafe, the road soon climbs into subtropical forest, dominated by giant kauri – a complete contrast to the coast. After a small descent, you'll arrive at the car park and takeaways caravan that herald the 1-minute walk to Tane Mahuta, Lord of the Forest and one of New Zealand's largest trees.

Stage 2: Tane Mahuta to Kauri Coast Holiday Park
31 km, 2–3 hours

From Tane Mahuta, the road weaves through the gracious Waipoua Kauri Forest, mostly downhill for 10 km, past amazing trees, including a squeeze between "Darby and Joan".

End-of-day cycling at its best beside the Hokianga Harbour.

Just after crossing the Waipoua River bridge, we recommend turning right off the highway and taking a 1-km smooth gravel road to the Waipoua Forest Cafe and information site. Set in a large sunny clearing at a bend in the Waipoua River, this information centre (with camping and cabin options) is a good place to regroup and catch your breath. Then head back to the highway and straight into another 5-km climb through forest and across farmland.

About 8 km from the cafe, turn left on to the quiet, gravelled Katui Road.

After about 4.5 km you will reach Donnelly's Crossing. Turn right on to Trounson Park Road and ride another 3.5 km to Trounson Kauri Park – a great place to dismount and explore for a while.

From the Kauri Park, Trounson Park Road is sealed. Turn right at the intersection 200 metres from the park entrance. In another 200 metres there is a small DOC camping area. Trounson Park Road continues 4.5 km to the lovely Kauri Coast Top Ten Holiday Park (22.5 km from Waipoua Forest Cafe, at a junction of the Waima and Kaihu rivers). This holiday park provides cabins, camping options, good swimming opportunities and a small shop.

Stage 3: Kauri Coast Holiday Park to Dargaville
31.5 km, 3–4 hours

From the holiday park take Trounson Park Road a further 2.5 km to Highway 12, where you turn left. Within 2.5 km you'll pass Kaihu Tavern and, a little later, a service station.

Four kilometres down the highway turn left again onto Ahikiwi Road. 1.5 kilometres later, turn left on to Maropiu Road, cross Kaihu River, and turn right onto Maropiu Settlement Road. After another 2 km, veer right again to stay on this road. When you reach a 'T' intersection at Waihue Road turn left and 200 metres later turn right onto Opanake Road. After 12 km, turn left onto the sealed Parore West Road. After 700 metres turn right and let Waihue Road lead you 2.5 km into Dargaville.

FACT FILE

Overview The west coast of Northland is poles apart from its sister coast on the east. The roads are much quieter, town life is slower and the beaches are wilder and emptier. It has a special unassuming quality that is ideal for a holiday.

How to get there Bus from Auckland to Kaitaia and follow the Far North Cycle Trail down to Rawene. Alternatively, bus to Dargaville and ride north.

Riding surface 90% sealed road, 10% gravel road

History The vast felling of the Northland kauri forests is well documented along this route, as is Maori and recent European history. Also check out the Dargaville Pioneer Museum.

Special considerations "Waipoua" roughly translates to "rainfall of the night": this is rainforest, and you should carry a good raincoat. Free drinkable water is available at the Dargaville museum, and free internet is available at the library.

Special features A night tour of the Waipoua Kauri Forest with the Footprints guided tour company is a magical experience.

Maps Kiwimap *Northland* or Google Maps

SUPPORT SERVICES

Rawene Cafe, shops, accommodation: Rawene Holiday Park: ☎ 09 405 7720, www.raweneholidaypark.co.nz, The Masonic Hotel: ☎ 09 405 7822

Opononi and **Omapere** Food and accommodation (the Copthorne hotel is a lovely treat): www.hokiangatourism.org.nz

Waipoua Campground, cabins and cafe: ☎ 09 439 6441

Trounson Kauri Park DOC campground: www.doc.govt.nz/parks-and-recreation/places-to-stay

Kauri Coast Top Ten Holiday Park ☎ 0800 807 200, www.kauricoasttop10.co.nz

Kaihu Tavern: ☎ 09 439 0722, and a petrol station a bit further on

Dargaville A range of food and accommodation (the Commercial Hotel has indoor storage for bikes): www.dargaville.co.nz

Dargaville Information Centre, 4 Murdoch Street, ☎ 0800 234 636

Time To bike shop, 45 Normanby Street, ☎ 09 439 0100

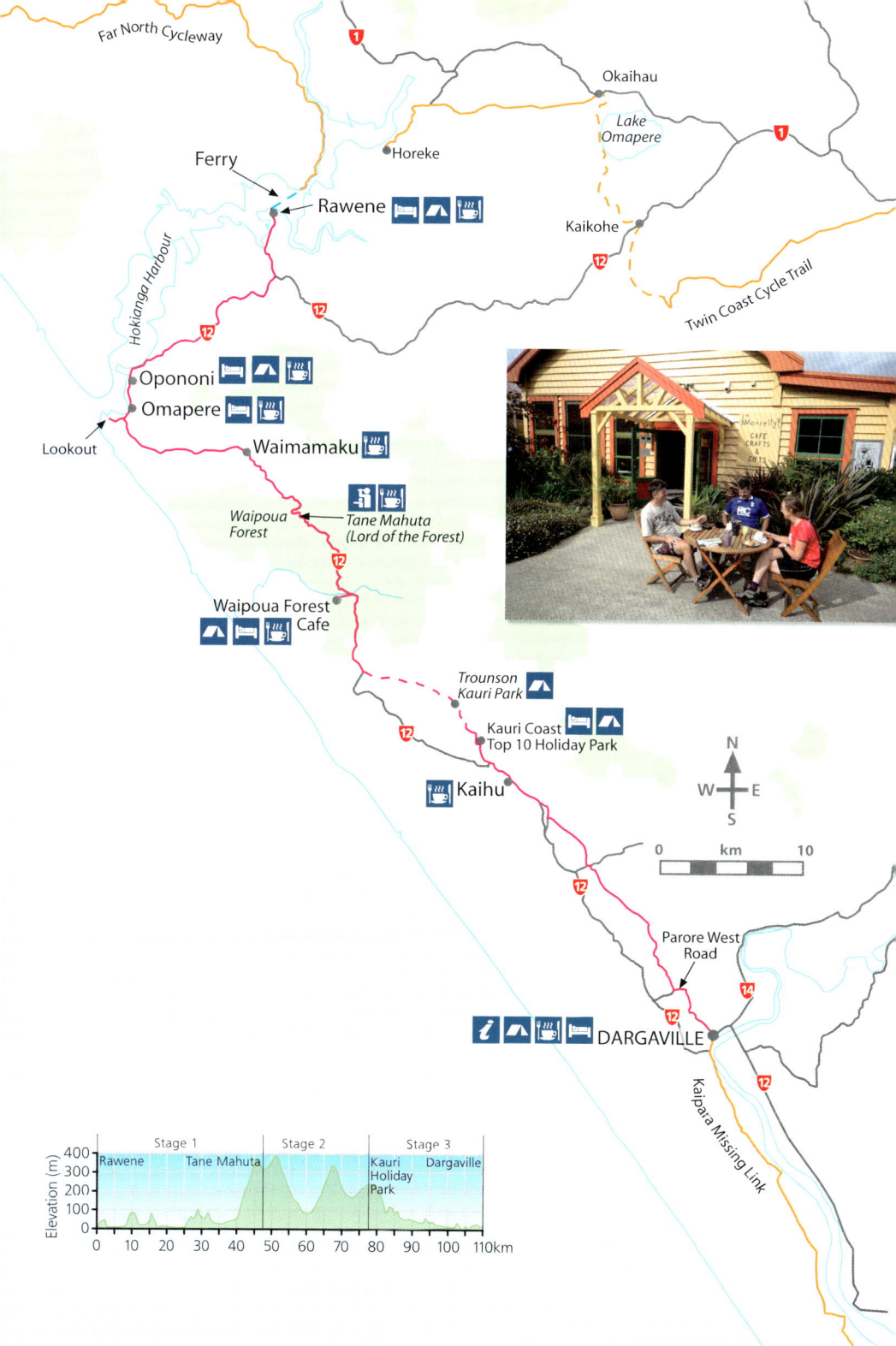

> **HEARTLAND RIDE**

Kaipara Missing Link
Dargaville to Auckland
Distance 118 km riding   Time 2–3 days   Grade 3 (Intermediate)

Sweep along the spine of the Pouto peninsula with vistas of rolling farmland before coasting to the mouth of the Kaipara, New Zealand's largest inland harbour, to follow a cunning route into the centre of Auckland.

Heading south from Dargaville, the road leads to Pouto Point, a wonderful hideaway at the mouth of the harbour. You'll want to spend a while exploring the towering white sand dunes, the historic lighthouse and the beautiful coastline of this area.

The missing link in this holiday is solved by taking a fascinating boat trip across the harbour. The history of the area, both ancient and recent, is totally absorbing. The boat drops you off at the Parakai hot pools. After a soak, you can take a surprisingly quiet and enjoyable route along back roads and cycle paths into the very centre of Auckland City.

ITINERARY

Stage 1: Dargaville to Pouto Point
65 km, 4–7 hours

Head south from Dargaville on River Road, which becomes Pouto Road. The first diversion is Ernie's Kumara Box Show, just 6 km out of town on Poutu Road and about 100 metres past the smallest church in New Zealand. It's amazing how entertaining a 1-hour show about a vegetable can be.

Just 10 km from town, the Te Kopuru dairy and takeways is the last food outlet before Poutu Point.

Choose between continuing along Pouto Road directly to Pouto Point or turning right onto West Coast Road, then left onto Redhill Road, right onto Glinks Road and out to the coast to ride south all the way down the beach. This latter option can only be completed 2½ hours either side of low tide.

If you choose to continue along Pouto Road, at the 45-km mark from Dargaville you'll be faced with another decision – hang a left to drop down a gravel road to Kellys Bay for a swim or continue straight ahead, rolling through farmland on a sealed road. The drop to Kellys Bay requires a stiff gravel-road climb back up to Pouto Road again 5 km on from where you left it.

Continue southeast for about 15 km to reach Pouto Point (the last 25 km is a

Boarding the boat Pouto style.

gravel road). Pouto Point is a timeless Kiwi bach town, where visitors often stay much longer than originally planned.

Stage 2: Pouto Point to Auckland CBD
A boat trip followed by 53 km riding, 7–9 hours

The boat trip across the harbour from Pouto Point village to Parakai (famous for its hot pools, and only 3 km from Helensville) takes 2–3 hours depending on weather conditions. On stormy days the trip will be postponed.

A plethora of cafes and accommodation options and an i-SITE are available at Helensville. From the main street, head east up any side street to reach Garfield Road. Turn right along Garfield, which becomes Wishart Road and then Old North Road where Inland Road heads off to the left. Keep on Old North Road, passing the well-known mountain biking area of Riverhead Forest as you strike out for Nixon Road (also known as Taupaki Road), which becomes Red Hills Road as it leads you directly to the west-Auckland suburb of Massey (19 km from downtown Auckland).

To cycle into the centre of the most car-crazy city in New Zealand, get yourself a copy of the Auckland Transport Cycle Route maps and follow the commuting cycle paths and lanes from Massey to the top of Queen Street. It is signposted most of the way as North West Cycle Route. What could be easier?

FACT FILE

Overview The Kaipara harbour is one of the largest harbours in the world but is notorious for the ever-shifting sandbars that can ground even the best sailors.

How to get there Bus to Dargaville. Connects to the Kauri Coast Cycleway.

Riding surface 86% sealed road, 9% cycle path, 5% gravel road

History Kauri forest removal at the turn of the 20th century saw the Kaipara Harbour develop as a humming port for kauri timber and gum, but once the trees had all been cut down, the area reverted to a quiet, overlooked backwater – ideal for cycle tourers.

Special considerations If the boat is unavailable, there is an alternative route around the east side Kaipara Harbour detailed in the Tour Aotearoa Official Guide books (see www.kennett.co.nz). This route is 100 km longer and quite hilly.

Special features Pouto Point is a cluster of baches nestled at Kaipara Head. You can take a horse trek or a 4WD trip out to the lighthouse or just spend hours beachcombing the coastline. It warrants a day for exploring and enjoying. Pouto Point has 1/3 of the rainfall found further inland.

Maps Kiwimap *Northland Rural Road Map*, Auckland Transport Cycle Route Map

SUPPORT SERVICES

Dargaville Many accommodation options available: www.dargaville.co.nz, Dargaville Information Centre for details on weather and boat/accommodation bookings: ☎ 09 439 8360.

6 km south of Dargaville Ernie and the Kumara Box, entertainment and campground (morning tea, lunch and afternoon tea available by arrangement): ☎ 09 439 7018, www.kumarabox.co.nz

Pouto Point No shops, purchase supplies at Dargaville: www.pouto.co.nz Camping and backpacker accommodation at the Pouto Point Marine Hall or bed and breakfast with Anne and Brian Malam at the Pouto Hideaway. They have details on weather and ferry bookings: ☎ 09 439 0199. Activities: horse trekking (Steven Nathan of Kahuparere Pouto Horse Treks: ☎ 09 439 6633, www.poutohorsetrek.homestead.com) or quad-bike trips (Sand Safaris with Jock: ☎ 09 439 6678)

Kaipara Harbour crossings Shamrock Charters Kaipara, Rod and Cheryl: ☎ 09 420 7061/(mob) 027 568 2447

Parakai Springs hot pools www.parakaisprings.co.nz

Helensville Shops, food, accommodation: www.helensville.co.nz

Auckland All the services you could possibly want and then some.

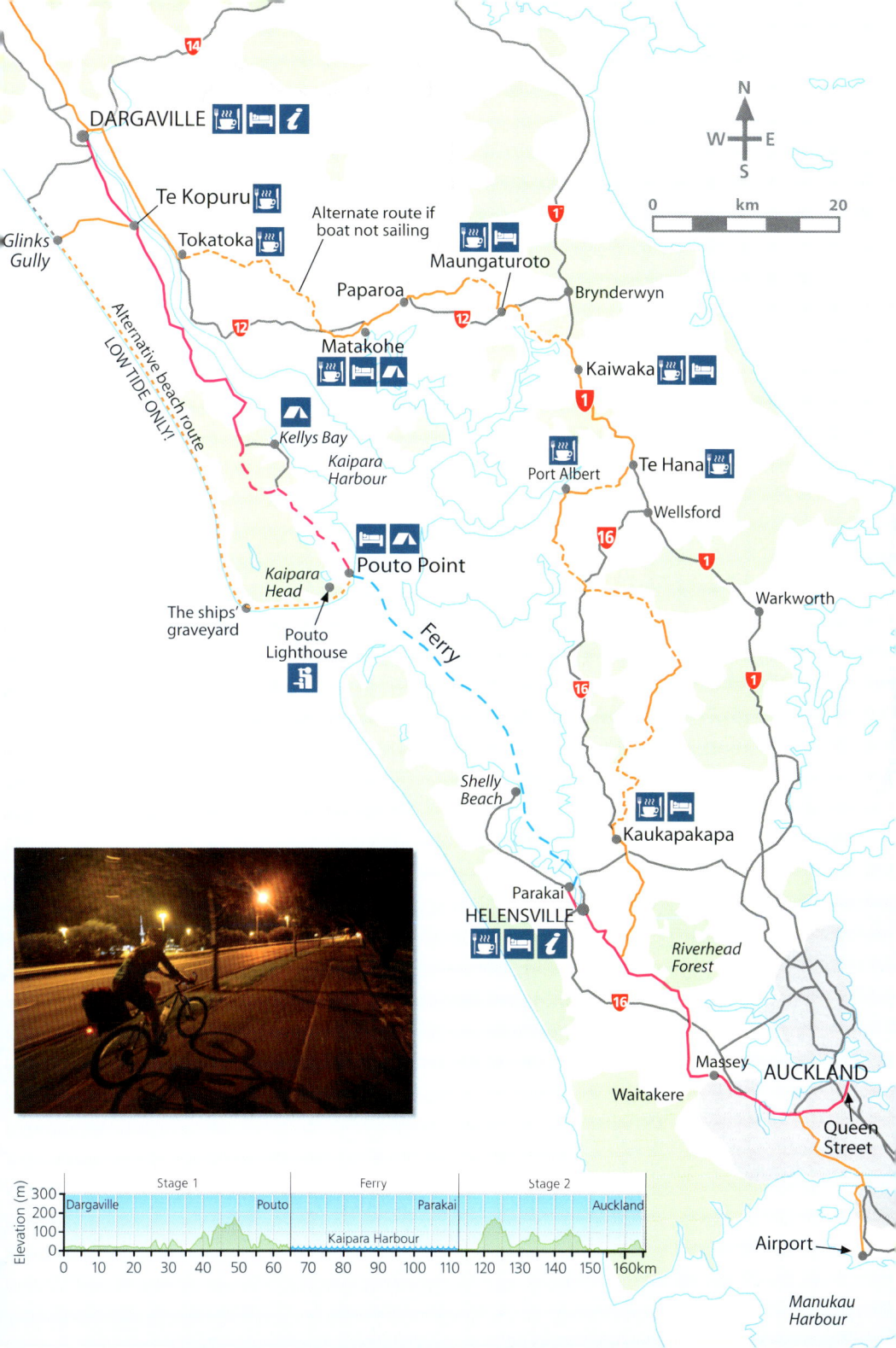

CONNECTOR RIDE

AUCKLAND AIRPORT TO CITY
Distance 29 km   Time 2 hours   Grade 3 (Intermediate)

If cycling from Auckland Airport to the inner city sounds crazy, then you'll be surprised to learn that Auckland has more cycle paths and lanes than anywhere else in the country. This is actually a pleasant ride.

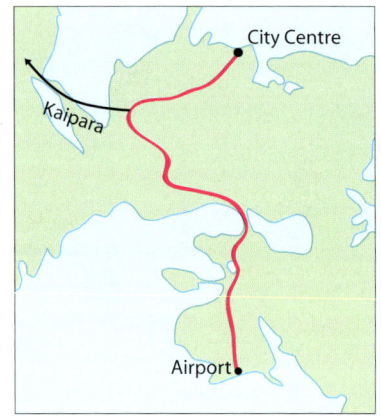

This route is not the shortest way into the CBD, but it is the safest and most enjoyable, and work is being done to make it even better. The alternatives are to take a shuttle van ($85/person) or pedal to Onehunga and catch a commuter train, but why not enjoy stretching your legs after all that time in a plane?

The route below is complicated, and you'll find Google Maps or an Auckland Transport Cycling Map helpful. Most of it is flat, but there is one short steep hill at the 12-km mark.

If you arrive at the International terminal, look for bike stands at the west end of the terminal. After building up your bike, head out on Tom Pearce Drive, turn left at Tahinga Lane, right at Manu Tapu Drive and left at Highway 20A (George Bolt Memorial Drive). Just 20 metres around the corner, head left onto an off-road path which runs parallel to the highway. It crosses Landing Drive, Montgomerie Road, Kirkbridge Road and Bader Drive.

The path forks just before a bridge – turn left and ride around Moyle Park, across Elmdon St and beside Tararata Creek to Hinau Road. Turn right at McKenzie Road and then left along Coronation Street, through the Mangere Bridge shopping centre and straight ahead to the old Mangere Bridge.

Cross the bridge and turn left to follow Orpheus Drive beside the coast. Take a short cycle path to connect with Hendry Avenue and then hop onto a much longer cycle path that runs parallel to the South Western Motorway. After 1.2 km, at Keith Hay Park, turn right and take the spiral bridge over motorway and make a hard right onto a cycle path beside Sommerset Road. Now follow the NZCT signs, to, and through, War Memorial Park to Mcgehan Close. You'll end up riding down Mt Albert Road, and eventually to the North-Western Motorway. Just 100

Breeze into Auckland with the help of the new bridge over the South Western Motorway.

metres before the motorway, turn right down Sutherland Road. At the end of this short road, you will find another cycle path (the North Western Cycle Route), which leads 4.5 km to the top of Queen Street, 27 km from the airport.

Hop off your bike at the Queen Street lights and cross as a pedestrian before taking the Grafton Gully Cycleway down to Anzac Ave, where the cycle route leads to the waterfront, just along from the bottom of Queen Street, the ferry terminal and Britomart.

Riding surface 100% sealed roads and cycle paths.

Maps Go to www.bikeauckland.org.nz/maps-rides/cycle-maps/ and look at the Auckland Transport *Southern* and *Central Cycle Maps*. Google Maps is also helpful.

Alternative Tour Aotearoa route There is a more direct route (only 20 km) via Mt Eden and Cornwall Park, but it uses some busy roads and is only suitable for traffic-savvy riders. Check it out at www.kennett.co.nz/maps/tour-aotearoa/

HEARTLAND RIDE

Bike Waiheke
Island escape
Distance 23–55 km   Time 1–2 days   Grade 3 (Intermediate)

Only 40 minutes east of Auckland by ferry lies Waiheke, an island of two halves. The first is buzzing with quirky shops, renowned vineyards and popular beaches. The second offers quiet roads through a scenic and hilly landscape.

Just jump on your bike and go! Everything you need is there – food, accommodation, even clothes. Fullers Ferries welcome bikes on their boats, which leave from the bottom of Queen Street, Auckland City.

There are two popular circuits on Waiheke. Some people stick to the shops and beaches. They might only cover 24 km in a restful two-day holiday (stages 1 and 3 below). Others fill their lungs with the sea air by exploring the whole island (stages 1, 2 and 3). There are steep hills, but none are too long, and there is always a park bench waiting at the top.

ITINERARY

Stage 1: Matiatia Bay (ferry) to Onetangi Bay
11 km, 1 hour, hilly roads

From the ferry at Matiatia Bay, wait 10 minutes for the ferry traffic to clear and then head up Ocean View Road for 2 km to the shops above Oneroa Bay. This is where you can get a great coffee and delicious food, then browse the interesting boutiques, galleries and fascinating Whittaker's musical museum.

From the Oneroa Village shops, descend Ocean View Road and turn left up Goodwin Ave to follow the less travelled route along Queens Drive, Hauraki Road, Cory Road and Hill Road, almost to the Palm Beach shops. Then continue from Palm Beach on Bay Road, Crescent Road West, View Road, Seaview Road and down Seventh Avenue to The Strand at Onetangi Bay. This is a stunning beach, and there are good cafes at the far end.

Stage 2 (optional): Onetangi Bay to the far end and back
32 km, 3–5 hours, hilly sealed and gravel roads

To complete this stage, take Third Avenue out of Onetangi Bay, turn left onto Waiheke Road and enjoy the quiet half of Waiheke Island!

Turn left at Man O'War Bay Road to do a long loop around to Stony Batter Lookout (optional side trip to the historic gun emplacements), Man O' War Bay, Cowes Bay Road and Orapiu Road back to Waiheke Road and Onetangi. Even

Don't forget to pack your togs!

though these roads have a 100 kph speed limit, they are relatively quiet and a joy to cycle – unless you detest hills.

Stage 3: Onetangi to Matiatia Bay (ferry)
12 km, 1.5–2 hours, sealed roads and gravel path

Once back at Onetangi, head south on Onetangi Road, which becomes Ostend Road, and then Belgium Street. Turn left at the end of Belgium Street, then right onto a walkway leading directly to Wilma Road.

From the southern end of Wilma Road, follow the main road west to the Surfdale shops before turning left onto Blake Street, and following the narrow Esplanade around the coast.

Turn right at Moa Ave, then left at Nikau Road, right at Tui Street and left to follow Mako Street up to Church Bay Road. Turn right at Church Bay Road and then left at Ocean View Road to coast back down to Matiatia Bay and the ferry terminal.

FACT FILE

Overview Waiheke Island has 8000 permanent residents, with the number more than doubling during summer holidays when festivities are in full swing. The quietest time to visit is during a working week.

How to get there Fullers Ferries depart for the island from 99 Quay Street, downtown Auckland (bottom of Queen Street) roughly every half hour throughout the day. A return trip takes up to an hour and costs around $38 (free to anyone over the age of 65 with a Gold Card on the weekends and public holidays and after 9am on weekdays). Bikes are carried free. Check www.fullers.co.nz for a timetable. Fullers also run a bus service on the island, with bike racks, should you wish to pedal only part of the way.

Riding surface 70% sealed road, 28% gravel road, 2% gravel path

History The island became a refuge for counter-culture in the 1960s and 70s, which has imbued it with a unique and refreshingly laid-back way of life. It was the first community in New Zealand to declare itself nuclear free and is now home to a range of artists, organic food growers, wineries and great cooks.

Special considerations The island is hilly, so you might just have to walk some hills or hire an e-bike from Oneroa (see below).

SUPPORT SERVICES

Fullers Ferry services (for ferry and bus details) www.fullers.co.nz/destinations/waiheke-island/ ☎ 0800 385 5377 or 09 367 9111

Waiheke Island information www.waiheke.co.nz

The Waiheke Mountain Bike Club has built tracks suitable for all grades of off-road rider: www.wmbc.co.nz

Matiatia Ferry terminal and cafe

Oneroa Village Cafes, restaurants, galleries, supermarket, movie theatre. Bike hire from E-CyclesNZ: ☎ 022 050 2233, www.ecyclesnz.com

Onetangi Beach Cafes, restaurants, accommodation

Onetangi Road Takeaways and dairy

Ostend and **Surfdale** have shopping centres.

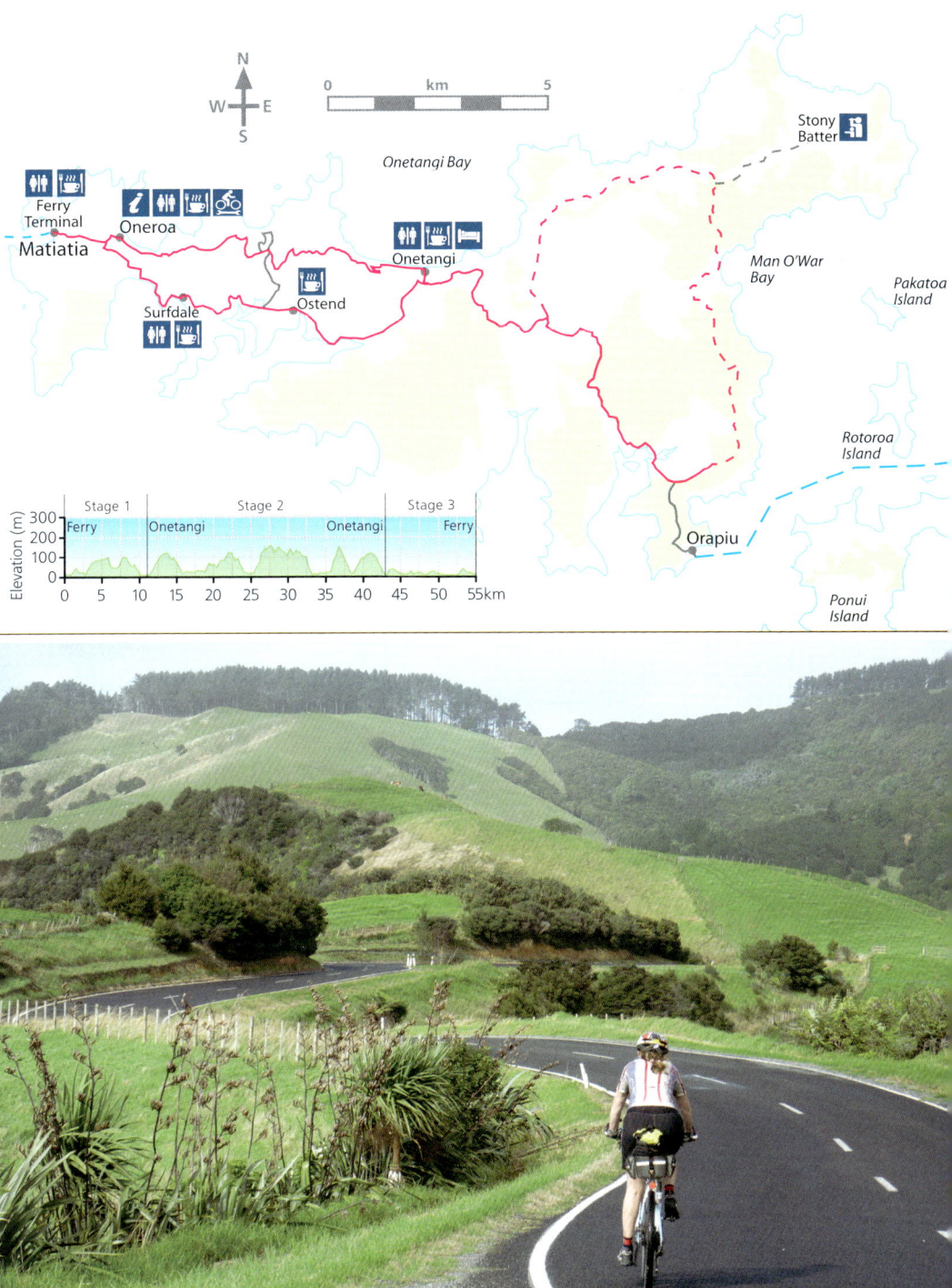

Classic New Zealand Cycle Trails 41

> HEARTLAND RIDE

Auckland's Great Escape
Auckland to Raglan
Distance 110 km   Time 2 days   Grade 3 (Intermediate)

With a little help from a commuter train, this ride soon has you exploring surprisingly remote and peaceful countryside en route to the popular surfing town of Raglan.

Catching the train out of the metropolis is a lot quicker and easier than tunnelling out of Fort Knox, and once you're spinning through the scenic reserves and farmland south of Port Waikato, you'll wonder why you didn't escape sooner.

South of the port, the road climbs over several moderate hills, each leading to valleys with dramatic limestone outcrops.

Although the ride is feasible in one long day, most people choose to stay a night at Nikau Cave and Café, making the next day an easy ride to Raglan with plenty of time for looking around and a leisurely swim in Raglan Harbour.

ITINERARY

Stage 1: Pukekohe to Nikau Cave and Café
70 km riding, 8–10 hours including train and sightseeing time
Take a two-stage commuter train ride from Auckland to Pukekohe (see page 44 for an alternative pedaling route). Allow 1.5–2 hours, including a train change-over at Papakura.

From the terminus at Pukekohe station, head south on Station Road for 500 metres, then right down Subway Road for 400 metres and left onto Manukau Road, which soon becomes Buckland Road and heads out of town. After 10 km you'll roll through Tuakau, where Ed Hillary grew up.

Take the main road through town, which becomes River Road. Just before crossing the Waikato (NZ's longest river), you'll pass Les Batkin Reserve, where there are toilets and picnic tables. This is 14 km into the ride.

Cross the bridge (carefully waiting for a gap in traffic) and then turn right, onto the Port Waikato Road.

Port Waikato is 38 km from Pukekohe. The first sign of it is the wharf and a small store beside a car park on your right. Another few hundred metres and you can turn right down Maunsell Street to go to Maraetai Bay Reserve (39 km, toilets and picnic tables), and the Holiday Park and takeaways (39.7 km). The road finally comes to an end at the beach (41 km), where there is good surfing and Sylvia's Café (great food and second-hand books).

Sylvia's Café is worth checking out, but then back track 2 km and continue south on Waikaretu Road. The road is sealed for several kilometres as it climbs away from the coast. Then it drops into a sunken valley bordered by cliffs at Limestone Downs (52 km). You'll pass a couple more scenic reserves, including Eric Baker Scenic Reserve, which has large kauri trees and an old picnic table (keep away from the base of the kauri trees to avoid infecting them with disease). Shortly after, the road becomes sealed again.

At the 69 km mark, turn onto Waikaretu Valley Road, and ride an easy 1.5 km to Nikau Cave and Café.

Stage 2: Nikau Cave to Raglan
40 km, 2–3 hours

From Nikau Cave, head back down Waikaretu Valley Road for 1.5 km, before turning left (south) on Pukerewa Road, which becomes Te Akau Coast Road. It's all gravel and narrows to a county lane approaching Raglan Harbour. Make sure you take Te Akau South Road, followed by Te Akau Wharf Road. Then 38.5 km from Nikau Cave, veer left down a road with no name to the harbour a few hundred metres away.

The back road to Raglan.

The concrete landing ramp at the end of the road is sheltered by an amphitheatre of low limestone cliffs and is a great spot for a swim. You can get cell phone coverage here – but there are no shops or any amenities. You need to have prearranged for the boat to take you across to Raglan (a 10-minute trip), where there are lots of shops and accommodation, toilets, etc.

FACT FILE
Overview This makes for a great weekend trip and, quite simply, it's the best way to start a long tour of the North Island. Once a busy shipping destination, Port Waikato is now a laid-back holiday town at the mouth of New Zealand's longest river, the Waikato. Raglan is a larger town, famous for surfing and creative arts, and the Orca Café opposite the jetty is highly recommended.

How to get there Catch a commuter train from the Britomart Transport Centre in central Auckland to Papakura (1 hour), then another train to Pukekohe (30 mins). Avoid evening rush hour, as the trains may have no spare space for bikes.

Die-hard cyclists can start from Auckland if they wish by riding the Tour Aotearoa course most of the way to Papakura, then heading south along Great South Road to Drury. After passing under the motorway, turn left onto Old Great South Road. Continue south to Bombay, turn right onto Mill Road, then left at Harrisville Road to arrive at Tuakau. That's 75 km, and thousands of vehicles.

Riding surface 50% sealed road, 50% gravel road

Special considerations There is no cell phone coverage at Nikau Cave. Take lots of water as this is a remote ride. You will need to book the Raglan Harbour boat in advance (phone Iain Hardy on 027 481 215).

Alternative route Traditionally, cycle tourists have ridden from Pukekohe straight down the old Highway 22 to Raglan. That's the route we've had in previous editions. It's 108 km and all sealed but has a lot more traffic, so we prefer this new route. But the old Highway 22 route could be combined with the ride above to create a worthy 3–4 day loop from Auckland.

Maps Kiwimap *Waikato-Bay of Plenty Rural Road Map*

SUPPORT SERVICES

Auckland Transport info ☎ 0800 10 30 80, http://at.govt.nz/bus-train-ferry

Pukekohe Large town with food (Kaos Café is recommended) and accommodation: www.franklincountry.com

Tuakau 4 Square supermarket

Port Waikato Stretched-out village with a small store at the jetty, Port Waikato Holiday Park in the middle offering drinks and ice creams as well as cabins and campsites, phone 09 232 9857, http://www.portwaikatoholidaypark.co.nz/ and Sylvia's Café at the far end of the road to the beach with great food and a relaxed ambiance.

Nikau Cave and Café Food, award-winning coffee, good food and accommodation, www.nikaucave.co.nz, ☎ 09 233 3199. Bookings essential as accommodation is limited. They also run 2-hour cave tours.

Raglan Accommodation, shops, food: www.raglan.net.nz, www.raglan23.co.nz, Cyclery Raglan is a real cyclist's bike shop! Also offers bike hire: 10 Bankart Street, phone 021 238 0818, www.cycleryraglan.co.nz

Book the boat across the Raglan Harbour in advance. It's a short trip, in a small boat, which cost $10 per person in 2017. Phone Iain Hardy on 027 481 215.

CONNECTOR RIDE

AUCKLAND TO HAURAKI RAIL TRAIL

Downtown Auckland to Miranda Hot Springs
Distance 112 km Time 1–2 days   Grade 5 (Expert) because of traffic

Hard-core cyclists may be determined to ride from Auckland to Hauraki despite having to run the gauntlet on a few busy roads. If you are one of them, we salute you! We'll even provide the best advice on how to get there.

This is part of the Tour Aotearoa route. The navigation is complicated, but this is the best route local cyclists recommend.

From the Upper Queen Street end of the Northwestern Cycle Route, follow Alex Evans Street, then turn right onto Symonds Street and left onto Mt Eden Road. You'll pass shops, including Mt Eden Cycles.

At the entrance to Mt Eden Domain, take the 10-minute side trip up to the Maungawhau/Mt Eden volcanic cone for 360-degree views of Auckland.

Back on the route, continue along Mt Eden Road, turn left onto Stokes Road, right onto Epsom Ave, right onto Gillies Ave, left onto Ranfurly Road and right onto Manukau Road.

One block down Manukau Road, turn left onto Campbell Cres, then take the second left to ride right through Cornwall Park on Puriri Drive (which becomes Pohutukawa Drive), Twin Oaks Drive and, after turning left beside a gate in a rock wall, Grand Drive. Grand Drive exits the park at the top of Onehunga Mall.

Ride all the way down Onehunga Mall, past lots of shops, and veer right 200 metres after crossing Neilson Street to get to the end of the mall. From the cul-de-sac, follow a cycle path to Old Mangere Bridge.

Cross the bridge and follow NZCT signs, along Kiwi Esplanade, Shortt Ave, Wallace Road, Creamery Road, Greenwood Road, left at Ascot Road, and along Kirkbride Road (use the path if busy), Westney Road, Timberly Road, Verissimo Drive, then take the path to a new shopping centre with a Countdown supermarket, and 100 metres further on, a good cafe with a car-shaped bike stand, on Leonard Isitt Drive. You are now very close to Auckland Airport.

Turn left at Tom Pearce Drive, left again at Puhinui Road. Go left-right-left at Kenderdine Road, Bridge Street and Cambridge Terrace to get across the railway lines and back onto Puhinui Road.

The last shops before leaving Auckland are on your left where you cross Great South Road (takeaways, fruit shop, general store, etc).

After crossing Great South Road, continue straight ahead onto Reagan Road. Veer right onto Boundary Road and Hollyford Drive. Turn left at Aspiring, right onto Rakaia Rise, cut through a pedestrian path between numbers 19 and 21, then left on Santa Monica Place, and left onto Redoubt Road at the T junction.

Turn right into Totara Park and ride the main Bridle Track through the park. You'll pass public toilets and a picnic area just before you reach Wairere Road.

At the end of Wairere Road, turn right onto Hill Road and left onto Stratford Road, then continue straight onto Alfriston Road. Turn right onto Alfriston-Ardmore Road, and straight onto Mullins Road.

Coastal option: *At this point, if traffic volumes are low, you may prefer to ride east via Clevedon to the coast and around the Firth of Thames to Miranda. It takes an hour longer but is more scenic. However, the roads are narrow and there is too much traffic during weekends and holidays to make this a pleasant option at these times.*

To continue along the main cycle route, at the end of Mullins Road, turn left at Papakura-Clevedon Road, then right onto Ardmore Quarry Road. Go left onto Creightons Road, right at Jones Road, left onto Garvie Road, right at John Hill Road then left at Hunua Road.

Ride through the village of Hunua (there is a dairy and an Indian restaurant), and stay on Hunua Road. It becomes Paparimu Road. After a few kilometres, turn right onto Lyons Road, left onto Mangatawhiri Road and veer left onto Mangatangi Road, which becomes Miranda Road and leads to Miranda. Veer left at East Coast Road and, after 350 metres, turn right onto the Hauraki Rail Trail. Follow it for 3.3 km to Front Miranda Road. Cross the road and head right to go to Miranda Holiday Park and Hot Springs. If you turn left you'll be following the Haurakai Rail Trail to Thames.

Notes Mt Eden Cycles, ☎ 09 630 1201 or see www.mtedencycles.co.nz

Accommodation There are several motels on Kirkbridge Road, and a backpackers near the airport (see www.kiwiairportbackpackers.co.nz). There's also a campground at Ambury Regional Park (2.5 km off the route – lovely ride) 43 Ambury Road, ☎ 09 301 0101 for bookings.

Hunua accommodation and camping. 'The Bike Bunker' at 66 Head Road Hunua. Contact Sally ☎ 021 0231 3706 or email sal.freebairn@gmail.com

Miranda Holiday Park and Hot Springs ☎ 0800 833 144, www.mirandaholidaypark.co.nz

See also www.kennett.co.nz/maps/tour-aotearoa/ for a detailed map.

HEARTLAND RIDE

Raglan to Waitomo Caves

Raglan Harbour to Waitomo Caves
Distance 142–158 km   Time 2 days
Grade 4 (Advanced – for fitness)

Quiet roads, beautiful holiday destinations and fabulous scenery combine to make Kawhia one of the best cycling regions in the country. It is hilly though, so fitness is essential.

From the coastal holiday town of Raglan, the ride heads south on scenic and sometimes narrow roads, past Aotea Harbour and around Kawhia Harbour to the picturesque village of Kawhia. Both Raglan and Kawhia are the sorts of small towns you could easily fall in love with. At the very least, they deserve a one-night stand.

The trail then passes several stunning scenic reserves, with cliffs, caves, forests and waterfalls, all within a stone's throw of the road. There is the option of a side trip to one of New Zealand's classic coastal camping grounds – Marokopa. The final buzz is the long downhill to Waitomo Caves, home to a wide range of caving tours.

ITINERARY

Stage 1: Raglan to Kawhia
55 km, 4–6 hours

From the Bow Street shops in the centre of Raglan, head down to the wharf to take the large pedestrian bridge across the inlet to ride along Marine Parade to Wainui Road. Turn right up Wainui Road for 300 metres then turn left onto Te Hutewai Road.

About 11 km from Raglan, turn right on Waimaunga Road and follow it for 2.5 km before veering left onto Ruapuke Road. At the end of Ruapuke Road, turn right and after 200 metres you will reach a picnic table under some trees in the village of Te Mata (19 km from Raglan).

From Te Mata, head south on Te Mata Road. After 2 km, you will pass a turn-off to Bridal Veil Falls (4 km away).

Continue south on Te Papatapu Road, over low hills and then around the head of Aotea Harbour. At the 34 km mark out of Raglan, the road name will change to Kawhia Road. Continue south to Highway 31, which is 50 km from Raglan and 5 km from Kawhia. Turn right to go to the harbourside village of Kawhia.

Slipping over an inlet at Kawhia Harbour.

Stage 2: Kawhia to Waitomo Caves
87 km, 6–9 hours

From Kawhia, head back up Highway 31, past Kawhia-Raglan Road, to the Oparau Roadhouse and picnic area (13 km from Kawhia).

Continue past the roadhouse for another 2 km and turn right to follow Harbour Road for 18 km to the southern end of Kawhia Harbour. There is a nice picnic area at Willow Point (35 km). After another 4 km you will reach a T-intersection, where you should turn left to follow Te Waitere Road towards Te Anga. Turn left again at the next T-intersection to follow Taharoa Rd down to Te Anga, 55 km from Kawhia.

From the intersection at Te Anga, you can ride 15 km down to the beautiful coastal village of Marokopa, which has a camping ground and a small store. Alternatively, head left and climb for almost 2 km to the Marokopa Falls (a 500-metre walk from the road).

After checking out the falls, continue following Te Anga Road for another 2 km and you will reach another short walk to the Mangapohue Natural Bridge. There are picnic tables and toilets just off the road. From here, there is a fair bit of climbing to the top of a hill, and just over the top is Haggas Lookout, with a picnic table and interpretation board.

It's mostly downhill from Haggas Lookout to Waitomo Caves, 10 km away, where there are cafes, accommodation, an information centre, and of course, caves.

Optional extra stage: Waitomo Caves to Te Kuiti
16 km, 1–1.5 hours

From Waitomo Caves, the best way to Te Kuiti (16 km away) is over Fullerton Road and left down Oparure Road. When you reach Highway 3, 11 km from Waitomo, turn right for 300 metres and then left down Te Kumi Station Road. Straight after crossing the railway line, turn right down Somerville Road, which leads into Te Kuiti via the Esplanade and King Street East.

FACT FILE

Overview The quintessential quiet backcountry road tour. Great scenery, cool towns and several short side walks.

How to get there Ride via Auckland's Great Escape (1–2 days)

Riding surface 80% sealed road, 20% gravel road

Special considerations These are very isolated roads, so you will need to be reasonably self-sufficient.

Maps Kiwimap *Waikato-Bay of Plenty*

SUPPORT SERVICES

Raglan Accommodation, shops, food: www.raglan.net.nz, www.raglan23.co.nz, Cyclery Raglan is a real cyclist's bike shop! Also offers bike hire: 10 Bankart Street, ☎ 021 238 0818, www.cycleryraglan.co.nz

Kawhia Harbour Shops and accommodation: www.kawhiaharbour.co.nz

Oparau Roadhouse Shop, cafe, petrol station and accommodation: www.oparauroadhouse.com

Marokopa Accommodation and food: Marokopa Campground and Village Snack Bar: ☎ 07 876 7444 or 027 918 3751, www.marakopa.co.nz. Marokopa holiday homes: www.bookabach.co.nz

Waitomo Caves A few shops and accommodation: www.waitomo.org.nz

Te Kuiti Lots of shops and accommodation: www.waitomo.org.nz

GREAT RIDE

Hauraki Rail Trail
Kaiaua to Waihi and Te Aroha
Distance Up to 101 km   Time 1–3 days   Grade 1 (Very Easy)

This trail follows historic railway lines across the Hauraki plains and through the stunning Karangahake Gorge. The smooth surface and gentle gradient makes it one of the cushiest trails in the North Island.

This is a trail is a triple treat. The Seabird Coast section from Kaiaua to Thames is a bird watchers dream. It is followed by a railtrail to Paeroa and on to Te Aroha which marches between dairy farms – flat and green, but not exactly clean (watch out for the cow pats).

The section from Paeroa to Waihi snakes through the scenic Karangahake Gorge, crosses unusual bridges, dives through a long tunnel, passes the remains of historic buildings and includes a stretch of regenerating native forest.

ITINERARY

Stage 1: Kaiaua to Thames
45 km, 3–5 hours

From the seaside village of Kaiaua, ride south on East Coast Road (note, that there are plans to build an off-road cycle path from here to Miranda in 2018). This is the seabird coast, and is famous among ornithologists.

After 9 km, there is an off-road trail on your left, which leads to Miranda Hot Springs, where there is food and accommodation, as well as soothing hot pools.

From Miranda Hot Springs, continue following the trail, now beside Front Miranda Road to the town of Waitakaruru and then around the coast to a suburb called Kopu. From there, you can turn left and ride to Thames (4 km away) or right and head to Paeroa.

Stage 2: Thames to Paeroa
34 km, 2–4 hours

The Thames i-SITE and most shops are on Pollen Street. From the shops, take any side street to the west and ride to the coast. At the Thames Coastal Walkway – a smooth path – turn left and ride down to the trail at the wharf.

From The Wharf cafe, the trail generally runs beside the main road out of town, then across farm paddocks and under the main highway. After 12 km, there is a sign inviting you to visit The Cheese Barn cafe, 200 metres off the trail at Matatoki. It's a great spot for your first rest.

Satisfy your 'inner mouse' at The Cheese Barn.

From The Cheese Barn, ride back to the trail and continue south for 10 km to Hikutaia, where there is another popular cafe, The Convenient Cow – be careful crossing the highway here.

It is 12 km from the Cow cafe to the world-famous-in-New Zealand L&P soft-drink town of Paeroa. This is the hub of the trail. You have to pay careful attention to the signs as you pass through Paeroa or you may get lost.

Stage 3: Paeroa to Waihi
22 km, 2–4 hours

This is the most popular section of the trail and over summer is likely to become crowded. This section is so darned good, you may want to ride it there and back.

From the Paeroa info centre, cross the road and follow the trail south along the stopbank to a road bridge on your right. Cross the bridge on the pedestrian path.

Once you are across the Ohinemuri River bridge, cross the road on your left to follow the path down Rotokohu Road past a school (the path to the right goes to Te Aroha). After a few kilometres, you will enter Karangahake Gorge. There are bridges, bush, heritage sites and even a long tunnel on the way to the lovely Waikino Railway Station. A vintage train runs from Waikino to Waihi at 2:30 pm over summer and during holidays. It takes bikes.

Alternatively, backtrack 200 metres from Waikino and continue on to Waihi 8 km further on. This section is a grade harder due to short steep hills.

Classic New Zealand Cycle Trails

Stage 4: Paeroa to Te Aroha
21 km, 2 hours

From the far side of the bridge on the outskirts of Paeroa, head south on the rail trail. You can't get lost. It is flat and straight. You can stop for devonshire tea at the lovely Depot Gardens. The trail ends at the old railway station in Te Aroha, two blocks from the main street. Te Aroha has wonderful hot pools and good mountain bike tracks.

FACT FILE

Overview Another stage is planned from Te Aroha south to Matamata.

How to get there To bike to the trail from Auckland see Connector: Auckland to Hauraki Rail Trail, page 46.

Riding surface Smooth gravel rail trail with a few short sections on quiet roads.

History The environment around this trail is dominated by mining and farming. The most fascinating historic mine relics are located at the Victoria Battery Site near Waikino.

Special features There is an amazing 'windows walk' that you can do in the Karangahake Gorge. We recommend you pick up the DOC pamphlet about the gorge from any of the local information centres.

Maps Pick up a trail map from an information centre in Thames, Paeroa, Te Aroha or Waihi, or from the trail website.

Trail website www.haurakirailtrail.co.nz

SUPPORT SERVICES

Two businesses offer transport, bike hire and trip itineraries: Hauraki Cycle Trail Ltd ☎ 027 203 9719, www.haurakicycletrail.co.nz, and Jolly Bikes ☎ 07 867 9026 or 021 0816 5000, www.jollybikes.co.nz

Kaiaua Accommodation, diary and takeways

Miranda Hot Springs Accommodation and takeways, ☎ 0800 833 144

Thames Accommodation, shops, food: www.thamesinfo.co.nz

Matatoki The Cheese Barn, open seven days: www.thecheesebarn.co.nz

Hikutaia Thames Valley Homestay: ☎ 07 862 4827/(mob) 027 437 6458, www.thamesvalleyhomestay.co.nz

Paeroa Accommodation, shops, food: www.paeroa.org.nz

Waikino The railway station has a lovely cafe.

Waihi Food, accommodation: www.waihi.org.nz

Tirohia Devonshire tea at the Depot Garden, ☎ 07 862 7900

Te Aroha Food, accommodation: www.tearohanz.co.nz

CONNECTOR RIDE

HAURAKI RAIL TRAIL TO WAIKATO RIVER TRAIL

Te Aroha to Horahora Road
Distance 64 km   Time 1 day   Grade 4 (Advanced – because of traffic)

This route has been designed for cyclists to get from Hauraki Rail Trail to the Waikato River Trail.

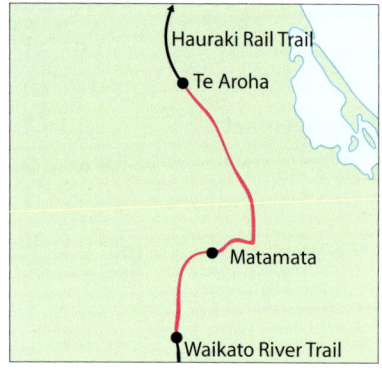

From Te Aroha Station, ride 200 metres to near the south corner of Terminus Street and take the path across the river to Spur Street. At the end of Spur Street, turn left down Stanley Road and ride out of town, past the Te Aroha Holiday Park.

Stanley Road road turns into Alexandra Road. Veer left down Manawaru Road, cruise through Manawaru. At the crossroads, 8 km further on, go straight onto Tower Road. From the historic Firth Tower, the last 2 km into Matamata (36 km from Te Aroha) are on a cycle path beside the road. Turn right off Tower Road, and cruise 1 km down Broadway to the i-SITE (on your left).

Matamata is rebranding itself as Hobbiton – as you can tell from the amazing i-SITE. There are plenty of shops in town, including a bike shop at 47 Firth Street (phone 07 888 7262), just around the corner from the i-SITE.

From the i-SITE, ride south down Hetana Street, which becomes Arawa Street, right down Tainui, which turns into Farmers Road, then left down Smith Street.

At the end of Smith, turn right onto Station Road and head out of town. Five kilometres from town, turn left at Matai Road, then 3 km later, turn right at Puketutu Road. At Highway 29 (12 km from Matamata), turn right and stick in the shoulder lane for the next 9 km, then turn left onto Highway 1. Again, stay in the shoulder for 1 km, before crossing the highway at Horahora Road. The Waikato River Trail starts 4.4 km down this country road and is clearly signposted.

Notes

Te Aroha Food, accommodation: www.tearohanz.co.nz. Te Aroha Holiday Park, 217 Stanley Road, ☎ 07 884 9567, www.tearohaholidaypark.co.nz

Firth Tower museum, toilets, drinks and ice creams

Matamata Accommodation: www.matamata.co.nz; On the trail is Broadway Motel, 128 Broadway, ☎ 07 888 8482 and Horse and Jockey Inn, 81 Arawa St, ☎ 07 888 9972, www.horseandjockeyinn.co.nz

Okauia Accommodation: Opal Hot Springs (motel and camping), 2.5 km from the trail at 257 Okauia Springs Road, ☎ 07 888 8198

CONNECTOR RIDE

CAMBRIDGE TO WAIKATO RIVER TRAIL

Cambridge to Arapuni
Distance 40 km   Time 2–3 hours   Grade 3 (Intermediate)

From Cambridge, a mix of cycle lanes, separate paths and country roads provides an excellent link to the Waikato River Trail. This connector glances past Lake Karapiro (famous for rowing events) and skirts around Maungatautari Scenic Reserve. It's very pleasant cycling with no hills over 100 m high.

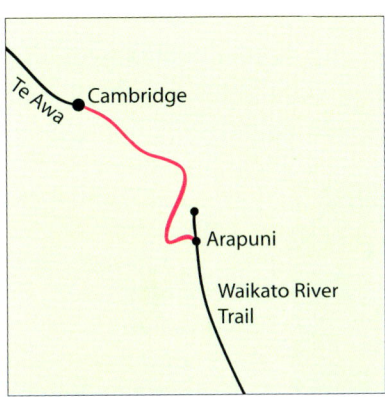

From Cambridge information centre, on the corner of Queen and Lake streets, ride south on Lake Street followed by Victoria Street. After 1.1 km, cross the Waikato River on Victoria Bridge and turn east onto Cook Street. Ride down Cook Street for 500 metres before turning right onto Shakespeare Street. Follow Shakespeare Street for 600 metres, then turn left onto Raleigh Street and ride for a further 600 metres to the start of the off-road Te Awa River Ride path at the Leamington Football Club. From here, there is an 8-km cycle path beside Maungatautari Road to Lake Karapiro Domain and on beside the lake to the start of the Karapiro rowing course.

From Lake Karapiro, the route jumps onto Maungatautari Road and continues along it for 13 km before turning right onto Oreipunga Road. It follows Oreipunga Road for 14.4 km, then turns left onto Arapuni Road. After crossing the first of two bridges over the Waikato River (right next to each other), turn left onto Powerhouse Road (there is a rest area with toilets at this intersection). This is a private road owned by Mighty River Power. Go down Powerhouse Road for 1.4 km before crossing New Zealand's longest swing bridge (151 metres) on your right. The Waikato River Trail is at the far end, and 80 metres further on is the main street of Arapuni. Turn left down the main street to reach the scrummy Rhubarb Cafe.

The small village of Arapuni is 13 km from the northern end of the Waikato River Trail.

GREAT RIDE

Te Awa River Ride

Ngaruawahia, Hamilton and Cambridge
Distance 58 km   Time 1 hour–2 days
Grades 2 and 3 (Easy and Intermediate)

Think Te Awa and think wide, flat paths flowing beside the lazy Waikato River. As easy as drifting in a boat down the river, this ride is perfect for everyone.

Te Awa is still under construction, but it's shaping up well, with two easy stages, from Ngaruwahia to Hamilton and Cambridge to Karapiro, ready to ride right now. The trail goes straight through Hamilton City, along the south side of the mighty Waikato River and provides beautiful views as it meanders through parks and gardens. You would hardly know you were in a city, except that the path is so well used by walkers, runners and cyclists.

The second completed stage runs from the south-eastern edge of Cambridge to the large public domain on Lake Karapiro, the home of a multitude of rowing regattas.

ITINERARY

Stage 1: Ngaruawahia to Hamilton
20-25 km, 2–3 hours, Grade 2 (Easy)

From Lower Waikato Esplanade in Ngaruawahia, the trail follows the Waikato River for 4.5 km before crossing the impressive 130-metre long Perry Bridge. If you're desperate for food, there is an option, at the 8.7 km mark, to divert for 500 m to a shopping village right next to the Perry Bike Park.

The path is mostly concrete and paved stone, with lots of walkers close to Hamilton. Continue following the trail towards Hamilton. There are numerous access/exit points to the CBD, which is 20 km from Ngaruawahia.

After about 24 km, cross the Waikato River on the major Highway 1 bridge - there is a cycle path leading all the way to the Hamilton Gardens (toilets, cafe and car parking).

Stage 2: Hamilton to Cambridge
25 km, 2 hours, Grade 3 (Intermediate)

In future, the off-road path will be completed between Hamilton and Cambridge, but for now confident cyclist are riding the following roads. From the gardens, ride east to the end of Hungerford Crescent and then follow a path to Howell Ave. At the end of Howell Ave, turn right at Highway 1, and follow a bike path for 650 metres before turning right again down Newell Road. After pedalling

Lake Karapiro Domain, Te Awa River Ride

down Newell Road for 3.5 km, continue on Devine Road and soon after turn right onto Wiremu Tamihana Drive, left down Highway 21 and then right onto Tamahere Drive. After another 3 km, turn left onto Pickering Road, go under the highway, and then right down Strawberry Fields Lane, which becomes Hautapu Road. Turn right down Peake Road, which ends at Cambridge Road. Turn right and ride to the Avantidrome, from where the off-road trail resumes and goes to Cambridge a few kilometres away.

Stage 3: Cambridge to Lake Karapiro
8 km, 1–2 hours, Grade 2 (Easy)

This stage starts from the corner of Raleigh and Carlyle Streets by the Leamington Clubrooms. To get there from the centre of Cambridge, head south on Victoria St, across the bridge, left along Cook St, right up Shakespeare St left at Raleigh St, which ends opposite the clubrooms (2.7 km from the centre of town).

From Carlyle Street, a gentle, 3-metre-wide concrete path leads to Lake Karapiro Domain, 5.5 km away. Absolutely anyone can give this sort of cycle path a go. It's as easy as, well, riding a bike, and the Lake Karapiro Domain is a great destination, especially if you like rowing, rivers or picnics.

From the Domain, a 2.5 km section heads east to the start of the famous Karapiro Rowing Course. It features an amazing lakeside boardwalk.

The colourful Perry Bridge spans the mighty Waikato River.

FACT FILE

Overview This will possibly the most popular trail in the country when completed. Stage 1 and 3 make a great short rides in their own right. Stage 2 from Hamilton to Cambridge has yet to be built at the time of writing (in 2018) but the on-road option is good for confident cyclists.

Status Te Awa is not (yet) an official Great Ride.

How to get there Hamilton is 125 km south of Auckland (1 hr 40 mins drive).

Riding surface Smooth concrete and paving stones.

History This section of the Waikato River is steeped in Maori history, and its stories are being told alongside the trail as it is being developed.

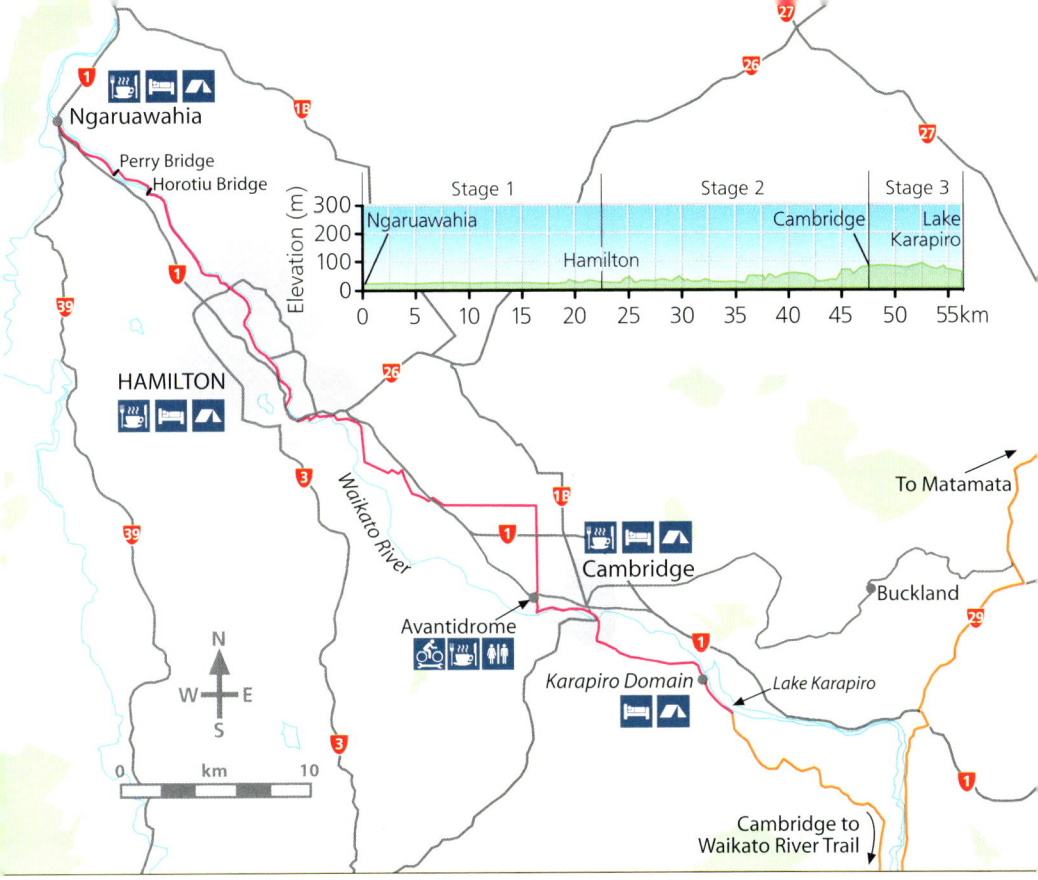

Special considerations One of the key goals of the trail is to enhance the environment between Hakarimata Reserve in the north and Maungatautari Ecological Island in the south.

Special features There are ample signs and interpretation boards along the trail.

Trail website www.te-awa.org.nz

SUPPORT SERVICES

Ngaruawahia Plenty of shops, a supermarket, cafes, accommodation

Hamilton New Zealand's fourth largest city. Plenty of accommodation, shops, restaurants, cafes and a range of bike shops: www.visithamilton.co.nz

Cambridge Large picturesque town, with a good range of accommodation and shops: www.cambridge.co.nz

Cambridge Bike Shop: ☎ 07 827 0485, www.evolutioncycles.co.nz

Lake Karapiro Accommodation and camping available at the Karapiro Domain: www.lakekarapiro.co.nz ☎ 07 827 4178

GREAT RIDE

Waikato River Trail
Between Cambridge and Taupo
Distance 105 km   Time 1 hour to 3 days
Grades 2, 3 and 4 (Easy, Intermediate and Advanced)

Nicknamed 'the Hidden Trail', this is a little-known gem that runs beside New Zealand's longest river. It reveals a series of hydro lakes and dramatic volcanic landscapes as it passes through forest and farmland.

The Waikato River Trail is made up of five stages, stretching from a car park north of the settlement of Arapuni down to Atiamuri, near Lake Taupo. The trail can be ridden in either direction. Some stages flow along easy, gravelled paths suitable for all ages, while others are rough mountain bike tracks, complete with tight switchbacks and steep hills.

Cycle tourers with loaded bikes (especially trailers) should only ride the easy stages. There are on-road alternatives to all intermediate and advanced sections.

Highlights include long boardwalks across wetlands and towering swing bridges spanning beautiful forested ravines.

ITINERARY

Each stage of the trail is named after the lake it follows and starts, or stops, at a hydro dam. All stages can be ridden in both directions.

Stage 1: Karapiro (Arapuni village to Pokaiwhenua Bridge)
13 km one way, 1–2 hours, Grade 2+ (Easy)

Because of the good trail construction and the satisfying destination of the Rhubarb Cafe at the northern end of Arapuni village, this is the most popular stage of the trail and is usually ridden as a there-and-back from Arapuni. The trail is signposted from the corner of Arapuni Road and Rabone Street.

Ride 80 metres towards the river and then turn right at a track fork – make sure you check out the amazing Arapuni swing bridge (New Zealand's longest!).

Ride north for 8 km, including along the 500-metre-long boardwalk through the Huihuitaha Wetlands, to reach the Little Waipa Reserve. This beautiful section of trail offers stunning views of the river.

From the reserve, the trail runs north beside Horahora Road. After 5 km, you'll reach a car park at the northern tip of the Waikato River Trail (this is 4 km south of Highway 1) and just south of Pokaiwhenua Stream. Turn around here for a fast pedal back to the good coffee and cake at the Rhubarb.

An easy morning spin along the Arapuni to Pokaiwhenua Bridge stage.

Stage 2: Arapuni (Arapuni village to Waipapa Dam)
34 km, 4–6 hours, Grade 4 (Advanced)

The 5-km section of trail from Arapuni south to Jones Landing is narrow single track with tight switchbacks. Jones Landing is a recreation/camping reserve.

From Jones Landing, the trail follows a sealed road for 15 km. Continue south on Lake Arapuni Road for 8 km, at which point the road curves to the right and becomes Wiltsdown Road. After another few hundred metres, turn right onto Waotu South Road and follow a 600-metre-long path to Jim Barnett Reserve, a welcome distraction – the trail then heads off road through a small patch of forest for 1.5 km. It rejoins the road at the main entrance to the reserve where there is information on the history of the forest. You can also camp here.

About 22 km from Arapuni, you will reach the end of the long sealed-road climb on Waotu South Road. Here the trail leaves the road and heads down to the river via a series of 37 (!) tight switchbacks. At the bottom, the riding improves a lot as the trail heads through regenerating forest and across a huge swing bridge. About 2 km before the Waipapa Dam, at the end of the stage, is a grunty little climb followed by a flight of wooden steps (to be replaced by a massive bridge in future).

Waipapa Dam is quite impressive and a great spot to stop for a rest.

Stage 3: Waipapa (Waipapa Dam to Mangakino Lakefront Reserve)
20 km, 3-4 hours, Grade 4- (Advanced)

From Waipapa Dam, continue south on an easy section of trail running beside Waipapa Road for almost 2 km. The trail then branches away and heads through forest, where there are a number of difficult steep climbs.

The trail rejoins Waipapa Road near Maraetai Dam and stays on road to Mangakino Lakefront Reserve at the end of Lake Road. Here there are toilets, a cafe and camping areas. Some of this 3-km on-road section may be taken off road in future.

Stage 4: Maraetai (Mangakino Lakefront Reserve to Whakamaru Dam)
13 km, 1.5–2 hours, Grade 3- (Intermediate)

This is one of the best stages of the Waikato River Trail. The gravel surface is generally well compacted, there are very few hills and there is an amazing swing bridge with sweeping views – well worth riding both ways. When you reach Whakamaru Dam, turn right and travel a few hundred metres to reach The Dam Cafe. Alternatively, turn left and cross the dam to ride the final stage.

Stage 5: Whakamaru Dam to Atiamuri
25 km, 2–3 hours, Grade 3- (Intermediate)

The trail starts on the northern side of Whakamaru Dam, so if you have just ridden from Mangakino, you'll need to cross the dam first. At the dam, check out the signboard and then head onto the trail. Early on, the trail follows a gravel road for a bit as it passes a popular camping reserve. Later, you must bypass the 'Stairway to Heaven' by riding on Highway 30 for 300 metres.

The trail ends at a nondescript parking area beside Ongaroto Road, only 100 metres from Highway 1. Eventually the trail will safely cross the highway and continue to Atiamuri village, 1 km away – possibly in late 2018.

FACT FILE

Overview This trail started out in 2004 as a walking track. That's why some stages didn't ride well when it was officially opened in 2011. However, it is being steadily improved. Sections are being re-routed, and thousands of trees are being planted along its flanks.

Further downstream, another trust is constructing Te Awa River Ride. This is currently a 58 km trail between Lake Karapiro, Hamilton and Ngaruawahia (see page 58).

How to get there Most people drive to and from various stages of the trail or arrange shuttle transport with the Waikato River Trails Trust.

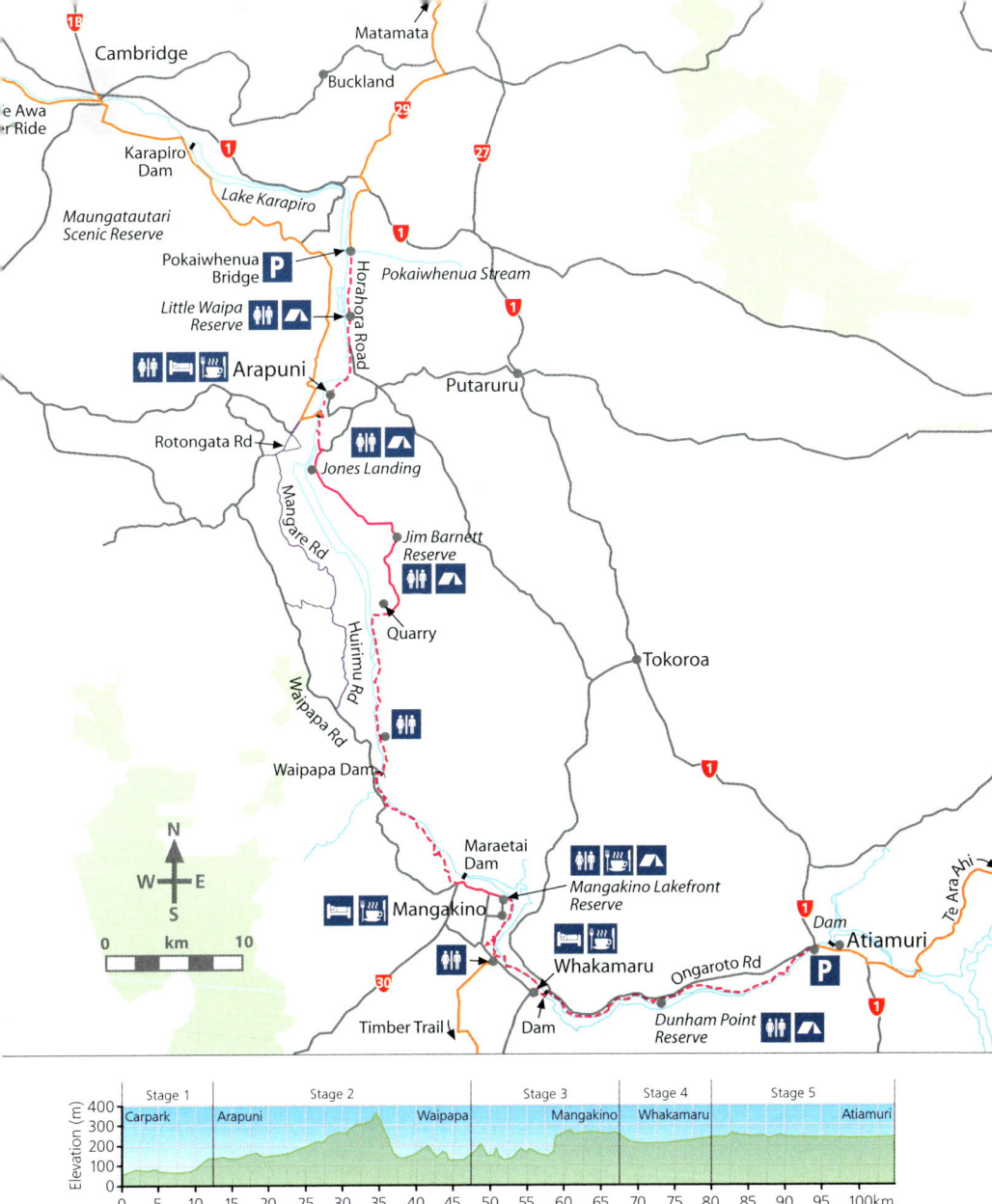

Riding surface *Stage 1:* 99% easy gravel path, 1% sealed road; *Stage 2:* 45% sealed road, 1% unrideable, 54% off-road trail; *Stage 3:* 45% forestry road, 45% off-road trail, 10% sealed road; *Stage 4:* 100% off-road trail; *Stage 5:* 90% off-road trail, 9% gravel road, 1% sealed road

History The Waikato River is 425 km long. It flows from Lake Taupo, over the

Huka Falls and finally enters the Tasman Sea just south of Auckland. It was largely formed by a massive volcanic eruption 1800 years ago. The river has been significantly modified by the construction of eight hydro dams between 1929 and 1971.

Special considerations There is very little difference in elevation from one end of the trail to the other, so it can be ridden just as well in either direction. There are only a few villages along the way, and while the remoteness is something to relish, travellers must be reasonably self-sufficient.

Special features The dominant features are the hydro dams and the long lakes they have created.

Important contacts Excellent information and services are provided by Waikato River Trails, ☎ 07 883 3720, www.waikatorivertrails.com

Maps The trail is well signposted, and there is also a map on the trail website.

Trail website www.waikatorivertrails.com

SUPPORT SERVICES

Waikato River Trails Transport and accommodation bookings: ☎ 07 883 3720, www.waikatorivertrails.com

Pokaiwhenua carpark (start of trail) Lake District Adventures, bike hire and accommodation: ☎ 0800 287 448, www.lakedistrictadventures.co.nz

Arapuni Food, bike hire and guided tours: Rhubarb Cafe: 6 Arapuni Road, ☎ 07 883 5722/(mob) 027 4317 207

Accommodation: Arapuni Backpackers ☎ 021 178 9332, www.arapuni.co.nz Camping along the trail at; Jim Barnett Reserve, www.southwaikato.govt.nz, Little Waipa Reserve, Horahora Road; and Jones Landing, Lake Arapuni Road.

Mangakino Shops and accommodation, www.mangakino.net.nz. Lake Maraetai Lodge: ☎ 0800 882 282, www.lake-maraetai-lodge.co.nz, Mangakino Hotel, ☎ 07 882 8276, www.mangakinohotel.co.nz, Mangakino Lakeside Village Inn (in the old Mangakino Hospital building), ☎ 07 882 8321

Camping available: Mangakino lakefront, Lake Road

Whakamaru Food: The Dam Cafe, Fred's Pizzeria, Whakamaru Store Accommodation: Arataki Farm: ☎ 07 882 8857/(mob) 021 069 5667, www.aratakifarm.com, That Dam Lodge: ☎ 07 882 8292/(mob) 021 0272 5567, www.thatdamlodge.co.nz

CONNECTOR RIDE

WAIKATO RIVER TRAIL TO TE ARA AHI
Atiamuri to Te Kopia Road
Distance 25 km   Time 2 hours   Grade 3 (Intermediate)

This is a scenic corner of the country that hardly anyone would ever think of exploring … unless they wanted to pedal between two Great Rides.

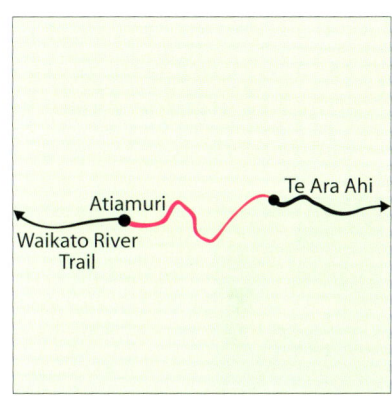

The Waikato River Trail ends on the side of Highway 30, only 100 metres from Highway 1. At the highway, turn right and ride across the Waikato River on the new Highway 1 bridge clip-on.

Ride down Highway 1 for 4 km (the shoulder is good) and then turn left onto Ohakuri Road. Follow Ohakuri Road for 4 km and cross the Lake Ohakuri dam.

Just 1 km after the dam, turn right onto Maleme Road and follow it 8 km to Galatos Road. Turn right at Galatos and veer right at Poutakataka Road to descend to Lake Ohakuri. Turn right to follow Whirinaki Valley Road for 1 km, then turn left at Mangatete Road. After another 4 km later, turn right onto Waikite Valley Road and ride 11 km to Waikite Hot Springs – the end of the Te Ara Ahi Cycle Trail.

Note There are several kilometres of gravel road on this connector route.

GREAT RIDE

Te Ara Ahi, Thermal by Bike
Rotorua
Distance 50 km   Time 1–2 days   Grades 2–3 (Easy–Intermediate)

This trail transports riders through unique geothermal sites, active with geysers and bubbling mud-pools. Highlights include cultural shows, bush walks and the lure of long soaks in soothing hot pools.

The trail is humming with interesting attractions both on and off the bike; so don't expect to cover more than 5 km an hour. The first day, you could just ride to Waimangu Volcanic Valley and back or continue to Waikite Valley Thermal Pools, where you could camp or get a shuttle back to Rotorua.

ITINERARY

Stage 1: Rotorua to Waimangu Volcanic Valley
30 km, 3–4 hours, Grade 2 (Easy)

From the Lake Rotorua i-SITE on Fenton Street, ride east on Queens Drive to Princes Gate Archway where the trail starts. There is an art gallery and museum with lots of parking. Carefully follow blue trail markers past the Polynesian Spa and the end of Amohau Place then through the Sulphur Bay section of the trail. You are heading for Sala Street, and can take the scenic route or the direct route – the signposted scenic route is longer but more interesting.

Just before Sala Street, the trail goes under Highway 5 and then weaves through trees beside a stream. When you are about 6 km out of town, you will pass a few shops at the entrance to the Whakarewarewa Maori Village and thermal area. It's only $40 for a guided tour of this fascinating thermal region.

From Whakarewarewa Village, the trail continues south, past Te Puia, another much larger cultural centre, and onto a new off-road track that leads through Hemo Gorge to the Whakarewarewa Mountain Bike Park car-parking area. This has a cool cafe nestled in an area throbbing with bike culture. You could easily get diverted into the 130-km maze of mountain bike tracks here or just kick back with a flat white and enjoy the vibe.

From the park entrance, head towards Highway 5, a stone's throw away, and you'll pick up a concrete cycle path that glides south beside the highway. It's easy cycling for several kilometres before you nip onto Highlands Loop Road.

Classic New Zealand Cycle Trails

Leaving Rotorua on the path less travelled.

This soon brings you back to a separate cycle path and then leads you away from the highway to Waimangu Road. A few kilometres along this road, you'll reach the entrance to Waimangu Volcanic Valley. There is a great cafe and various walks and tours available here at one of the most impressive thermal areas on the trail.

From this geothermal area, backtrack to Rotorua (mostly downhill) or ride on to stage 2 and the Waikite Valley Thermal Pools.

Stage 2: Waimangu Volcanic Valley to Waikite Valley Thermal Pools
17–21 km, 2–3 hours, Grade 3 (Intermediate)

From Waimangu, continue along Waimangu Road, past Lake Okaro picnic area, to a T-intersection at Highway 38. Cross the highway and pick up an off-road path that leads around Rainbow Mountain (Maungakakaramea) to Waiotapu. You can detour 2 km off to Te Ranga (Kerosene Creek), which is popular for its free hot pools.

At Waiotapu, there is an old-school Kiwi pub (with accommodation), a petrol station and a cafe/store attached to a large honey factory. It's worth diverting to the huge mud pool and the Waiotapu Thermal Wonderland (2 km).

Ride west from the pub along Waikite Valley Road for 6 km to the Waikite Valley Thermal Pools. Open 10 am to 9 pm daily with cafe and camping.

Classic New Zealand Cycle Trails

From Waikite Valley Thermal Pools, you have three choices:
1. Ride back the way you came.
2. Arrange for a shuttle to take you back to Rotorua.
3. Loop back to Rotorua via quiet back roads and the cycle trail (29 km).

Loop return to Rotorua

Head southwest along Waikite Valley Road for 500 metres, then turn right onto Corbett Road. After 4 km, turn right to stay on Corbett Road. Then 2.5 km later (at the bottom of a downhill), turn hard right onto Tumunui Road. Ride 9 km to Highway 5, carefully cross the highway and follow the Te Ara Ahi cycle trail back to Rotorua (12 km away).

FACT FILE

Overview The first two-thirds of this ride, from Rotorua to Waiotapu hot pools, is mostly off road and packed full of features. The rest is all on road, albeit quiet country roads, and there are no points of interest to visit along this stretch until the Waikite Valley Thermal Pools.

How to get there The trail starts in Rotorua. Buses and planes travel there daily. It is 230 km from Auckland.

Riding surface You name it, this trail has it! Cycle paths and lanes, sealed and gravel roads, boardwalks, even some mountain bike tracks.

History For centuries, Maori have been attracted to the thermal hot pools around this trail, and it is rich in culture and heritage. A tour at the Whakarewarewa Maori Village or Te Puia is enlightening.

Special considerations You will need a mountain bike for the few kilometres around Rainbow Mountain to Waiotapu. Alternatively, just ride on the highway shoulder.

Special features The geothermal activity is what makes this ride special – mudpools, geysers, steaming hillsides and hot pools that you can soak in.

Trail website www.nzcycletrail.com

SUPPORT SERVICES

All the geothermal areas are well established with a wide range of amenities such as cafes, souvenir shops, toilets and bike storage facilities.

For transport around the trail, contact Thermal Land Shuttle, ☎ 0800 894 287, www.thermalshuttle.co.nz

Rotorua Lots of accommodation, shops and cultural tours: www.rotoruanz.com

Te Puia Cafe, geysers, culture, ☎ 07 348 9047, www.tepuia.com

Whakarewarewa Cafe, bike hire: ☎ 0800 682 768, www.mtbrotorua.co.nz

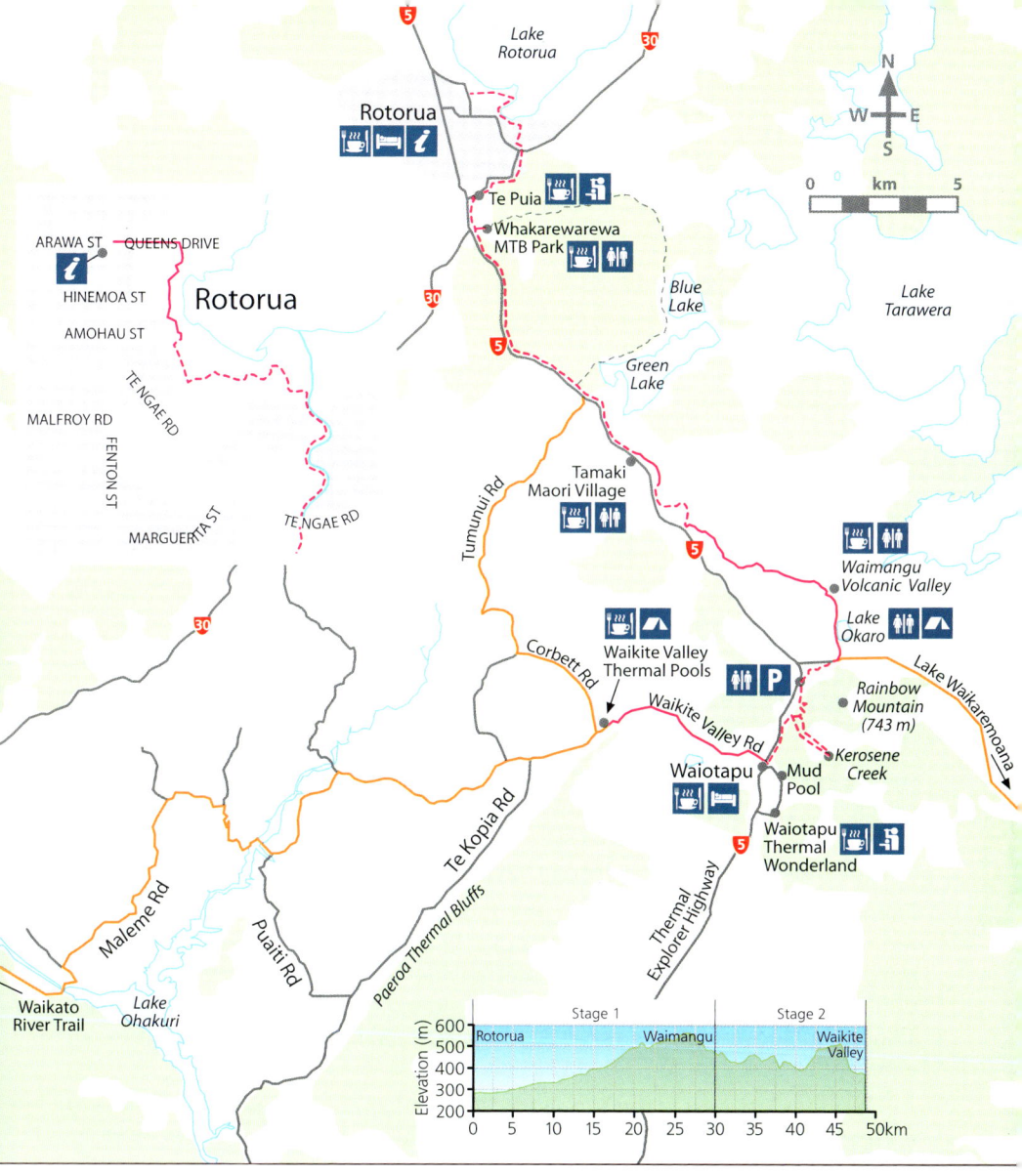

Waimangu Volcanic Valley Cafe, tours: ☎ 07 366 6137, www.waimangu.com

Waiotapu Food, accommodation: Waiotapu Tavern (pub meals and cheap accommodation): ☎ 07 366 6640, www.waiotaputavern.co.nz, Waiotapu Thermal Wonderland is only 2 km away: ☎ 07 366 6333, www.waiotapu.co.nz

Waikite Valley Thermal Pools Great hot pools and camping: ☎ 07 333 1861, www.hotpools.co.nz

GREAT RIDE

The Motu Trails
Opotiki, Bay of Plenty
Distance 10–90 km   Time 1–8 hours
Grades 2 and 3 (Easy and intermediate)

Opotiki has leapt onto the radar as a fabulous cycling destination with the development of a package of three impressive tracks – a platter that offers a range of rides to suit everyone's tastes.

The Dunes Trail is the easiest. Most people do it as a there-and-back ride. It gives great views across the eastern Bay of Plenty and up to the bush-clad peaks of the Raukumara Range.

The Motu Coach Road is ideal for those with an appetite for exercise. It is a narrow gravel road, used by only a few cars a day. In places, the trees meet overhead, and we saw a deer on the road.

For experienced mountain bikers, the Pakihi Track provides the icing on the cake. It's a historic stock route that passes through the beautiful Urutawa Conservation Area.

ITINERARY

Stage 1: Dunes Trail, Opotiki
11 km one way, 1.5–2.5 hours, Grade 2 (Easy)

From the centre of Opotiki, cycle north to the end of St John Street and cross the celebrated Pakowhai-ki-Otutaopuku Bridge (impossible to miss). As the trail's name suggests, the 10-km, 2-metre-wide Dunes Trail rolls along the sand dunes of the Bay of Plenty coast. There are no big hills, and the gravel surface is smooth but loose in places. This is an ideal warm-up for the big loop or makes an excellent easy ride for families and beginners.

The Dunes Trail passes the Tirohanga Holiday Park (a great spot for bikers) and finishes at the main highway, opposite Jackson Road. Head back from here, or follow the directions below to try out the Motu Road and Pakihi Track.

Stage 2: Motu Road to Pakihi Track
38 km, 3–5 hours, Grade 3 (Intermediate)

To link up with Motu Road (also referred to as the 'Old Coach Road'), you'll need to be on your toes for the following tricky little manoeuvre … head up Jackson Road for 860 metres and then, just before the road starts to climb, take a left onto a minor track. Within seconds, you'll cross a cycling bridge and pop onto Motu Road.

Opotiki's popular Dunes Trail.

Motu Road leads to the top of the Pakihi Track (and beyond to Matawai if you are heading that way). There are two big hills to climb. The first is Meremere Hill (447 m), which passes through Meremere Scenic Reserve. From there, you will ride to Toatoa. From Toatoa, the road climbs into Toatoa Scenic Reserve, topping out at 625 m on Papamoa Hill summit. Only 12 km beyond Toatoa, you will reach a large sign, a shelter and a toilet at the top of the Pakihi Track.

For a description of the full Motu Road ride in the reverse direction, see Rere Falls Trail on page 76.

Stage 3: The Pakihi Track to Opotiki
41 km, 3–4 hours, Grade 3 (Intermediate)

The Pakihi Track has virtually no uphills, and the track surface is generally easy. However, there are some vertical drops along the sides of the narrow track.

From the signpost beside Motu Road, dive off into the tall forest. A benched single track descends to Pakihi Hut 10 km away. Almost 1 km past the hut, cross the river on a large suspension bridge and continue down valley on single track. You will reach the track end next to a second swing bridge about 9 km down valley from the hut.

Most people ride from here back to Opotiki. The first 7 km is gravel, with plenty of potholes to dodge. Then it's gently downhill on the sealed Otara Road. Turn right onto Te Rere Pa Road for 500 metres, then left onto the stop bank trail. It leads back to the swing bridge at the start of the Dunes Trail.

FACT FILE

Overview The old Motu Road and the Pakihi Track have no cellphone coverage.

How to get there Drive to the Opotiki information centre on Bridge Street (Highway 2) and ask about their secure parking. Otherwise, fly/bus to Gisborne and ride the Rere Falls Trail to the Motu Trails (highly recommended, page 76).

Shuttle services are available for drop off/pick up, from any part of the trail.

Riding surface The Dunes Trail is 100% gravel path, Motu Road is 30% sealed road and 70% gravel road, the Pakihi Track to Opotiki is 55% single track, 30% sealed road and 15% gravel road.

History Built around 1914, the Motu Coach Road was the original road from the East Coast to the Bay of Plenty. The Pakihi Track was built as a stock route. A local has boasted that the Pakihi took more dynamite per metre to build than any other track in the country. The Dunes Trail was opened in 2012.

Special considerations Motu Road is prone to slips after storms, which close it to motor vehicles – cyclists can usually still sneak through. The Dunes Trail is not good for a fully loaded touring bike because of a series of motorbike squeeze barriers. Try to minimise your load.

Important contacts Department of Conservation in Opotiki, ☎ 07 315 1001

Maps NZTopo BE41 Opotiki and BF41 Oponae are recommended.

Trail website www.motutrails.co.nz

SUPPORT SERVICES

Opotiki Food, accommodation, shops: www.opotikinz.com

Bike shops: Hickeys Opotiki (bike shop, rentals, shuttle): ☎ 07 315 6238, Motu Trails Ltd. (bike hire, shuttles, secure parking): ☎ 07 315 5864, www.motucycletrails.com

Tirohanga Cafe, petrol, accommodation: Tirohanga Beach Motor Camp: ☎ 07 315 7942, www.tirohangabeachmotorcamp.co.nz

Toatoa Accommodation: Toatoa Farmstay: www.toatoaaccommodation.co.nz

Bushaven (near the bottom of the Pakihi Track) Accommodation: Bushaven and Motu Trails Hire and Shuttle: ☎ 0800 668 887, 027 287 4283, www.bushaven.co.nz, Weka Wilds: ☎ 021 142 1515, www.wekawilds.co.nz

Pakihi DOC hut: www.doc.govt.nz/parks-and-recreation/places-to-stay/

Motu Limited accommodation: Motu Community House: ☎ 06 863 5804 or 06 862 8736, email: rakanui@xtra.co.nz. Cafe: Motu-Vation Cafe, ☎ 06 863 5045

Matawai Cafe, accommodation: Matawai Campground: ☎ 06 862 4800

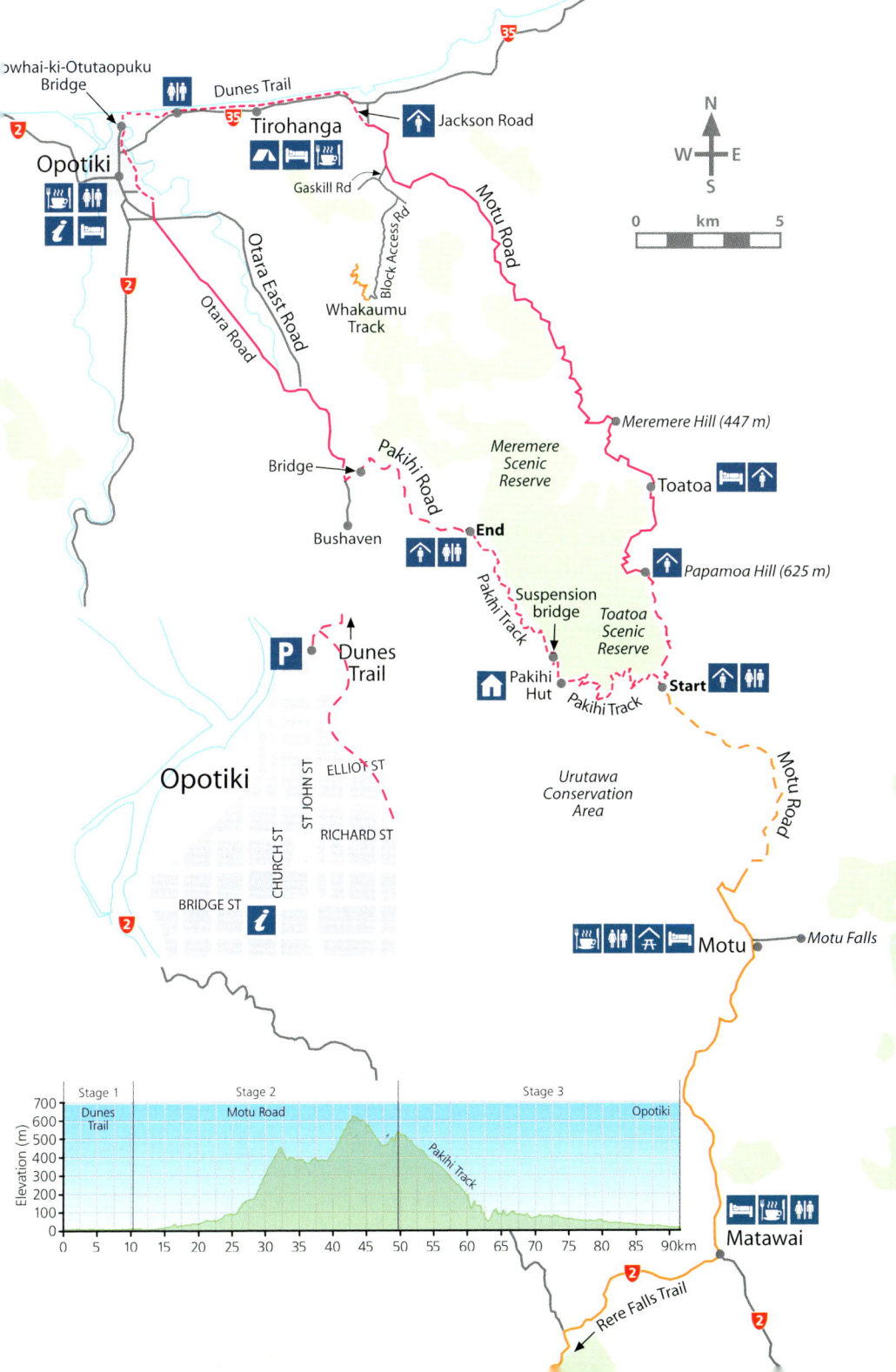

HEARTLAND RIDE

Rere Falls Trail
Gisborne to Bay of Plenty
Distance 181 km   Time 2–3 days   Grade 3 (Intermediate)

The Rere Falls Trail and the Motu Trail combined provide the ideal cycle link between Gisborne and the Bay of Plenty. Either could be completed as a day trip through beautiful country.

From Gisborne, the route follows sealed roads through farms and vineyards to the famous Eastwoodhill Arboretum. Next comes the Rere Falls and Rere Rock Slide – natural features to view or jump in and experience first hand!

Beyond Rere, the road passes farms and forest reserves on its way to Matawai. From here, the ride traverses a wild landscape. In places, the forest arches over the road, and if you pedal quietly, you may encounter a wild pig or deer. The Motu Road trail meets the Bay of Plenty at the new Dunes Trail (see Motu Trails, page 72), which leads directly to Opotiki.

ITINERARY

Stage 1: Gisborne to Eastwoodhill Arboretum
40 km, 3–4 hours

From the Gisborne i-SITE, ride north up Grey Street, across the main shopping street to Taruheru River. Turn left and cross the river on the Derby Street pedestrian bridge 100 metres away. Alternatively, the official route heads south from the i-SITE and follows the scenic riverside path around to the same bridge.

On the other side of the river, turn left and follow Stout Street, which becomes Nelson Road. At a T-intersection, 7 km from the town centre, turn left onto Tucker Road, and just over 1 km later, left again onto Pilmer Road.

Almost 10 km from town, at the end of Pilmer Road, carefully cross Highway 2, onto Farmer Road (just to your right). A few minutes later, turn right onto Bushmere Road, then after another few minutes, left onto Bloomfield Road. This takes you down to another part of Highway 2, where you turn right and ride across a long bridge, on the pedestrian path. At the end of the bridge, go through the roundabout to Tiniroto Road. You are now 14.4 km from Gisborne.

Ride west on Tiniroto Road for 3 km, then turn right onto Kaimoe Road and, at the next intersection, left onto Wharekopae Road. This leads all the way to Eastwoodhill Arboretum, signposted on your right, about 40 km from Gisborne. A stunning driveway welcomes you to the cafe and accommodation.

A family trip to the Bay of Plenty.

Stage 2: Eastwoodhill to Rere Falls
12 km, 1 hour

From Eastwoodhill, continue westwards along Wharekopae Road to Rere Falls, signposted on your left (52 km from Gisborne). A 100-metre gravel side road leads to a shelter in front of the falls and great spot for a picnic. A couple of kilometres beyond the falls is Rere Rock Slide (on your right), a natural water slide into a deep pool. You'll probably want a lilo or boogie board to cushion you on the slide (we found an abandoned one at the picnic area).

Stage 3: Rere Falls to Matawai
51 km, 3–5 hours

Just keep following Wharekopae Road. This is a wonderfully quiet ride (only one car passed us). You'll soon hit 28 km of smooth gravel road. Just after passing a stand of tall native trees, you'll reach Mutuera Stream. Below the bridge are some bizarre round boulders that look like giant marbles, discarded mid-game. Make sure you follow Tahora Road when Wharekopae Road ends. Later Tahora Road becomes Te Wera Road and skirts past Matawai Conservation Area where the road becomes sealed again before meeting Highway 2. Turn right and ride the final 7 km of this stage to Matawai.

Stage 4: Matawai to Tirohanga
70 km, 4–6 hours

From Matawai, the Motu Road is well signposted opposite the historic pub. The road is virtually flat for the first 11 km to Motu, where there is a shelter and toilets. Then it climbs into the hills and becomes gravel, and very narrow, twisty and even more scenic. You'll pass the start of the Pakihi Track and a toilet. Those who love mountain biking should take that route to Opotiki – it's a fun track but rough in places with daunting drop-offs.

Alternatively, carry on along Motu Coach Road, out to the coast. Less than 1 km from the end, a short track on your left leads to Jackson Road, 100 metres away. Jackson Road meets the highway across the road from the Dunes Trail, which leads to Tirohanga.

Stage 5: Tirohanga to Opotiki via the Dunes Trail
8 km, 1 hour

The Dunes Trail skirts around the back of the Tirohanga Holiday Park and goes right to Opotiki. If you want to go to the Tirohanga cafe, you have to ride through the middle of the holiday park. There are a couple of obvious routes through.

See page 75 for a map of these last two stages.

FACT FILE

Overview This two-day tour is often combined with the East Cape (see page 80).

How to get there Buses go to both Opotiki and Gisborne. There is also an airport at Gisborne, and transport can be arranged with the Gisborne Cycle Tour Company (see Support Services).

Riding surface 52% sealed road, 40% gravel road, 8% gravel path

Special features Don't miss Eastwoodhill Arboretum or Rere Rock Slide.

Maps Kiwimap *Gisborne & Eastern Towns*

Trail website www.motutrails.co.nz

SUPPORT SERVICES

Gisborne Accommodation, shops, including bike shops: www.gisbornenz.com

Gisborne Cycle Tour Company: bike hire, transport, organised tours around the region: ☎ 06 927 7021, www.cyclegisborne.com

Eastwoodhill Arboretum: Refreshments and accommodation (catering by prior arrangement): 06 863 9003, www.eastwoodhill.org.nz

Wharehopae Road Shearers Quarters (14 km west of Rere Falls) Stephen/Rene Pellett have comfortable and basic accommodation. ☎ 06 8639811 or email stephen.rene@yrless.co.nz

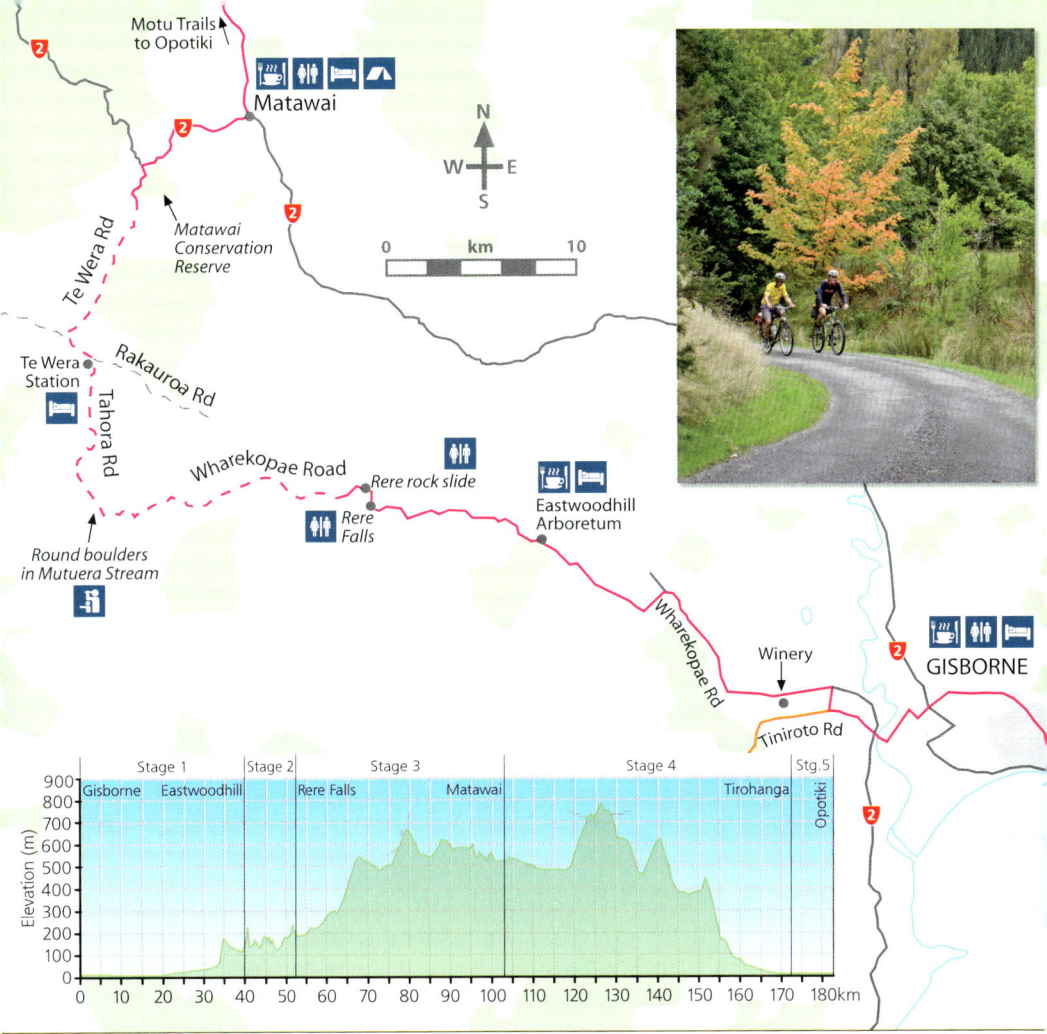

Te Wera Station junction of Rakauroa Road and Te Wera Road. Loretta and Mark O'Neil: Phone 06 868 3436 or email tewerastn@gmail.com. Sleeps up to 10 people, $40 per person per night; meals available on request.

Matawai Cafe, store, accommodation: Matawai Campground: ☎ 06 862 4800

Motu Limited accommodation: Motu Community House: ☎ 06 863 5804 or 06 862 8736, email: rakanui@xtra.co.nz. Cafe: Motu-Vation Cafe, ☎ 06 863 5045

Toatoa Accommodation and bike hire, secure parking and luggage transfers at Toatoa Farmstay: www.toatoaaccommodation.co.nz

Tirohanga Cafe, accommodation: Tirohanga Beach Motor Camp: ☎ 07 315 7942, www.tirohangabeachmotorcamp.co.nz

Opotiki Food, shops, accommodation: www.opotikinz.com

Classic New Zealand Cycle Trails

CONNECTOR RIDE

EAST CAPE

Opotiki to Gisborne via the East Cape
Distance 333 km   Time 3–5 days   Grade 4 (Advanced)

The great touring route of the East Cape has seen a steady increase in logging trucks. If that doesn't faze you, it's still a fantastic adventure.

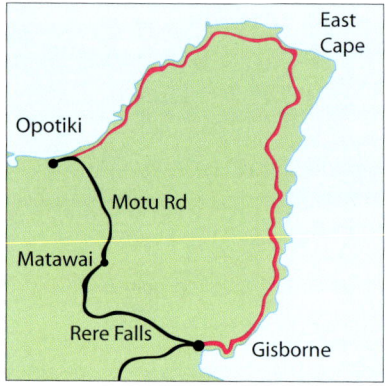

The route follows Highway 35 from Opotiki to Gisborne. At either end, drop into an i-SITE and pick up a free route guide. We have divided this ride into stages based on good options for accommodation and food.

Stage 1: Opotiki to Omaio, 56 km
Beautiful rolling terrain; you could start with the Dunes Trail, but if you are fully loaded for touring, the vehicle barriers will be difficult to get around.

Stage 2: Omaio to Whanarua Bay, 32 km
Te Kaha on the way has a cafe, store, camping ground and nice beach, followed about 10 km later by the wonderful Macadamia Cafe at Whanarua Bay.

Stage 3: Whanarua Bay to Hicks Bay, 63 km
Waihau Bay has a great pub and a dairy. The last 30 km follows an inland route.

Stage 4: Hicks Bay to Tikitiki, 36 hilly km
Hicks Bay has a dairy. On the way to Te Araroa, you'll pass a great camping ground and a fish 'n' chips caravan. The Te Araroa shop is closed at New Year. From Te Araroa to Tikitiki, you'll hit big hills!

Stage 5: Tikitiki to Te Puia Springs, 45 km
Tikitiki is a bit run down now and is not a good stopover spot, but it does have a beautiful church. Ruatoria is 2.5 km off the highway and has a proper supermarket. Te Puia Springs has a hotel and a shop that sells great ice creams.

Stage 6: Te Puia Springs to Tolaga Bay, 47 km
Tokomaru Bay has a restaurant, dairy and a backpackers. There is a big hill just south of the village and then it's flat for miles. If you feel like diverting 7 km, Anaura Bay has a great beach and a B&B. Tolaga Bay has Maria's amazing cafe, a supermarket, a pub and the country's best Holiday Park just down the road.

Stage 7: Tolaga Bay to Gisborne, 54 km
This last stretch suddenly throws in a load more traffic and trucks. Enjoy an East Coast sunrise and knock it out early.

CONNECTOR RIDE

RERE FALLS TRAIL TO FRASERTOWN

Gisborne to Frasertown
Distance 98 km   Time 1–2 days   Grade 3 (Intermediate)

The relaxing Tiniroto Road is the best way to link Rere Falls with Lake Waikaremoana.

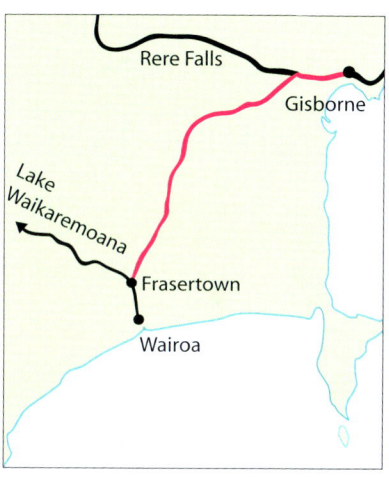

Stage 1: Gisborne to Tiniroto, 63 km

From Gisborne, follow the Rere Falls Trail for 17 km to the corner of Tiniroto and Kaimoe roads. If you are hooking into this connector from Rere Falls, this is 17 km you won't have to ride.

Instead of turning down Kaimoe Road, to get to Eastwoodhill Arboretum, follow Tiniroto Road up to the summit of Gentle Annie hill (360 m). Then cruise along to Waerenga-o-kuri (30 km from Gisborne).

Continue west on Tiniroto Road, for another 23 km (about 54 km from Gisborne), and then turn right down Ruakaka Road for 1 km to Donneraille Park on the banks of the Hangaroa River. This native bush reserve has picnic areas, swimming holes and camping facilities.

From Doneraille Park, ride back out to Tiniroto Road and continue south to Tiniroto, where there is a tavern that sells takeaways and has Eftpos. Hackfalls Arboretum on Berry Road, 4 km from Tiniroto, is set beside Tiniroto Lakes and includes accommodation (www.hackfalls.org.nz).

Stage 2: Tiniroto to Frasertown, 35 km

From Tiniroto, it is mostly downhill to Te Reinga Falls, which has bushwalks. Then it's time to tackle the only climb in this stage, which is only 140 m above sea level.

Tiniroto meets Highway 38 at Frasertown, which is 7 km from Wairoa. Or you can turn right and ride to Lake Waikaremoana (see page 82).

HEARTLAND RIDE

Te Urewera Rainforest
Hawke's Bay to Rotorua
Distance 198 km   Time 3 days   Grade 4 (Advanced)

This classic cycle touring trip has changed little over the last 50 years. For those who love quiet roads and amazing scenery, a tour through Te Urewera may be the trip of a lifetime.

This tour can be done in either direction. It starts/finishes in Hawke's Bay and passes the beautiful forest-lined Lake Waikaremoana before meeting the Te Ara Ahi ride 33 km from Rotorua. There are a few villages and one small town along the route, otherwise it is a very quiet and scenic narrow road (much like the best parts of the Forgotten World Highway). Te Urewera is Tuhoe country – home of the 'People of the Mist'. There are many unique signs of Maori culture in this isolated area.

ITINERARY

Stage 1: Wairoa to Lake Waikaremoana
67 km, 4–6 hours

From the centre of Wairoa (116 km north of Napier), head north across the Wairoa River, and out of town on Carroll Street, which becomes Frasertown Road. This is actually a highway, although you would hardly think so. It is very quiet and becomes gravel 37 km from Wairoa.

When you reach Piripaua, the lowest of three hydro stations below Lake Waikaremoana, you have the option to take the back road into Tuai. Turn right onto Piripaua Road and enjoy the brilliant view out over Lake Whakamarino. You are now at the 50-km mark and are 380 m above sea level. Check out the historic Lake Whakamarino lodge here if you feel like a shortish day.

From Tuai, ride out to the highway again and continue climbing steadily for several kilometres to Lake Waikaremoana (600 m altitude). Ride northeast around the lake on Lake Road for about 10 km, and you will reach Lake Waikaremoana Motorcamp, which has both food and accommodation – and it's a great swimming spot. The visitor centre is 2 km further on.

Stage 2: Lake Waikaremoana to Murupara
95 km, 6–9 hours

From Waikaremoana, the road continues as gravel most of the way to Ruatahuna, about 47 km away. This whole section through Te Urewera is stunningly scenic

It was at this moment that Simon realised he'd forgotten to pack one thing – his matador cape.

and tranquil. You will pass two camping areas en route and possibly meet trampers heading to and away from the Lake Waikaremoana Great Walk.

From Ruatahuna, the road is a mix of seal and gravel until near the 75 km mark, just before Minginui Road, 20 km short of Murupara. Then it is sealed all the way.

Stage 3: Murupara to Rainbow Mountain
36 km, 2–3 hours

From Murupara, it is only 36 km to the Te Ara Ahi ride, however, it is mostly uphill and logging trucks use this route during the week. Much of it doesn't have a wide shoulder either. Best to ride it in the weekend or very early or late in the day.

When you reach Okaro Road, you are at the Te Ara Ahi trail, and you are spoilt for choice. Turn right to ride 30 km to Rotorua, mostly downhill on a mix of on- and off-road trail. Or follow Te Ara Ahi south towards Taupo (see Te Ara Ahi page 68). If you are on a skinny tired bike take the highway rather than Te Ara Ahi towards Taupo (the off-road track around Rainbow Mountain is a mountain bike track).

FACT FILE

How to get there There is a daily Intercity Bus going to/from Wairoa, and several buses going to/from Rotorua.

Riding surface 40% gravel road and 60% sealed road

History Lake Waikaremoana was formed around 2200 years ago by a massive landslide that blocked a river.

Special considerations The only time this road is busy and dusty is during summer public holidays. Watch out for stray stock and horses on the road. You can create a fantastic week-long tour by combining this ride with the Motu and Rere Falls trails. Also, a great side trip for real bush lovers is the Moerangi Track (see *Classic New Zealand Mountain Bike Rides* for details).

Special features Te Urewera is the largest tract of native bush in the North Island.

Maps Kiwimaps *East Cape Rural Road Map* and *Rotorua*

SUPPORT SERVICES

Wairoa Accommodation, supermarkets, cafes: www.visitwairoa.co.nz, Riverside Motor Camp: ☎ 06 838 6301, www.riversidemotorcamp.com, Three Oaks Motel: ☎ 06 838 8204, www.threeoaksmotel.co.nz, Vista Motor Lodge: ☎ 06 838 8279 or ☎ 0800 284 782, www.vistamotorlodge.co.nz

Orangihikoia Campsite: www.doc.govt.nz

Tuai Accommodation, general store, petrol, postal facilities: The Tuai Suite: ☎ 06 837 3779, www.waikaremoana.ollyfuntree.com, Lake Whakamarino Lodge: ☎ 0800 837 387, www.lakelodge.co.nz

Big Bush Holiday Park (1 km on from Tuai) ☎ 0800 525 392 or 06 837 3777, www.lakewaikaremoana.co.nz

Lake Waikaremoana DOC Holiday Park, general store and fuel (closes 5:30 or 6pm): 06 837 3826

Te Whaiti (1 km off-route) Whirinaki Forest Holidays and Jailhouse Shuttles: ☎ 07 366 3235, www.whirinakiforestholidays.co.nz

Murupara Accommodation, cafes, shops: Kohutapu Lodge: www.kohutapulodge.co.nz. Flaxy Lodge Motel: ☎ 07 366 5583, www.flaxylodge.co.nz, Murupara Motor Camp: ☎ 07 366 5365, 021 565 246

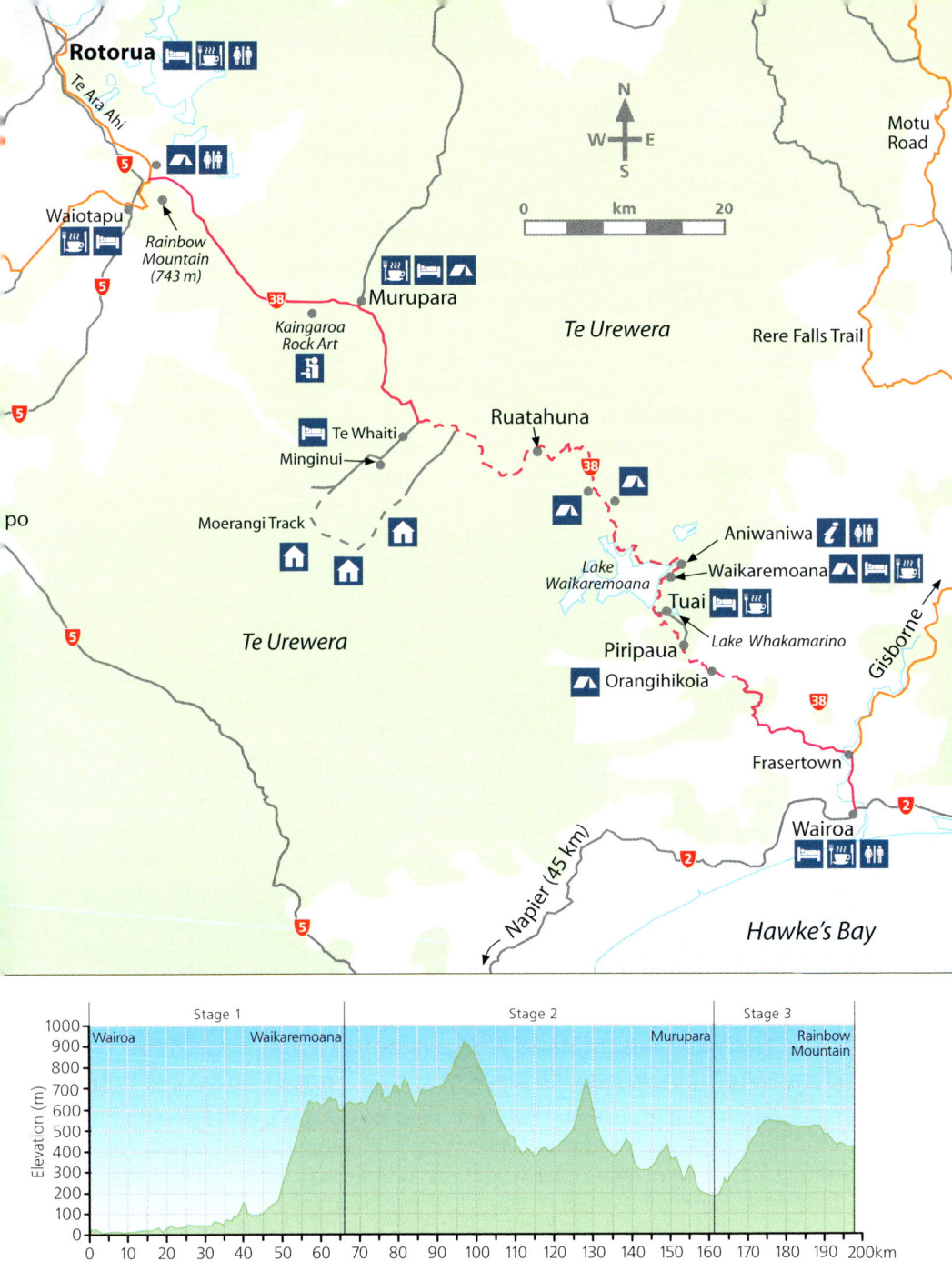

GREAT RIDE

Great Lake Trail
Northern Lake Taupo
Distance 15–73 km   Time 2 hours–2 days   Grade 3 (Intermediate)

With stunning lookouts and beautiful bays for swimming or picnicking, this track is simply the best land-based way to explore the northern half of Lake Taupo.

From Taupo township, the adventure begins with a short drive to one of three trailheads. Choose to bike one, two, or all three stages of the Great Lake Trail depending on how much time you have. All three provide relatively easy mountain biking through an interesting volcanic landscape of native forest, large rock outcrops and welcoming bays on the shores of New Zealand's largest lake.

Those keen to ride the Great Lake Trail from the Western Bays Road to Taupo township need to arrange a boat to take them between two sections. The whole journey is 61 km of fantastic single track plus 12 km of road riding via Acacia Bay back into Taupo.

ITINERARY

Stage 1: W2K and the Headland Loop, Kinloch
24 km (or 15 km without the Headland loop), 2–4 hours

This section has been open for a few years now, and it's just got better with time! From Kinloch Domain, carefully follow the W2K marker posts through the marina and out of the village. Climb gently for about 7 km onto the shoulder of Te Tuhi Point. At a signposted intersection, turn right to do the Headland Loop. It is 10 km long, and there are two good lookout spots of Lake Taupo along the way. When you rejoin the W2K track, turn left and fly back down to Kinloch. Alternatively, you could turn right and head down to Whakaipo Bay, but you'd have to be prepared for a long slog back or have arranged a pick-up.

Stage 2: Whangamata Road to Kawakawa Bay and Kinloch
18 km single track, plus 10 km if you ride from Kinloch, 2–4 hours

There is no firm consensus on the best direction to ride this stage. If you love single track and hate road riding, then ride it there and back from Kinloch or arrange a shuttle. We made it a loop trip by road riding from Kinloch to the start of the track 30 minutes away.

From Kinloch, follow the road you drove in on back to Whangamata Road – that's 2.6 km, but you could take the Whangamata Track instead (hook into it as you head out of town, 200 metres down Lisland Drive). At Whangamata Road,

Looking out over Lake Taupo on the way to Waihora Bay.

turn left and ride 8 km to a car park and shelter on your left. There is a squeeze barrier to negotiate, and then it's 10 km of sweet single track down to Kawakawa Bay. Apart from a couple of off-camber corners, it is just a perfect grade-3 trail.

From Kawakawa Bay, the Bike Taupo pixies have upgraded an old tramping track to Kinloch, re-routing everything that was too steep. It used to be tough going; now it's an easy 3-km climb to a magnificent rocky lookout followed by a sweeping downhill ride. The single track for this stage totals 18 km, and there are several good stopping points en route.

Stage 3: Western Bays Road to Waihora Bay
31 km, 3–6 hours

From Taupo, drive 54 km to the Waihaha River bridge on Western Bays Road. The track starts from the car park at the southern end of the bridge. Ride towards the lake before weaving north through bush to Waihora Bay (where Kotukutuku Stream joins the lake). That is 31 km of awesome single track. There is a rest area, shelter and toilets at the bay.

Hopefully you've arranged for a water taxi to take you from Waihora Bay to Kawakawa Bay because the track ends here. Otherwise it's a long way back to the road.

Sweet single track on the way to Kawakawa Bay.

FACT FILE

Overview At first, it's not obvious how to tackle the Great Lake Trail. It is being marketed as one track, but you'll soon figure out that it has three distinct sections. In future the trail may be extended.

How to get there For stages 1 and 2, it is easiest to drive to Kinloch village, 22 km from Taupo. Kinloch Domain has plenty of parking, and there are toilets and a cafe/store on the lake front. To do all three stages, or even possibly stages 1 and 2 sequentially, arrange a shuttle with Tread Routes or Great Lake Shuttles (see Support Services).

Boat transport can be arranged to and from Taupo with Bay2Bay Ltd (see Support Services)

Riding surface 100% pumice single track

History Almost all the single track has been specifically built with cycling in mind by the volunteer group Bike Taupo.

Special features Lake Taupo is one of the largest volcanic lakes in the world. It is a popular holiday destination for all sorts of activities, including boating, rock climbing and slothing.

Maps Waterproof maps for $3 from Top Gear Cycles in Runanga St, Taupo.

Trail website www.biketaupo.org.nz

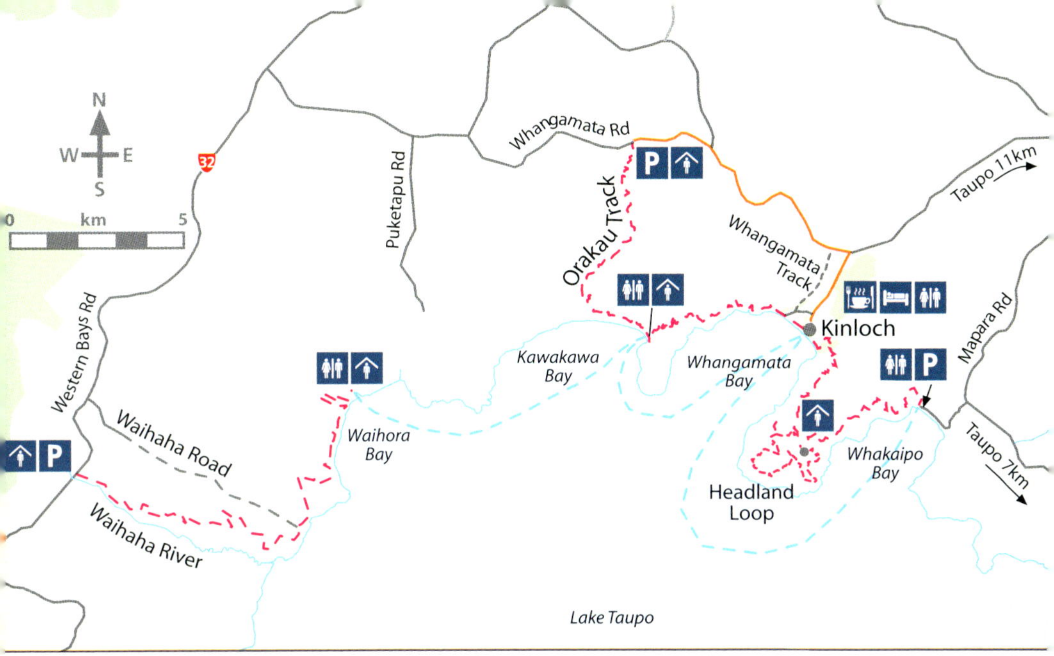

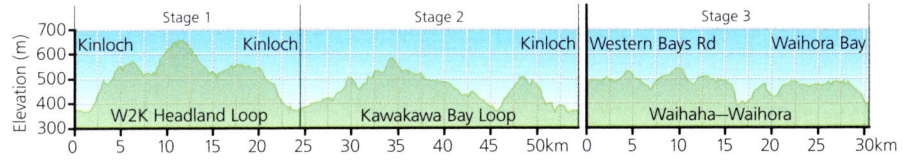

SUPPORT SERVICES

Taupo Plenty of accommodation and shops: www.greatlaketaupo.com

Taupo bike shops: Top Gear Cycles 40 Runanga St, ☎ 07 377 0552, Phoenix Cyclery, 5 Tamamutu St, ☎ 07 378 7381

Tread Routes for transport and guides, ☎ 07 377 8319 or 027 446 2408 or www.treadroutes.co.nz.

Great Lake Shuttles can take you from Taupo to the start of the trail: ☎ 021 656 424, www.greatlakeshuttles.co.nz (about $60 to take you and your bike from Whakaipo Bay to Whangamata Road, minimum number 4 people)

Adventure Shuttles also provide transport to the trails around Taupo, www.adventureshuttles.co.nz or ☎ 022 547 0399

Bay2Bay Ltd boat can take 14 people and 11 bikes to the bays on this trail. Costs approximately $75 per person from Waihora Bay to Kawakawa Bay, ☎ 022 132 7449, email bay2bayltd@hotmail.com

Kinloch General store, cafe and a small range of accommodation options: www.kinloch.org.nz

Classic New Zealand Cycle Trails

GREAT RIDE

The Timber Trail
Pureora to Ongarue (between Te Kuiti and Taupo)
Distance 87 km   Time 2 days   Grades 2–3 (Easy–Intermediate)

The Timber Trail ushers you through majestic native forest, across the flanks of Mount Pureora, over long suspension bridges and down to the village of Ongarue on historic bush tramlines.

From Pureora, this trail heads south, through four ecologically significant areas, passing 800-year-old trees, a bush tramway and historic timber-milling sites along the way.

Although the full trail takes two days to cycle, there are several options for shorter rides, with trackside shelters, toilets and interpretation panels positioned at regular intervals along the way.

The Timber Trail has some of New Zealand's highest and longest suspension bridges (the biggest is 141 metres long and 60 m high!), a tunnel at the amazing Ongarue Spiral bush tramway and a sustained gentle downhill to the end at Ongarue.

ITINERARY

Stage 1: Pureora Information Centre to the first shelter
8.5 km, 1–2 hours, Grade 2+ (Easy)

This first section is ideal for those looking for a short there-and-back ride. From the Pureora Information Centre, ride 200 metres east and you will see the track signposted beside the road (opposite the picnic area).

Just follow the little signposts at every intersection, and you can't go wrong. The trail leads through ecologically important virgin forest for the first 4 km and then a mix of exotic and regenerating native forest. There is a track off to the left at the 3.4 km mark, leading to a historic bulldozer under a large shelter.

The trail climbs gently all the way towards Mt Pureora. The first trail shelter is right beside the track and affords expansive views of the area. Turn around here or carry on up the flanks of Mt Pureora into the cloud forest.

Stage 2: First shelter to Piropiro Flats (or Black Fern Lodge)
31.5 km, 3–5 hours, Grade 3 (Intermediate)

From the first shelter, the trail becomes steeper in places. With loaded bikes, some riders may have to walk short sections. The intensely green and twisted cloud forest on this section is absolutely stunning. After 14 km of climbing, you will reach the highest point of the ride.

Spanning 85 metres, this is one of the shorter swing bridges on The Timber Trail!

About 13 km from the first shelter, you'll cross a 115-metre suspension bridge over Bog Inn Creek, followed by a 109-metre bridge over Orauhora Creek. At Harrisons Creek, 2.5 km further on, you'll reach a rest area with a toilet.

Just over 13 km from the rest area, you will reach Piropiro Flats campsite. In 2017 a new lodge was opened (200 m before Piropiro Flats). It is well signposted from the trail.

Alternatively, if you don't mind cycling an extra 6 km, you can stay at the highly rated Black Fern Lodge (see Support Services). It is signposted from the Timber Trail, a few kilometres before Piropiro Flats, down Black Fern Road.

Stage 3: Piropiro Flats to Ongarue
47 km, 3–5 hours, Grade 3- (Intermediate)

From Piropiro Flats campsite, follow the markers along Piropiro Road for 2 km to a locked gate. Ride between the concrete bollards and into native forest on a new section of purpose-built trail. About 3 km from the bollards, you'll cross the huge Maramataha River on one of the highest and longest swing bridges in the country. If you suffer from vertigo, don't look down!

Ahead lies a 3-km climb, but otherwise the trail is quite easy (grade 2). From the old tramway terminus, it is mostly downhill all the way to Ongarue. There are old huts, more swing bridges and the fascinating Ongarue Spiral. From the spiral, an 8-km downhill takes you to Ongarue-Ngakonui Road where there is a

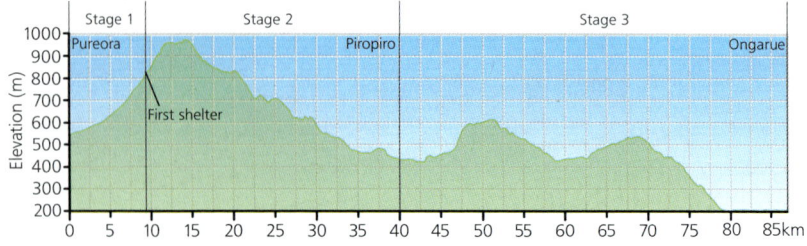

carpark. The last 2 km to Ongarue village are along a sealed road.

You may wish to ride from Ongarue to Taumarunui on the beautiful Ongarue Back Road. It's 24 km long and mostly flat (see Timber Trail Link, page 95).

FACT FILE

Overview A fantastic, but very remote ride for lovers of the great outdoors. The first 4–9 km from the Pureora Information Centre are ideal for families and day trippers. Trampers will enjoy a 50-minute side trip to a trig on top of Mt Pureora.

How to get there Pureora is in the middle of nowhere. That's part of its charm. From Te Kuiti, head southeast on Highway 30 for 55 km. Just past the Pa Harakeke Centre, on Maraeroa Road, turn left onto Barryville Road and travel another 2.5 km to the Pureora Information Centre.

Riding surface 40% old bush tramline, 35% new single track, 25% new and old logging roads

History The Ongarue mill processed trees from Pureora Forest from 1910 to the 1960s. A 16-wheel-drive bush locomotive brought out massive trunks. In the late 1970s, 'suicide squads' of conservationists risked their lives protesting from the tops of the tallest trees. Much of the remaining native forest was saved, and the Pureora Forest is once again home to a variety of endangered birds, such as the kokako and kiwi.

Special considerations This is kiwi country – leave your pets at home.

Maps Pick up a pamphlet map from the DOC Pureora Visitor Centre.

Trail websites www.doc.govt.nz/parks-and-recreation, www.timbertrail.net.nz

SUPPORT SERVICES

For trail transport, contact Pa Harakeke (based in Pureora) ☎ 07 929 8708 or 027 207 1500, www.paharakeke.co.nz, or Tread Routes (based in Taupo)

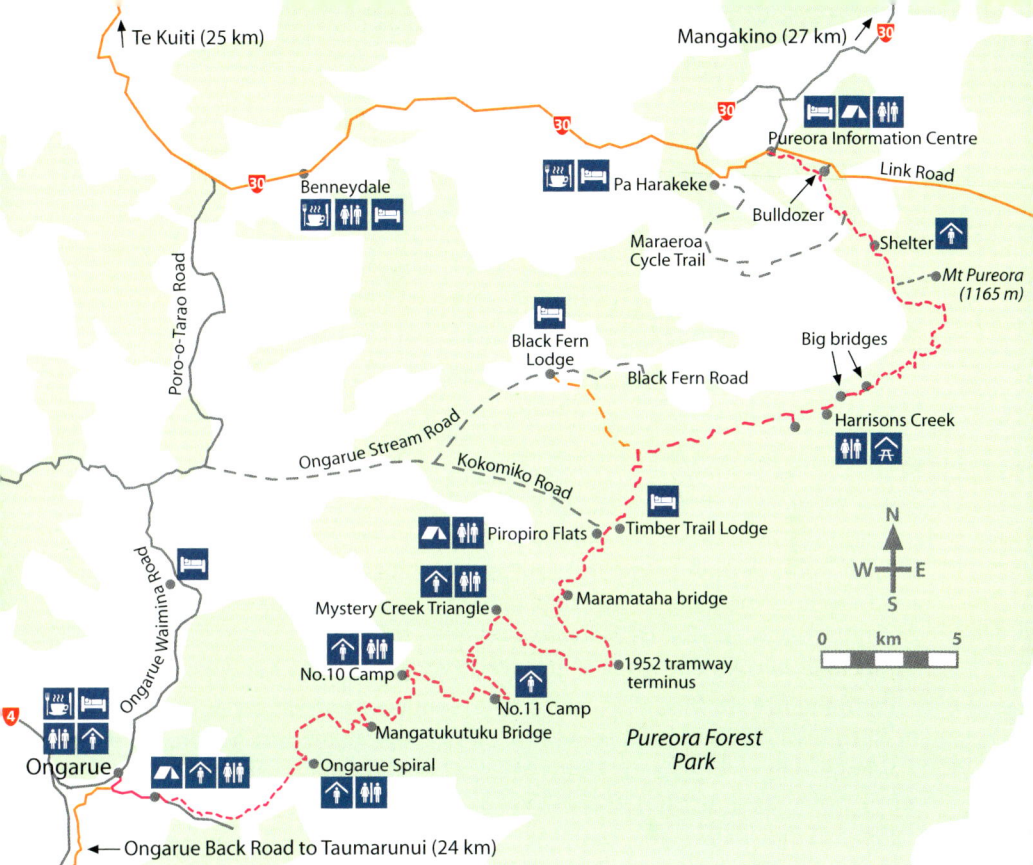

☎ 027 446 2408 or www.treadroutes.co.nz

The nearest facilities to the Pureora trailhead are at Benneydale and Mangakino.

Te Kuiti Lots of places to eat and stay, www.waitomo.govt.nz

Benneydale Cafe, general store, two places to stay: Benneydale Cafe and Lodge: ☎ 07 878 4708, www.benneydale.co.nz, or ArtDoc Sleepout: ☎ 07 878 4780, www.artdoc.co.nz

Pureora Cabins and campsites: www.thetimbertrail.com, Pa Harakeke chalets and cafe: ☎ 07 929 8708 or 07 878 4879, www.paharakeke.co.nz

Black Fern Lodge ☎ 07 894 7677, www.blackfernlodge.co.nz

Piropiro Timber Trail Lodge (200 m past Piropiro Flats) ☎ 0800 885 6343, www.timbertraillodge.co.nz. Epic Cycle Adventures for camping ☎ 022 023 7958, www.thetimbertrail.nz

Ongarue Flashpackers ☎ 027 321 6274, www.timbertrailhub.co.nz and Timber Trail Centre, www.timbertrailcentre.co.nz

Taumarunui Too many shops and accommodation places to list. Go to www.visitruapehu.co.nz or phone the i-SITE on ☎ 07 895 7494

CONNECTOR RIDES

TE KUITI TO THE TIMBER TRAIL

Te Kuiti to Pureora Information Centre
Distance 55 km   Time 3–4 hours   Grade 5 (Expert for traffic)

If you want to connect the dots between Te Kuiti, at the end of the Kawhia to Waitomo Caves heartland ride and The Timber Trail, this is the easiest route.

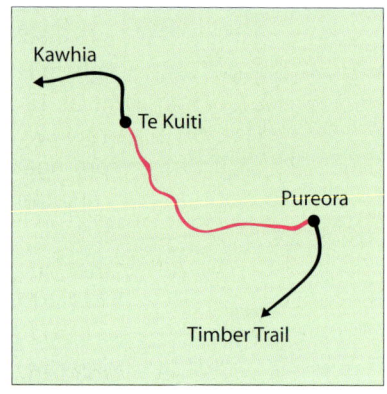

From Te Kuiti, there is only one direct route to Pureora – along Highway 30. It has about 700 vehicles per day (with 20% of that being logging trucks). There is no road shoulder most of the way, so you must be traffic savvy or ride in the weekend or during a public holiday when there will be virtually no trucks.

From the Te Kuiti shopping centre, head south-east on Highway 30 and follow it all the way to Benneydale, 34 km away. Benneydale has a store, cafe and accommodation. Check out Bennydale Lodge and Cafe, www.bennydale.co.nz, ☎ 07 8784708 or Artdoc Gallery ☎ 07 878 4780.

From Benneydale, follow Highway 30 for another 13 km before turning right onto Maraeroa Road. After passing the Pa Harakeke (cafe, chalet accommodation and cultural centre: ☎ 07 929 8708 www.paharakeke.co.nz), turn left and follow signs to the Pureora Information Centre (almost 55 km from Te Kuiti). The last 4 km from the highway are gravel.

A shuttle option is available from Bennydale Cafe ☎ 07 8784708.

WAIKATO RIVER TRAIL TO TIMBER TRAIL LINK

Mangakino to Pureora Information Centre
Distance 54 km   Time 5-6 hours   Grade 4 (Advanced)

Adventure cyclists will love this link for its remoteness and scenic beauty. It also passes the topographical centre of the North Island.

From the Mangakino Lakefront Reserve, follow the Waikato River Trail towards Whakamaru for approximately 6-7 km. A few minutes after crossing Mangakino Stream on a large swing bridge, turn right up a gravel road. Within a few hundred metres you will pass some public toilets and Whakamaru Reserve and then

CONNECTOR RIDES

reach the highway. Wait 'til there is no traffic and turn left and sprint down the highway till you pass around a blind corner. Just after the corner, carefully cross to McDonald Road.

Head up McDonald road for 7 km, turn left at Sandel Road, then right at Henderson, right at Arataki and right at Titiraupanga Track. This leads to a narrow swing bridge crossing Mangakino Stream again. On the far side, cross a small gully and take the next right along an old forestry road.

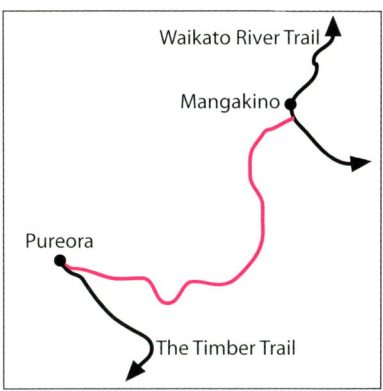

DOC have signposted the route to Pureora. 10.5 km from the Arataki swing bridge you'll see a 'Centre of the North Island' sign, turn right and ride 500 metres (including a cool singletrack) to the sign of topographical significance.

Head back to the main road and follow it to Link Road, 3.5 km away. Turn right at Link Road and stay on it all the way to the start of the Timber Trail at Pureora.

Note: You can short cut the few kilometres of the Timber Trail by turning left at the 'Historic Tractor' track sign. There is a shelter at the tractor.

TIMBER TRAIL LINK

Ongarue to Taumarunui
Distance 24 km   Time 1–2 hours   Grade 3 (Intermediate)

Here's an easy ride from The Timber Trail to the town of Taumarunui and various options for public transport homewards.

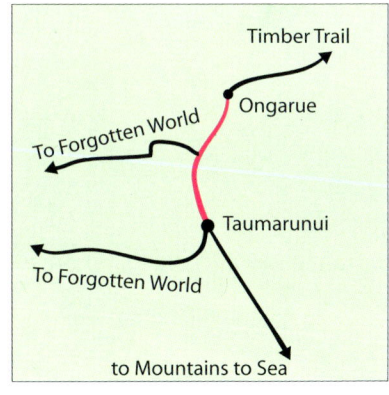

From Ongarue, at the southern end of The Timber Trail, ride south on Ongarue Back Road for 24 km. It is gravel for the first half with a few rolling hills. It is signposted with New Zealand Cycle Trail signs.

The Ongarue Back Road passes a marae, and then, on the outskirts of Taumarunui, it turns into Golf Road. Turn right into Short Street to ride underneath the main trunk railway line to the main street of town. The shops are on your left. There is a good cafe on the corner or, if you prefer, a big bakery further down the road.

CONNECTOR RIDE

THE PRISON BREAK

Ongarue to Forgotten World Highway
Distance 60 km   Time 3–4 hours   Grade 3 (Intermediate)

A series of beautiful and quiet country roads links the southern end of The Timber Trail with the northern end of the Forgotten World Highway and makes for a lovely ride in its own right.

From Ongarue, follow the Ongarue Back Road (gravel) south for 13 km. Then turn right at Okahukura and cross a double-decker road-rail bridge to Highway 4. Cross the highway and take Okahukura Saddle Road over a 200-m climb (all sealed now) to Ohura Road. Now turn left and follow Ohura Road to the ghost-like town of Ohura (perfect setting for a Coen Brothers' movie).

From Ohura, continue south on the main road for 10 km and you will connect with Highway 43 – the Forgotten World Highway – 40 km west of Taumarunui.

CONNECTOR RIDE

OWHANGO CONNECTION

Taumarunui to Whakahoro (Mountains to Sea)
Distance 67 km   Time 3–5 hours   Grade 3 (Intermediate)

This connector ride leads you away from the hustle and bustle of some central island highways and into the breathtaking backblocks of the volcanic plateau.

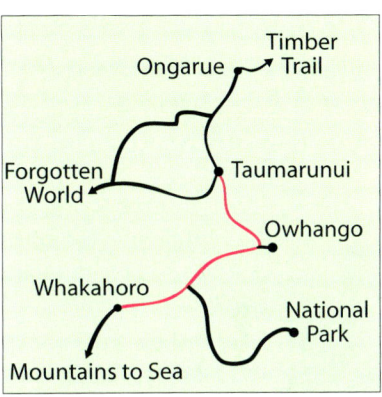

From opposite the railway station on the main street of Taumarunui, head south on Hikaia Street, then straight onto Morero Terrace and, a minute later, you'll cross the Whanganui River. On the other side, turn right to follow Hikumutu Road into the boonies.

About 10 km from Taumarunui (at the start of Whanganui Valley Road), veer left to stay on Hikumutu Road. It soon becomes a narrow gravel road that climbs for 300 m. You'll hit the seal again at a T-intersection with Kawautahi Road. Turn left to nip out 1 km to Owhango for supplies or accommodation. Alternatively, turn right to carry on to Whakahoro. Kawautahi Road is just perfect for cycling: narrow, windy, scenic and 90% downhill with virtually no traffic. It whisks you to Oio Road, 45.3 km from Taumarunui. This is part of the Mountains to Sea Great Ride as well as Tour Aotearoa.

Go right, down Oio Road for 21 km to get to Blue Duck Station 200 metres from the Whanganui River at Whakahoro, where there is a great cafe, accommodation and a DOC campsite and hut. We found this an inspiring place to stay due to its exceptional mix of good riding, great scenery and awesome hosts: ☎ 07 895 6276, www.blueduckstation.co.nz

From Blue Duck Station, you'd be mad not to ride on to the Bridge to Nowhere (see Mountains to Sea, page 102). It's one of those iconic rides you have to experience before you die.

Note At the time of writing, Google Maps showed that part of Hikumutu Road didn't exist. Trust us, it does. Take Kiwimap *Taranaki-Ruapehu Rural Road Map*.

HEARTLAND RIDE

Forgotten World Highway
Taumarunui to New Plymouth
Distance 185 km   Time 2–3 days   Grade 4 (Advanced)

One of New Zealand's best-loved cycle touring routes, this ride takes in the quiet Highway 43, rustic tunnels and the historic Bertrand Bridge before finishing along an award-winning coastal path to New Plymouth.

The Forgotten World Highway starts at Taumarunui, a railway town in the middle of the North Island. Don't be fooled by the term 'highway' as it has to be the quietest in New Zealand, with fewer than 200 cars a day.

From the classic backcountry Republic of Whangamomona, the ride veers west to follow the original coach road that provides a quiet road ride down to New Plymouth's stunning coastal path. Although a few operators offer accommodation along the route, there are currently limited options for purchasing supplies, and you will need to be self-sufficient.

ITINERARY

Stage 1: Taumarunui to Tahora Saddle
77 km, 5–8 hours

Highway 43, the Forgotten World Highway, is well signposted from Taumarunui. It tracks an undulating course west from the town, alongside the graceful Whanganui River then heads over hilly farmland for 30 kilometres before settling in for a steady climb to Paparata Saddle. Once down the other side, it weaves through the beautiful Tangarakau Gorge, which is thickly covered in native forest. Thirteen kilometres of this section is smooth gravel.

The road is sealed again beyond the gorge as it begins a moderate climb to the 'Hobbit Hole' tunnel. On the other side of the tunnel, it dives to Tahora village before tackling the stiff climb to Tahora Saddle (where there are stunning views from Ruapehu to Taranaki).

Stage 2: Tahora Saddle to Purangi
45 km, 3–5 hours

Tahora Saddle is followed by a 12-km gentle downhill to Whangamomona. This rustic town claims to be an independent republic. For a small fee, visitors can have their passports stamped at the Whangamomona Hotel.

Te Rewa Rewa Bridge, the icing on the cake for the popular New Plymouth coastal path.

An hour south of the republic, our recommended 'special' route peels off Highway 43 at Junction Road to head west along a historic coach road from Pohokura Saddle. There are a dozen kilometres of gravel to negotiate at the start of this deviation, but the effort is well rewarded as you follow Junction Road through Matau to Purangi where you can stay in the original schoolhouse. This is kiwi country, and you will notice dozens of stoat traps beside the road. Goats, domestic pigs, sheep and cattle also commonly wander along the verge. There are only three buildings at Purangi – blink and you'll miss it.

Stage 3: Purangi to New Plymouth
63 km, 4–6 hours

The 'special' route leads you over Tarata Saddle, through another tunnel and down to the historic Bertrand suspension bridge, which crosses the Waitara River.

Leaving Purangi, Junction Road soon changes name to Tarata Road. Follow this for 15 km before turning right onto Otaraoa Road. The next important turn is 31 km from Purangi and is often missed because it is at the bottom of a fast downhill – make sure you turn left onto Tikorangi Road. Then turn right at Ngatimaru Road and left at Bertrand Road to descend to the Bertrand Bridge.

From the bridge, climb up to Waitara Road, turn left and then right onto Cross Road. Take a right onto Kelly Road and then left at Manutahi Road to Lepperton for an ice cream.

From Lepperton, take Manutahi (squiggle across the highway), Corbett and left at De Havilland Drive to hook into the Mangati Walkway that leads under Highway 3. At the end, turn left up Parklands Ave and then right along Smeaton Road and left down St Andrews Drive to the Taranaki Cycle Park. There you will find the famous coastal path that leads from Bell Block to the centre of New Plymouth, 10 km away. This finale can't help but leave you with a smile on your dial, but remember to 'share with care' – it's also popular with walkers and families.

FACT FILE

Overview One of the top 10 cycle touring routes in New Zealand. Starting from Ohura is also a good option, as it has fewer hills and less traffic than the Taumarunui start (but is harder to get to).

How to get there There are regular bus connections between New Plymouth, Palmerston North and Wellington. You can also arrange a shuttle to take you to Ohura with Taumarunui Canoe Hire, ☎ 0800 226 634.

Left field Here's a great idea! Hire a modified rail bike from Forgotten World Adventures. Check out www.forgottenworldadventures.co.nz

Riding surface 70% sealed road, 25% gravel road, 5% cycle path

Special considerations The traditional Forgotten World Highway ends at Stratford. This cyclists' alternative avoids a bland section of road with moderate traffic volumes in favour of a pleasant back-country road, and an award-winning path into New Plymouth.

Cell phone coverage is limited between Taumarunui and Whangamomona.

Trail website www.nzcycletrail.com

SUPPORT SERVICES

Transport Eastern Taranaki Experience for shuttle service, bike hire and accommodation ☎ 027 471 7136 or 027 246 6383, www.eastern-taranaki.co.nz/cycle

Taumarunui Accommodation, shops, cafes and a supermarket: www.visitruapehu.com, Lauren's Lavender Farm and Cafe: lovely garden cafe (15 km from Taumarunui): www.laurenslavender.co.nz

Whangamomona Hotel: Takeaways and hot meals, as well as accommodation (must book ahead): ☎ 06 762 5823, www.whangamomonahotel.co.nz, Whangamomona Campground: camping and basic cabins, ☎ 06 762 5881

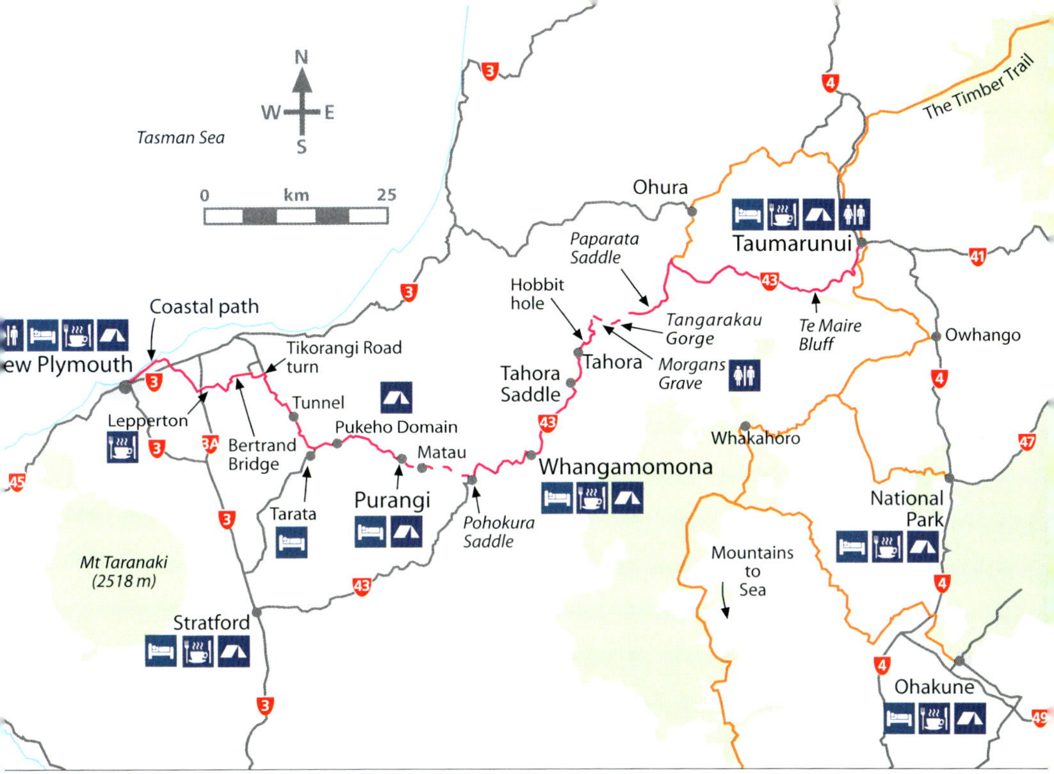

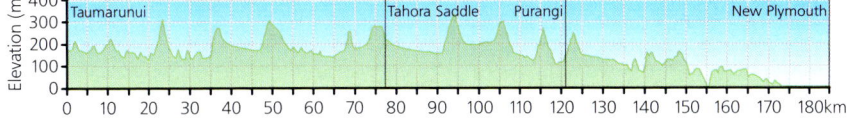

Purangi Orchard Beds and tent sites (can provide meals but must be pre-booked), ☎ 06 756 5569 email: ian.laurel@xtra.co.nz

Pukeho Domain camping ☎ 06 756 5537

Lepperton Dairy and Tawa Glen Cafe (open 9-3 most days)

New Plymouth Copious options for food and accommodation: www.visitnewplymouth.nz

Bike shops: Mitchell Cycles, 477 Devon Street East, ☎ 06 758 3813, www.mitchellcycles.co.nz. Cycle Inn, 133 Devon Street East, ☎ 06 758 7418, www.cycleinn.co.nz

GREAT RIDE

Mountains to Sea
Ohakune to Whanganui via the Bridge to Nowhere
Distance 208 km   Time 1–4 days   Grades 2–4 (Easy–Advanced)

A fantastic mountain bike adventure from the central plateau volcanoes, across massive viaducts and the Bridge to Nowhere and down through Whanganui National Park to the Tasman Sea

From Ohakune, at the foot of Mount Ruapehu, this trail takes the Ohakune Coach Road through forest and across a massive viaduct to Horopito. Country roads lead to the Whanganui National Park, where the trail follows an abandoned road, the Mangapurua Track, to the iconic Bridge to Nowhere.

A fun downhill leads from the bridge to the Whanganui River, where you can choose between a jetboat or canoe to carry you down to Pipiriki (or take both!) A wonderful road ride then leads down the Whanganui Valley and over the Gentle Annie hill to Whanganui township and the coast a hop, skip and a jump away. This ride can be done as separate sections or as one big trip.

ITINERARY

Stage 1: Ohakune Coach Road
14 km one way, 2–3 hours, Grade 2+ (Easy)

Ride northwest from Ohakune railway station under the New Zealand Cycle Trail sign and across a new cycle trail bridge. From there, the trail runs beside Old Station Road and Marshalls Road for 10 minutes before crossing a small bridge on your right and heading up into the hills. The track is rocky in places – remnants of the century-old cobbled road. There are fascinating interpretation panels along the way, massive rimu to admire and, just off the trail, two huge viaducts. The Hapuawhenua viaduct is 45 metres high! The last stretch to Horopito follows farm roads. If you choose to turn back to Ohakune, the return trip will be faster as it is mostly downhill. Otherwise continue on to Whanganui National Park.

Optional start: Ohakune Mountain Road – the top of New Zealand's biggest sealed road climb (1000 m above Ohakune! See Mtb Station page 106).

Stage 2: Horopito to Whanganui National Park
43 km, 3–4 hours, Grade 3 (Intermediate)

From Horopito, ride southwest beside Highway 4 for 800 metres, then turn right to follow Middle Road to Ruatiti Road, 14 km away. Turn right and follow Ruatiti

High above the trolls of the Hapuawhenua viaduct.

Road to Ruatiti Domain. It is mostly downhill – fast fun on a sealed road. Then the road narrows and breaks into gravel to the start of the Mangapurua Track. Ruatiti Backpackers is 3 km before the Mangapurua Track.

Stage 3: Mangapurua Track to Bridge to Nowhere
38 km cycling, 3–4 hours, Grade 3 (Intermediate) + 28 km on river

From the start of the 4WD track, head left through a gate and cruise up a well-graded 4-km climb. When you reach a second gate, near the top of the hill, take a look back; the views are stunning on a clear day. This is the only real climb of the day. After an hour, you'll reach a letterbox and see a 'National Park' sign ahead.

About 2 km after entering the national park, you will reach a Y-intersection and must go left (to the right is the Kaiwhakauka Track, down to Whakahoro). Continue rolling along the ridge, and you'll soon pass a steep walking track (signposted on your left) that goes up to the Mangapurua Trig.

The track is all downhill from here, and it will take fit riders about 1½ hours to get to the Bridge to Nowhere; it's a real hoot. Johnsons clearing, in the valley, is a good place for a rest and regroup.

The track follows the valley gently downhill all the way to the bridge; so gently, it's almost flat. There are many narrow swing bridges, a few bluffs and several large clearings en route.

The bridge itself, quite aptly, appears out of nowhere. Opened in 1936, it had become overgrown by 1948. DOC have restored it, and it now looks weirdly new.

There is a lookout track 100 metres on from the bridge and then toilets a few hundred metres further on again. The ride down to Mangapurua Landing at the Whanganui River takes about 15 minutes. There is a shelter 200 metres before the landing (not a bad place to camp if required).

Alternatives From the landing most people get a jetboat all the way down the river to Pipiriki (a 1-hour trip).

Otherwise you could catch a jetboat down to the Bridge to Nowhere Lodge and stay the night before canoeing down to Pipiriki. The bonus is a big dinner and breakfast at the lodge.

The paddle down the river takes about 5 hours from the lodge if you allow plenty of time for photos. Much of the river is like a long narrow lake, with hardly any flow at all, but there are several grade 2 rapids to negotiate.

From Pipiriki, keen cyclists ride 28 km up to Raetihi (2–3 hours), but the full Mountains to Sea journey continues down the valley.

Stage 4: Pipiriki to Whanganui City and the sea
85 km, 6–8 hours, Grade 3 (Intermediate)

From Pipiriki, the beautiful and quiet Whanganui River Road leads down past Jerusalem (12 km) and Koriniti (30 km), and finally over the ironically named Gentle Annie hill to Highway 4 at the 63-km mark. Carefully follow the highway south, past Upokongaro to Whanganui. Cross the first river bridge you reach and take Somme Parade further down valley to the Whanganui i-SITE (just by the next river bridge) where there is also a cafe. That is 77 km.

By now you'll have spotted the wide path beside the river. This path and a few signposted streets lead to the coast, 8 km away – a dramatic end to a spectacular journey.

Hot tip Take some breadcrumbs for finding your way back along the last few kilometres. The route is well signposted heading down to the sea but not in the other direction.

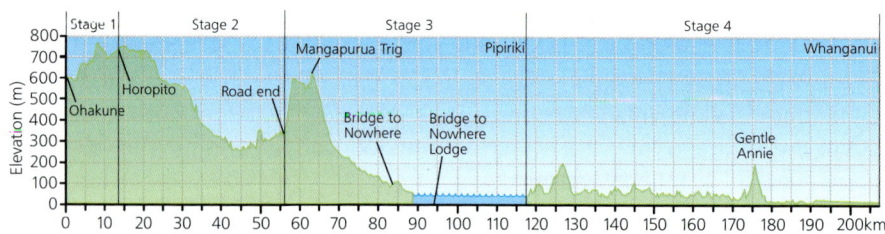

104   Classic New Zealand Cycle Trails

FACT FILE

Overview The most satisfying all-round biking adventure in the North Island.

How to get there You can catch the Northern Explorer train to Ohakune and bus back to any major city from Whanganui. Alternatively, have a rest day and then pedal The Three Rivers back to Ohakune to make this a loop trip!

Mountain Bike Station starts groups from the top of New Zealand's biggest sealed road climb – the Ohakune Mountain Road (1000 m above Ohakune!)

There is also a great option of riding to the Bridge to Nowhere from National Park and the Kaiwhakauka Track.

Riding surface 49% sealed road, 14% gravel road, 24% off-road trail, 13% river

History The history of this road is mind-boggling. After the First World War, returned servicemen were given a portion of the Mangapurua Valley to farm. The government assisted by building the impossible road to the Bridge to Nowhere. It didn't last long, and neither did most of the settlers.

Maps The best map to take is Whanganui Parkmap 273-05.

Trail websites www.nzcycletrail.com, www.doc.govt.nz

SUPPORT SERVICES

The jetboat/canoe, lodging, and meals cost about $300 per person. Transport only from Mangapurua Landing down the river and up to Raetihi costs about $130 per person. To organise transport and accommodation, contact Bridge to Nowhere: ☎ 0800 480 308, www.bridgetonowhere.co.nz or Whanganui River Adventures, ☎ 0800 862 743, www.whanganuiriveradventures.com

Other operators on the Whanganui River: www.whanganuiriver.co.nz/operators

Ohakune Plenty of cafes, restaurants and accommodation: www.ohakune.info

Bike hire and packages (including a shuttle up the Mountain Road) from Mountain Bike Station: ☎ 0800 385 879, www.mountainbikestation.co.nz, TCB Ski Board and Bike: ☎ 06 385 8433, www.tcbskiandboard.co.nz

Horopito Lahar Farm Log Cabin: ☎ 06 385 3384 or 027 651 5777

Raetihi Cafes and restaurants, grocery store, accommodation: www.raetihi.com, Raetihi Holiday Park: www.raetihiholidaypark.com or ☎ 0800 408 888

Ruatiti Backpackers ☎ 06 385 4266 evenings or email ruatitibtnw@farmside.co.nz

Mellonsfolly Ranch ☎ 027 702 3158, www.oldwesttown.co.nz

Bridge to Nowhere Lodge: ☎ 0800 480 308, www.bridgetonowhere.co.nz

Pipiriki Food, camping and accommodation: Whanganui River Adventures, ☎ 0800 862 743, www.whanganuiriveradventures.com

Koriniti The Flying Fox lodge, www.theflyingfox.co.nz or ☎ 06 927 6809

Whanganui Plenty of shops and accommodation: www.wanganui.com

CONNECTOR RIDE

FISHER ROAD AND KAIWHAKAUKA TRACK
National Park to Bridge to Nowhere
Distance 74 km   Time 4–6 hours Grade 3 (Intermediate)

This is an exciting alternative start to the Mountains to Sea trail. It involves 48 km of quiet gravel roads and 26 km of off-road trail. The scenery is fantastic, and the Blue Duck Lodge is a compelling destination.

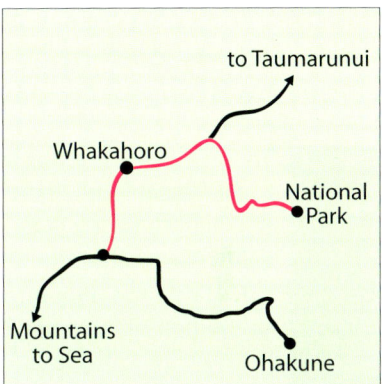

The Station Cafe on the corner of Findlay Road and Station Road in National Park is a good place to start.

Ride 400 metres north to the end of Station Road. Turn left across the railway tracks and follow Fisher Road west into the wilderness. This is mostly a narrow gravel road, but for 5 km it is an old grassy track. It is mostly down hill for 17 km.

At Upper Retaruke Road, turn right and pedal down to the war memorial at Oio Road, 12 km away. Now turn left and cruise 26 km down valley to Whakahoro, where you'll find the Blue Duck lodge and cafe.

From Whakahoro, take the 16 km Kaiwhakauka Track up to the Mangapurua Track (part of the Mountains to Sea trail, see page 102). At the top (2–3 hours from Whakahoro), turn right to ride past Mangapurua Trig and down to the Bridge to Nowhere, 2 hours away. The Kaiwhakauka Track includes 5 km of grade 4 mountain biking.

Notes Blue Duck lodge and cafe, ☎ 07 895 6276, www.blueduckstation.co.nz. We recommend staying here a night. It's a cool spot.

There is also a DOC camping site and cabin at Whakahoro.

HEARTLAND RIDE

The Three Rivers
Whanganui to Huterville and Ohakune
Distance 60–153 km   Time 1–2 days   Grade 3 (Intermediate)

Passing through heartland Rangitikei, the Three Rivers follows stock routes used by farmers for over a century as it weaves its way northward to the Volcanic Plateau.

The Three Rivers leads from Whanganui (at the end of the Mountains to Sea Great Ride) across to Hunterville. From there, you can continue north, back to the start of the Mountains to Sea ride or head east to Palmerston North and beyond.

This ride has a unique start: a tunnel followed by an elevator deals to the first hill in a blink of an eye. From there, country roads lead to Hunterville, a small rural town renowned for its burgers and big bark.

The ride then heads north via the lovely Turakina Valley on a narrow, windy road. Then comes a few kilometres along Highway 49 before the route hooks into one last back road to follow the main trunk line to Ohakune.

ITINERARY

Stage 1: Whanganui to Hunterville
60 km, 3–4 hours

Start from the Whanganui i-SITE, on the corner of Victoria Ave and Taupo Quay. (It's right beside the Whanganui River, and there is a good cycle path running along the river banks. There is also a cafe next door!)

From the i-SITE, ride across the big bridge and cross Anzac Parade at the far end. Just on your left is the entrance to the Durie Hill elevator. Ride into the well-lit tunnel and take the elevator to the top of the hill (you'll need some coins to pay the fare for the elevator ride). At the top, park your bikes and climb the tower to take in some impressive views over Whanganui.

Leaving the lookout, ride left down Rodney Street, right down Durie Street and then right down Portal Street to head out of town. This becomes No 2 Line and takes you to Fordell, a small village with a pub and garage, 13 km from Whanganui.

From Fordell, continue east on the main road for just over a kilometre to Denlair Road. Paloma Gardens is a 3.5-km side trip from here that offers accommodation and a series of amazing themed gardens to peruse (garden entry fee $10). This detour involves a short steep hill.

From the Denlair Road turn-off, continue east on Kauangaroa Road and

Freewheelin' fun on The Three Rivers.

descend to the Whangaehu River (23 km from Whanganui) before climbing back up and over to the Turakina Valley (37 km). When you see a sign that says 'Hunterville 27 km', we think you only have 23.5 km to go to reach the township. About 1 km past the sign, you will reach Sutherland Bush, which has a dilapidated picnic table, and then you need to veer right up Mangatipona Road. Carry on, past Mangahoe sheep station and the Turakina Valley, and take Ongo Road through to Hunterville. This small town on Highway 1 has a great juice/smoothie/ice cream bar (Revive) and good burgers at the Hunter Cafe on the corner.

Optional Stage 2: Hunterville to Ohakune
93 km (mostly uphill), 8–10 hours

Backtrack 6.5 km, almost all downhill, to the Turakina Valley Road intersection. Turn right and follow Turakina Valley Road up to Rangiwaea Junction (55 km from Hunterville). Turn left onto Owhakura Road and ride west to Whangaehu Valley Road (at the 67-km mark). Then head north to Highway 49 and carefully follow the highway west to the turn-off down to Rangataua before following Dreadnought Road into Ohakune. From Owhakura to Ohakune, you are following the first half of the Ohakune to Taihape Trail (OTT) in reverse (see below).

Alternative option Adventurous riders can head to Karioi and follow a 4WD track beside the railway line to Rangataua.

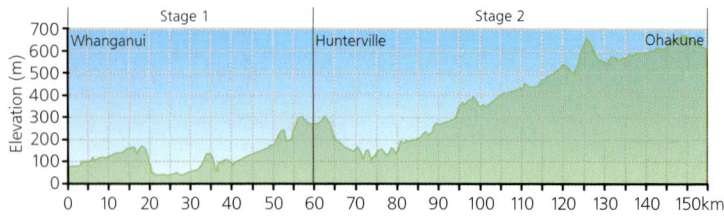

FACT FILE

Overview This trail is a great way to ride from the end of the Mountains to Sea Great Ride back to the start or makes a good link into the heartland rides of the Rangitikei and Manawatu. However, as a stand-alone ride, you should go from Ohakune to Whanganui – the elevation chart shows why.

How to get there Train to Ohakune and ride some or all of the Mountains to Sea trail.

Riding surface All sealed roads on the first half and a mix of seal and gravel in the second half.

History These roads were all built to give access to farming options. In the 1930s in particular, 'rovers' would wander the countryside, making their way from farm job to farm job.

Special considerations There are no shops and virtually no traffic along large sections of this trail, so go very well prepared.

Special features Quiet country roads, large rivers and lots of sheep

Important contacts None

Maps Kiwimap *Wanganui, Marton, Taihape*

SUPPORT SERVICES

Whanganui Plenty of supermarkets, shops, cafes, restaurants, takeaways, accommodation options: www.wanganui.com

Fordell: Hotel: ☎ 06 342 7896, Paloma Gardens (accommodation): ☎ 06 342 7857, www.paloma.co.nz

Hunterville Cafes, pubs, shops, accommodation: The Station Hotel: ☎ 06 322 8006, www.stationhotel.co.nz, Hunters Cafe and Motel: ☎ 06 322 8115, www.hunterscafe.co.nz

Ohakune Plenty of great cafes, bars, restaurants, shops and accommodation: www.ohakune.info, bike hire and packages available from Mountain Bike Station: www.mountainbikestation.co.nz, TCB Ski Board and Bike: ☎ 06 385 8433, www.tcbskiandboard.co.nz

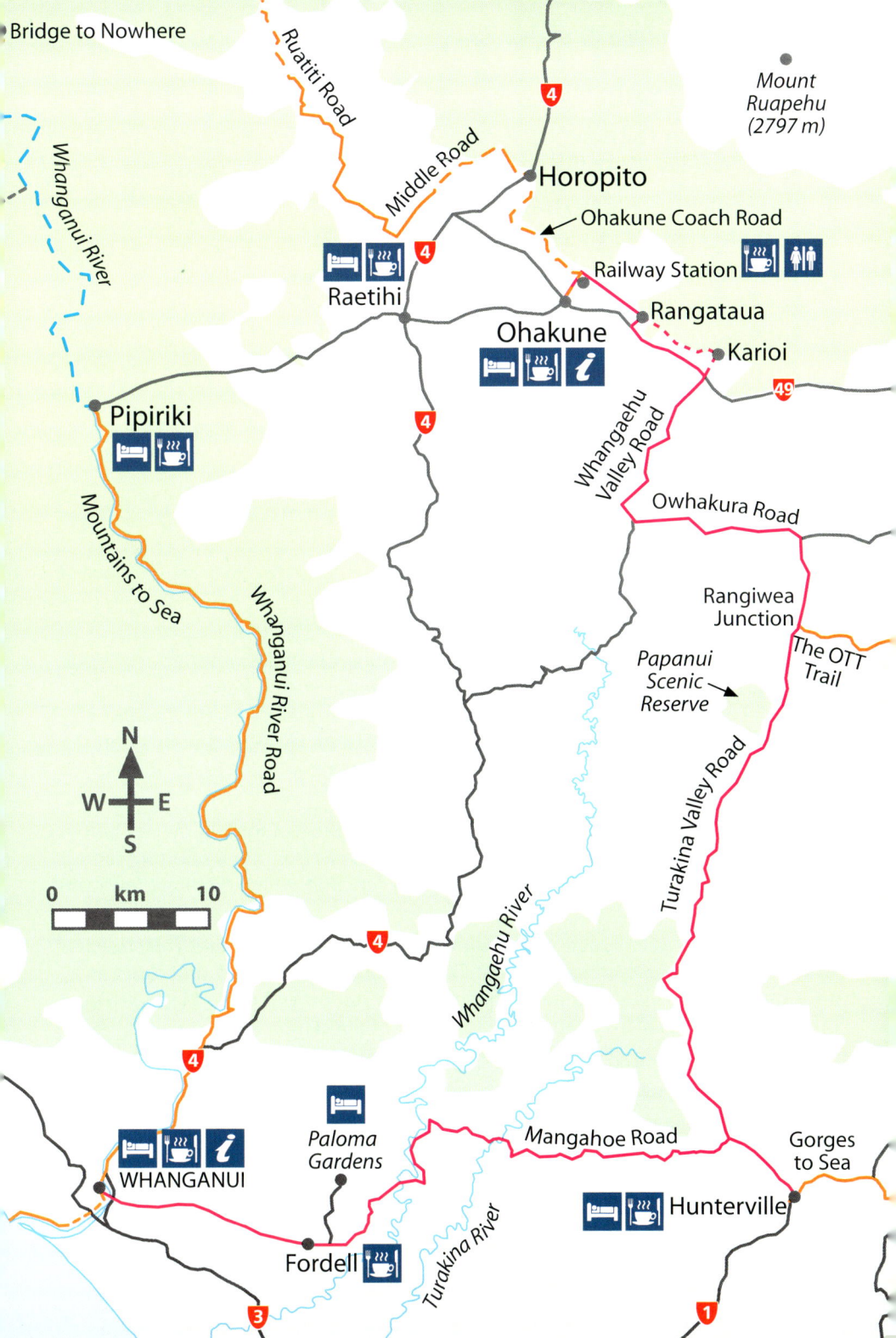

CONNECTOR RIDE

THE OTT TRAIL

Ohakune to Taihape
Distance 77 km   Time 5–7 hours   Grade 4 (Advanced)

The seldom-travelled Ohakune to Taihape (OTT) Trail provides excellent cycling for those who relish the chance to tackle a few hills across lumpy backcountry farmland. There are services at Ohakune and Taihape but nothing in between.

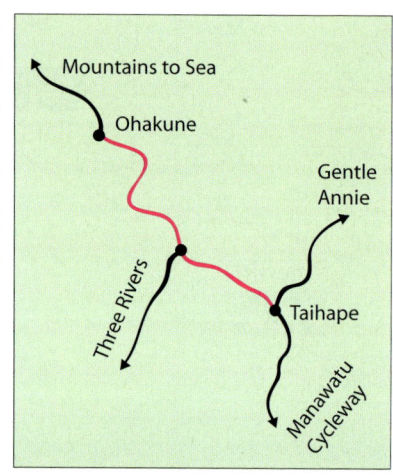

From the Ohakune Railway Station, cross the tracks on Ohakune Mountain Road and turn right on Railway Row. After 1 km, recross the tracks and turn left down Dreadnought Road. At Rangataua village, you have two choices: the adventurous way and the fast way.

The adventurous way is to cross the tracks again and follow a 4WD track beside the railway line to Karioi Station, then follow Karioi Station Road to Highway 49. This choice involves getting your feet wet at two stream crossings. The fast way is to ride from Rangataua, down Marino St to Highway 49 and then along the highway to Karioi Station Road. This highway is narrow in places, so ride early in the morning and take extra care.

From Karioi Station Road, take the highway southeast for 200 metres before turning into Whangaehu Valley Road. Just on 25 km from Ohakune, turn left up Owhakura Road and follow it to Rangiwaea Junction, where there are few farm houses.

From Rangiwaea Junction, turn right down Turakina Valley Road. This stretch is lovely; back-road cycling at its best. Turn left onto Ruanui Road, and climb away from the Turakina Valley past a hilltop sheep station and on to Mataroa. There are great views of Mt Ruapehu near the top of the climb.

Fine autumn riding along the Turakina Valley – nothing beats it.

Mataroa is a picturesque village with a postcard-perfect church. Ride through the village and follow Mataroa Road to Highway 1 almost 4 km away.

Ok, so you need to pedal along State Highway 1 in a 100 kph zone for 3 km to get to Taihape. It will take about 13 minutes. Pay attention and stick to the shoulder (it's generally very good).

The entrance to Taihape is heralded by a huge corrugated-iron gumboot, closely followed by a choice of delissimo cafes, made all the better by cycling to them.

How to get there Northern Explorer train, or bus to Ohakune.
Maps Kiwimap *Wanganui, Marton, Taihape*
Accommodation See www.taihape.co.nz

HEARTLAND RIDE

Gorges to Sea Cycleway
Taihape to the Tasman Sea
Distance 191 km   Time 2–4 days   Grade 4 (Advanced)

Four country roads transport you to a bygone era, when cars were rare and cyclists a novelty. You'll discover seldom-travelled Rangitikei roads at a pace perfect for this intricate landscape.

The four celebrated country road rides that make up this cycleway connect Taihape – gumboot capital of the world – with Himatangi Beach on the west coast. Apart from two short sections along Highway 1, the route follows quiet roads and becomes less hilly as it approaches the coast.

You could travel this route in two easy weekend trips: Taihape to Hunterville and Hunterville to Himatangi.

ITINERARY

Stage 1: Omatane Trail: Taihape to Mangaweka
40 km, 3–5 hours

From Taihape, ride south on Highway 1 for 6 km before turning left onto Gorge Road. This section of highway has a good shoulder most of the way.

You will meet your first gorge less than 20 metres from the start of Gorge Road, where a narrow bridge crosses Hautapu River. About 8 km further on are another two gorges at Omatane Scenic Reserve. The first is an amazing slot below the Omatane Bridge, then round the corner is the huge Rangitikei River bridge. The depths of some of New Zealand's most famous gorges are marked out along the edge of the bridge's downstream handrail.

Climb away from the bridge on Omatane South Road and Potaka Road to a T-intersection at Kawhatau Valley Road, 29 km from Taihape (parts of this section are gravel). Turn right and cruise along the huge terrace until you drop down to Mangawharariki River and cross another bridge. On the other side, a signpost flags a 5-minute walk to a power house built in 1913. A few hundred metres further on, you will reach Ruahine Road. Turn right to ride to Mangaweka, 2 km away.

Stage 2: Pemberton Trail: Mangaweka to Hunterville
63 km, 4–7 hours

From Mangaweka, backtrack 2 km, then continue east on Ruahine Road. You will be following the first 19 km of the Manawatu Cycleway.

Morning tea at Pemberton.

Branch off the Manawatu Cycleway to head to Rangiwahia, a small village with a camping/picnic area and toilets. Continue south on Rangiwahia Road for 4 km to the Pemberton picnic area and historic site.

Now turn right up Mangamako Road to climb over a small hill and begin a lovely section down a picturesque valley. After a while, the seal morphs into gravel, and then, about 43 km from Mangaweka, you will reach a T-intersection at the end of Mangamako Road where you turn right on Sandon Block Road. This leads to Highway 54 and the seal once more. Vinegar Hill camping ground is a few hundred metres to your right. This is about 55 km from Mangaweka, at the bottom of a brisk downhill.

From the camping area, it is 2 km uphill, to Highway 1. Then turn left and ride the good shoulder beside the highway towards Hunterville, 6 km away. There are two narrow bridges along this stretch that require special care. When you get to them, stop and look behind you. When, and only when, there is no traffic visible on your side of the road, will you have enough time to cycle across the bridge before any traffic can reach you.

After the second bridge, which is curved, you will soon be able to leave the main road by turning left down Kotukutuku Road. It's a lovely country lane that leads into Hunterville, 5 minutes away.

Stage 3: Mt Curl Trail: Hunterville to Marton
33 km, 2–3 hours

Cross Highway 1 and head west out of Hunterville on Bruce Street, which soon becomes Ongo Road. It's sweet riding almost straight away. After 3 km, turn left down Aldworth Road. This brings you around to the south end of the Bruce Park Scenic Reserve (with car park and a pleasant walk), just before Highway 1. Now you need to head south for 500 metres, and you can do this by either following an abandoned section of old highway (through a farm gate opposite the Bruce Park car park) or nipping out to the current Highway 1. Either way, shortly after, turn right up Mt Curl Road. A few hundred metres up this road, the route splits into an easy or a hard option.

The hard hilly option continues straight ahead and over Mt Curl – a tough climb, but rewarding, with great views. The easier option goes left and is fairly flat, making it 20 minutes faster. Both routes are signposted and meet again after 10–12 km.

Where they converge, Jeffersons Line and Tutaenui Road lead you across easy farmland to the rural centre of Marton.

Stage 4: Tangimoana Trail: Marton to the Tasman Sea
55 km, 3–5 hours

This is a day of flattish riding. Head south out of Marton on Wellington Road, then left at Makirikiri Road and, after 6 km, you will reach Highway 1. Carefully cross it and head right for 1 km before turning left onto Kakariki Road. Next, turn right onto Mingaroa Road – from now on, you will be riding roughly parallel to the Rangitikei River all the way to the Tasman Sea. Take Wilson Road South, Hurst Road and Wightman Road to the highway. Cross carefully and then follow Tangimoana Road to the coast.

You should plan to reach the beach two hours either side of low tide so that you can follow hard sand south to Himatangi Beach, a holiday village with a camp ground.

FACT FILE

Overview In 2009, this became the first heartland ride to be opened in the country. It passes through an interesting rural landscape, flanked by trees, both native and exotic.

How to get there Drive or bus to Taihape. Alternatively, you can ride to Taihape from Ohakune or Napier (see The OTT Trail and Gentle Annie).

Riding surface Mostly sealed roads, but there are several sections of gravel and 8 km of sand at the end.

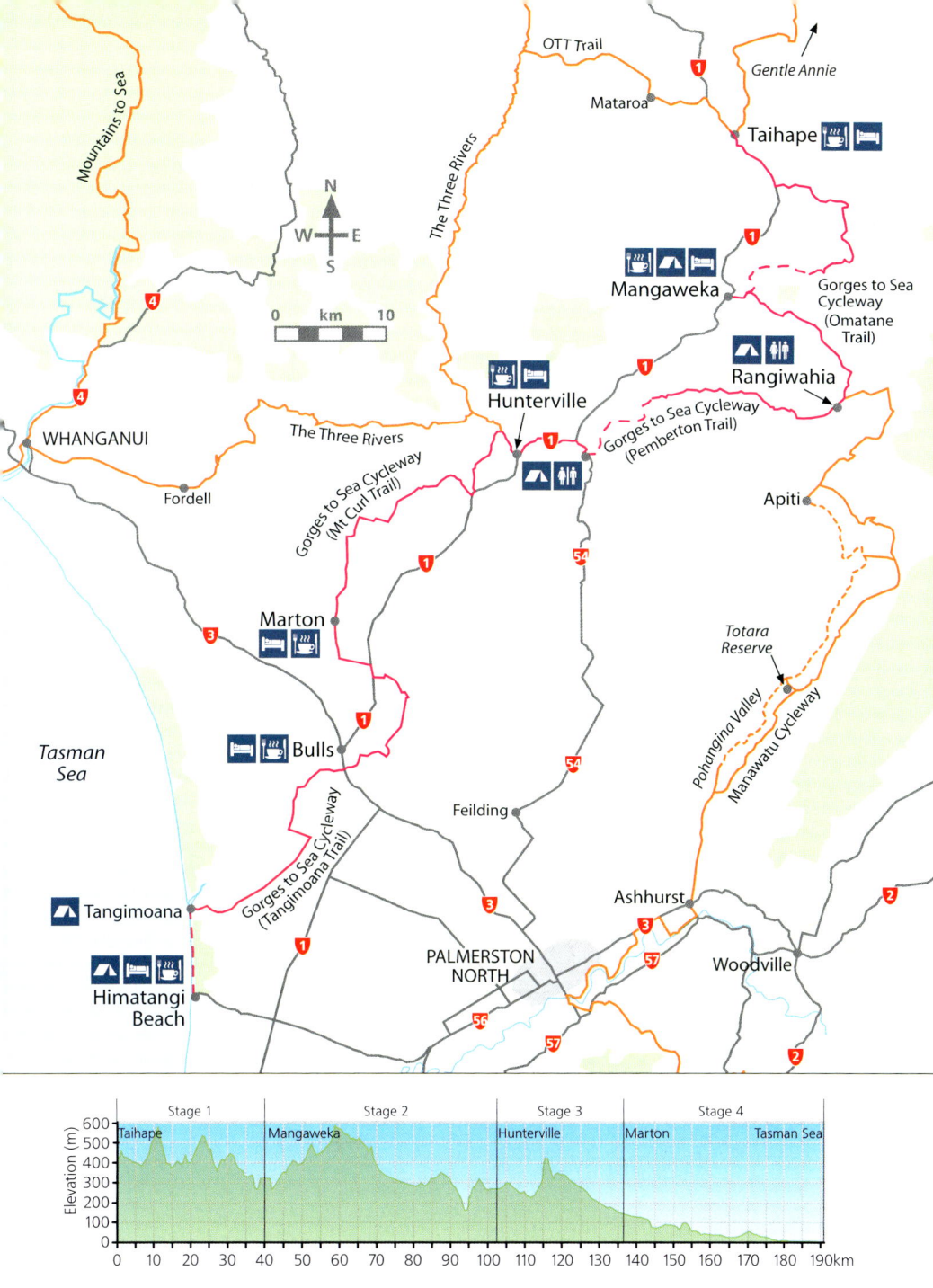

Classic New Zealand Cycle Trails

Special considerations We have graded this trail 4 (advanced) because of the two short sections that you have to take along Highway 1: if you ride sensibly, they should cause no problems. Without the highway sections, the ride is a grade 3 (intermediate).

Special features This is a hilly route, but the only real monster is Mt Curl, and there is a signposted alternative for those who wish to avoid it.

Vinegar Hill campground is usually empty, but over the summer holidays it is a popular camping destination.

Maps Pick up a map from the information centre in Taihape or go to the trail website below.

SUPPORT SERVICES

Taihape Food, shops, petrol, accommodation: www.taihape.co.nz

Mangaweka Accommodation, gallery and food: Papa Cliff Cafe, ☎ 06 382 5778, Mangaweka Homestay: ☎ 06 382 5774 or 027 526 6612, www.freewebs.com/mangawekagallery/, Mangaweka Camping Grounds for cabins and camping, ☎ 06 382 5744 or 0800 655 747, www.mangaweka.co.nz

Ruahine Road Mt Huia Farmstay: ☎ 06 382 5726, www.mthuia.co.nz and Mairenui Rural Retreat: ☎ 06 382 5564, www.mairenui.co.nz

Vinegar Hill Putai Ngahere Reserve/Vinegar Hill Camping Ground, www.manawatunz.co.nz

Rangiwahia Rangiwahia Domain available for camping, www.manawatunz.co.nz

Hunterville Cafes, pubs, shops, accommodation: The Station Hotel: ☎ 06 322 8006, www.stationhotel.co.nz, Hunters Cafe and Motel: ☎ 06 322 8115

Marton Food, accommodation: Marton Motel: ☎ 06 327 8499/0800 462 7866, www.martonmotel.co.nz, Cosy Oak B & B: ☎ 06 327 7980/0800 327 980, www.cosyoak.co.nz, Adobe Motel: ☎ 06 327 6111, www.adobemotelmarton.co.nz

Tangimoana Tangimoana Motor Camp, ☎ 06 324 8208

Himatangi Beach General store, takeaways, accommodation: Himatangi Beach Holiday Park, ☎ 06 329 9575, www.himatangi-beach-holiday-park.co.nz

HEARTLAND RIDE

Manawatu Cycleway
Mangaweka to Ashhurst and Palmerston North
Distance 124 km   Time 2–3 days   Grade 3 (Intermediate)

The Manawatu Cycleway provides an excellent weekend away, exploring a seldom-visited part of the Rangitikei. It is also a great alternative to Highway 1 for cycle tourists.

Starting from Mangaweka, the route quickly whisks you away from the main highway to follow quiet country roads to the village of Apiti before wiggling through to the scenic Pohangina Valley, down to Ashhurst and finally into Palmerston North via a state highway, back roads and an off-road path beside the Manawatu River.

The majority of the first half crosses a farmed plateau with several dips into river valleys carved deep into the region's famous mudstone. The second half rolls down the Pohangina Valley where the road is tree lined and passes three scenic reserves.

ITINERARY

Stage 1: Mangaweka to Apiti
42 km, 2–4 hours

From Mangaweka, head north up Highway 1 for 150 metres and turn right onto Ruahine Road. After 18 km of steady uphill, the route takes a left off Ruahine Road to follow Te Parapara Road. After 4 km, veer right down Main South Road, which becomes Oroua Valley Road and leads to the quaint village of Apiti. Apiti has a pub and camping area. Rangiwahia Domain (2 km off the route) also offers a camping area and public toilets.

This stage includes several small climbs out of gorges and two short sections of gravel road.

Stage 2: Apiti to Ashhurst
58 km, 3–6 hours

From Apiti, the ride is all sealed and follows a popular cycling route along Pohangina Valley, parallel to the Ruahine Range. Riders backtrack from Apiti for 2 km to take Pohangina Valley East Road. The road soon presents the only significant climb of the stage, then rolls through open farmland and lush native bush. A good stopping point is Totara Reserve, a lovely camping area with swimming holes, walking tracks and giant totara. From Totara Reserve, the route continues down the Pohangina Valley to Ashhurst.

It's all smiles when you're at the highest point of the ride.

Tour Aotearoa alternative Follow the uber quiet gravel roads directly from Apiti to Utuwai and down the west side of Pohangina Valley to Pohangina. This route rejoins the cycleway 4 km south of Pohangina.

Stage 3: Ashhurst to Palmerston North
24 km, 1.5–2 hours

From Ashhurst, the route into Palmerston North is flat but interesting. Head south on the main road, and turn left into Ashhurst Domain. Ten metres inside the entrance gates turn right onto a gravel path that skirts around the edge of the domain. When you reach the next sealed road turn right, exit the domain, turn left down the highway and left shortly afterwards to ride underneath the highway bridge. This is the start of the Manawatu River Pathway.

In 2018, there was still a gap in the pathway that requires you to cycle up Raukawa Road to Highway 3, then turn left and follow the highway to Te Matai Road to head back down to the river pathway. It follows the Manawatu River to Fitzherbert Park, where a cycle lane along Fitzherbert Avenue leads to the information centre in The Square.

FACT FILE

How to get there The cycleway makes an enjoyable weekend trip, with riders able to take advantage of public transport options (train or bus) to access either end.

Riding surface 91% sealed road; 6% gravel road; 3% cycle path

Maps Pick up an excellent map of this trail from local i-SITEs and businesses.

Trail websites www.nzcycletrail.com or to download an app of the cycleway for your smartphone: www.everytrail.com/guide/manawatu-cycleway-on-the-country-road

SUPPORT SERVICES

Mangaweka Accommodation, gallery and food: Papa Cliff Cafe, ☎ 06 382 5778, Mangaweka Homestay: ☎ 06 382 5774 or 027 526 6612, www.freewebs.com/mangawekagallery/, Mangaweka Camping Grounds for cabins and camping ☎ 06 382 5744 or 0800 655 747, www.mangaweka.co.nz

Cafe: plans are afoot to reopen the cafe at Mangaweka's iconic aeroplane.

Ruahine Road Mt Huia Farmstay: ☎ 06 382 5726, www.mthuia.co.nz and Mairenui Rural Retreat: ☎ 06 382 5564, www.mairenui.co.nz

Rangiwahia Rangiwahia Domain available for camping, www.manawatunz.co.nz

Apiti Accommodation, food: Apiti Tavern: ☎ 06 328 4848, Makoura Lodge (6 km from Apiti along the alternative gravel route): ☎ 06 328 4746, www.makouralodge.co.nz

Piripiri Campsite Small, basic DOC campsite: www.doc.govt.nz

Komako Food and accommodation: Springvale Gardens and B&B: ☎ 06 329 4891

Pohangina Valley Totara Reserve camping area: ☎ 06 329 4708; Pohangina Base: ☎ 06 350 9700, www.doc.govt.nz; Songbird Gardens (accommodation) ☎ 06 329 4822, www.songbirdgardens.co.nz

Ashhurst Cafes, general store, takeaways, accommodation: camping at Ashhurst Domain: ☎ 06 326 8203, www.manawatunz.co.nz

Palmerston North Plenty of supermarkets, shops, cafes, bars, restaurants, accommodation: www.manawatunz.co.nz

Bike shops: Crank It Cycles, 244 Cuba Street, ☎ 06 358 9810; Bike Barn Palmerston North, cnr Ferguson & Oxford Streets, ☎ 06 356 7987

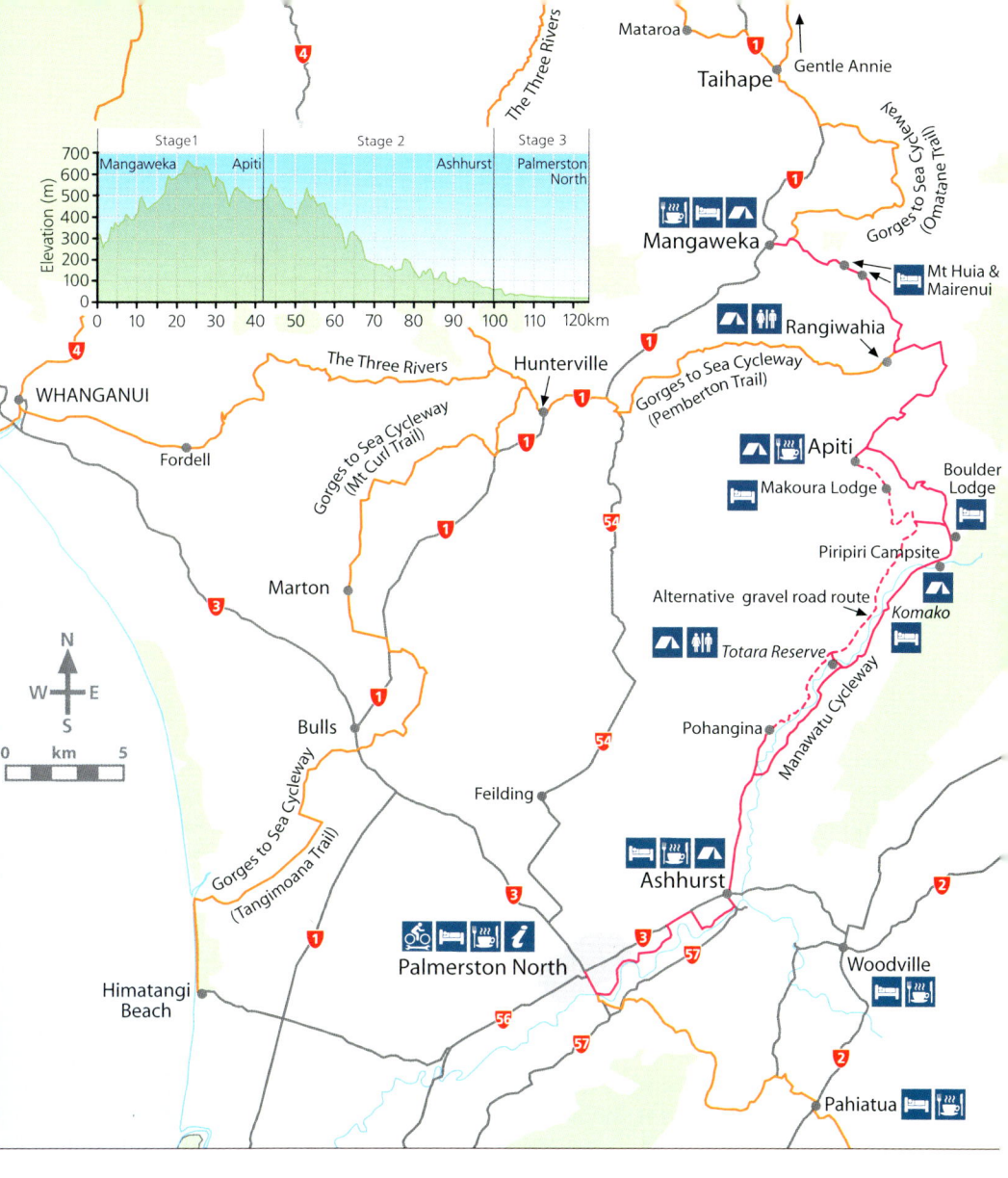

CONNECTOR RIDE

PALMERSTON NORTH TO MASTERTON
Manawatu and Wairarapa
Distance 106 km   Time 1–2 days   Grade 5 (Expert – because of traffic)

For cyclists with gravel ready tyres this is the best route across the ranges to the Wairarapa plains.

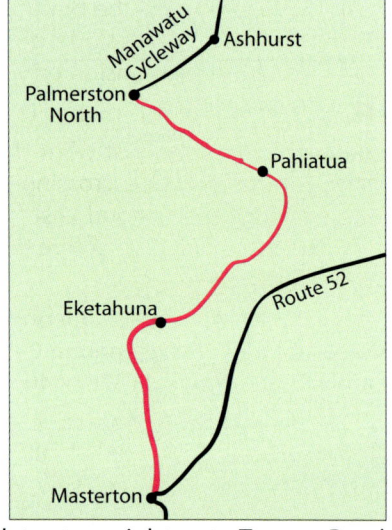

From Palmerston North, head southeast across the Manawatu River on Fitzherbert Ave, and continue up Summerhill Drive to Aokautere Drive (Highway 57) 4 km from town. Head north on Aokautere Drive for 2 km and, just after crossing a bridge, make a right-hand turn onto Polson Hill Drive. Polson Hill Drive and The Bush Track together are a short cut to the Pahiatua Track (a sealed road climb).

When you are 16 km from Palmerston North, veer left off the Pahiatua Track and onto Ballance Valley Road, and 300 metres later, turn right onto Tararua Road. At the bottom of this fast gravel downhill, turn right on Ballance Road and head south to cross the Mangahao River on Pahiatua Mangahao Road. Ride 6 km into Pahiatua, passing a railway museum, and taking a cycle path in to town.

From the south end of Pahiatua, take Tiraumea Road southeast. This becomes Kaitawa Road and then Mangaone Valley Road. When you meet Alfredton Road, 28 km from Pahiatua, veer right and ride a further 5 km to Eketahuna, a small town with food and accommodation. Cruise into town on Alfredton Road, go straight ahead across Jones Street, then left down Bengston and left onto Haswell Street to the main street of Eketahuna.

From the large Kiwi sculpture on the main street, head down Church Street. Turn left at Bridge Street, then left again at Stanly Street. About 3 km from town, make sure you veer left to stay on South Road. A radical gravel road downhill spits you out at the highway. Turn left again, along the highway for 300 metres before turning right onto Falkner Road. When you hit Opaki Kaiparoro Road, turn left then right 2 km later at North Road. Turn right into West Road, then left onto Jackson Line – a quiet, scenic gravel road alternative, which pops you back out on Opaki Kaiparoro Road. Follow Opaki Kaiparoro all the way to Highway 2, and ride south for 7 km to Masterton. There is just enough shoulder on this last stretch, except over a road rail bridge, where you need to take extra care. Don't start crossing the bridge until there is no traffic behind you.

A few blocks into Masterton, there is a corner dairy at First Street, and 30 metres around the corner is a takeaways, a cafe and a sandwich shop.

One block further south is a big Mobil petrol station opposite a pedestrian entrance to Mawley Holiday Park. Ahead is a big highway bridge over the river.

Just 5 metres before the bridge, at the Golden Shears sign, turn left and ride 20 metres down a grass slope, on to a lime-sand path. Follow it for 300 metres, before crossing a suspension bridge to Queen Elizabeth Park on your right.

Veer right though the park to Dixon Street, to a supermarket, café, i-SITE, etc.

Alternatively, if you just want to take the quickest and quietest route out of Masterton, turn left after crossing the suspension bridge and follow a lime-sand path beside the river southeast to Colombo Street. Turn right and ride down Colombo Street for 1 km before turning left on Johnstone Street and riding out of town towards Gladstone.

Notes Accommodation is plentiful in Pahiatua. We stayed at the Post Office Hotel, 164 Main Street, phone 06 376 7489. A cheaper option is the Pahiatua Carnival Park, phone 06 376 6340 or see www.carnivalpark.co.nz

In Eketahuna, there are a couple of options: Eketahuna Inn (food and rooms), 42 Main Street, phone 06 375 8000, or the Motor Campground, phone 06 375 8677, or 027 747 2111, see www.eketahunacamp.com

In Masterton, the first place is Mawley Holiday Park, phone 06 378 6454 or go to www.mawleypark.co.nz but there are also plenty of motels in town.

Death by kiwi in Eketahuna.

HEARTLAND RIDE

Gentle Annie
Taihape to Hawke's Bay
Distance 162 km   Time 2 days
Grade 4 (Advanced, purely because of the big hills)

This remote and scenic route follows an old Maori trail across rugged ranges and rivers through the Kaweka Forest Park. With virtually no traffic, this road is tempting for road racers and adventurous cycle tourers.

Starting from Taihape railway station, head for the shops and stock up: there are no shops from here on in. The road is gentle for an hour but then settles into a series of hills past the remote Erewhon sheep station, before dropping into the mighty Rangitikei River valley. It climbs again, passing exposed farmland to enter the Kaweka Range. This heralds the start of the infamous Gentle Annie climb, an anything-but-gentle ascent followed by an exhilarating downhill to the Kuripapango camping ground.

From here, the ride passes pine forests and farmland, with views of Hawke's Bay. The descents outnumber the ascents as you fly towards 'Mary of the Crossroads', at the end of the Taihape-Napier Road.

ITINERARY

Stage 1: Taihape to Rangitikei River
40 km, 2–4 hours

Head north out of Taihape on Hautapu Street. This morphs into Spooners Hill Road and, after 4 km, you will reach Kaiewe Junction. If you have an aversion to gravel, continue straight ahead, and you will meet the Taihape-Napier Road after another 4 km. However, the shorter and less hilly option is to turn right onto Pungatawa Road, then left at Waikakahi Road and left again at Moawhango Valley Road. This recommended short cut includes 10 km of gravel and meets the Taihape-Napier Road at Moawhango.

From Moawhango, the road is sealed all the way to Hawke's Bay. After passing the huge Erewhon ('nowhere' spelt backwards by a bad speller) Station stockyards, the road climbs to a high point that offers a breathtaking panorama of the Rangitikei Valley. The descent is wonderful but tempered by the view of the next climb! Sandwiched between lies a basic camping ground, toilet and the historic Springvale Suspension Bridge. The river offers good swimming and the possibility of brown trout for tea.

Viewing the Springvale Suspension Bridge over the Rangitikei River.

Stage 2: Rangitikei River to Kuripapango
36 km, 2–4 hours

The road ahead was laid down on the landscape as an obvious challenge to cyclists. It must be climbed, and climb you must. This is an exposed part of the trip. At Otupae Station, there is 'No.1' shed, which would provide good shelter in a northwesterly storm. Further on at Ngatoma Station, there is a shelterbelt of pine trees. However, there is little else until you drop down to Taruarau Valley, which is forested and has a few baches.

From there, the road enters Kaweka Forest Park and tackles the Gentle Annie. All the uphills on this tour are followed by fantastic downhills: the Gentle Annie is no exception. The climb takes at least 30 minutes with a loaded bike. The downhill side is steep and ends at the Ngaruroro bridge. Carry on for 2 km, gently uphill, to reach the DOC camp ground at Kuripapango.

Stage 3: Kuripapango to Fernhill, Hawke's Bay
60 km, 5–6 hours, including a 1-hour walking side trip

Naturally, this stage starts with a climb. It is through pine forest, and you should be prepared to meet logging trucks. The road is wide enough as long as you keep well left.

After 13 km, there is a turn-off to Blowhard Bush Reserve, about 600 metres down Lawrence Road (gravel), on your left. Just next to the small car park is a shelter, with drinking water supply and toilets. From here, you can do a neat 1-hour loop walk through native forest, past limestone formations and out to a stunning view of the Kaweka Range.

From Blowhard Bush, return to the main road, which continues up and down, down and up to a 'Panorama of Hawke's Bay' lookout, then massively down. If you have your day well planned, you might like to pop into the De la Terre Winery at the 46-km mark. The Taihape-Napier Road ends 60 km from Kuripapango at Mary of the Crossroads (Fernhill).

Stage 4: Fernhill to Napier
26 km, 2–3 hours

The most enjoyable way back to civilisation from here is via the Hawke's Bay Trails. Turn right onto Highway 50, a busy road, and follow it for 200 metres to cross the Ngaruroro River on the Fernhill Bridge. On the far side, turn left onto a lime-sand trail. This follows a stopbank all the way out to the coast. If you are heading to Hastings instead, then branch off down Oak Avenue.

From the coast, turn left to follow a smooth concrete path to Napier – a relaxing end to this rollercoaster tour.

FACT FILE

Overview If the hills start feeling a bit tough, think of the old timers who rode (and walked) over the Gentle Annie on single-speed bicycles when the road was rough gravel the whole way.

How to get there The Northern Explorer train will stop at Taihape for large groups, otherwise take a bus to Taihape. From Napier/Hastings, catch a bus or ride south on Route 52.

Riding surface 90–100% sealed road, 10–0% gravel road

Special considerations There is no cellphone coverage for most of the ride. **Be warned** if you leave your food unattended at the Kuripapango campground, it may be eaten by horses during the day or by possums at night.

SUPPORT SERVICES

Taihape Food, shops, accommodation: www.taihape.co.nz

Springvale Basic campground with toilets only

Kuripapango (Ox Bow) campground www.doc.govt.nz (no booking required)

Mangawhare Bed & Breakfast (23 km east of Kuripapango) ☎ 021 500 271, www.mangawhare.com, 72 Glenross Road. Will do lunches if you call ahead.

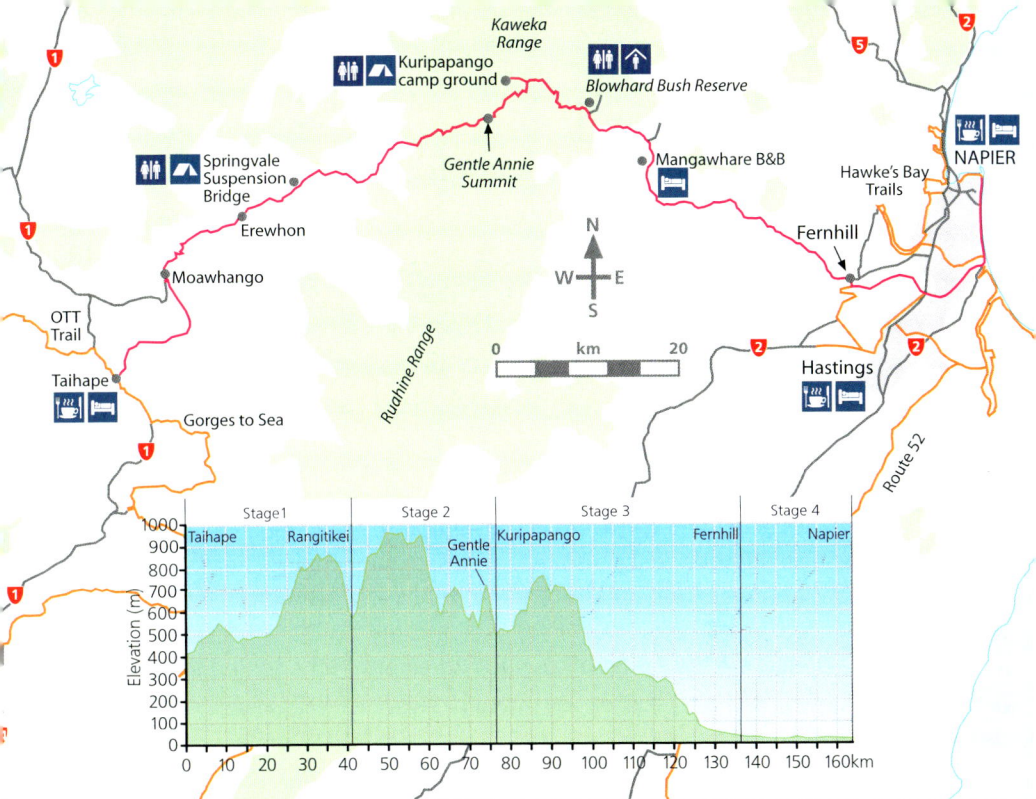

Fernhill Bridge (after Mary of the Crossroads) Farmhouse Lodge: ☎ 06 878 1288
Napier and Hastings Food, bike shops, accommodation: www.napiernz.com and hawkesbaynz.com/

GREAT RIDE

Hawke's Bay Trails
Napier, Hastings and Havelock North
Distance up to 180 km   Time 1 hour–1 week
Grades 1–3+ (Very Easy–Intermediate)

Hawke's Bay is the closest you can get to a European cycling holiday without travelling to Europe. It's all about gently absorbing fabulous coastal and rural scenery en route to award-winning vineyards and restaurants.

The extensive network of cycle paths link the well-known attractions between Napier, Hastings and Havelock North, including Mission Estate Winery, Splash Planet swimming pools and Cape Kidnappers wildlife tours. They also lead to lesser-known attractions, such as the Pheasants Nest (Rural Restaurant winner) in Puketapu and the restored wetlands of Ahuriri Estuary.

Cycling has taken off to such an extent in the region that Hawke's Bay now lays claim as the Cycling Capital of New Zealand. Many hotels hire bikes, and tour companies can help with itineraries ranging from a few hours to a week. Here is our pick of six of the best riding options.

ITINERARY

The Coastal Ride
27 km, 2–3 hours, Grade 1 (Very Easy)

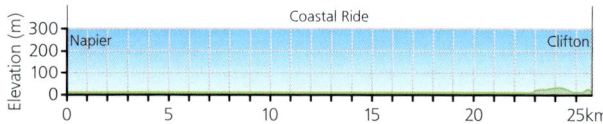

Nip around the back of the Napier i-SITE on Marine Parade and onto a smooth path following the Pacific coastline. Head south towards Cape Kidnappers. After 9 km, you'll ride through Waitangi Regional Park which has a large star compass worth checking out. Then you'll cross two rivers, the Tutaekuri and the Ngaruroro. At the 11 km mark, duck under the Clive River bridge to take a pedestrian path safely across the river. Once at the far end, you are 100 metres from Clive.

If you don't need a cafe stop, duck under the bridge again and continue along the main path towards Clifton. You will pass the beautiful East Clive Wetlands.

After riding 17 km from Napier, you'll reach another major bridge (Black Bridge) and will have to repeat the ducking process to safely cross via a pedestrian path to follow the path out to the coast. When you reach houses, take care to follow

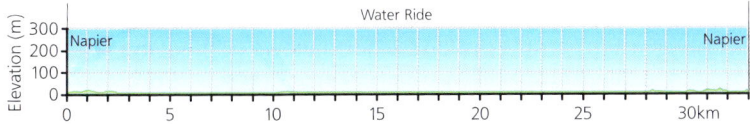

The Puketapu Loop - great for a hot summers day.

the pathway signs or you will get lost. The path ends at Clifton by the beach, where you can head to the cafe or arrange for a tour of the Gannet Colony. Nearby is the Clearview Winery.

The Water Ride (north end)
33 km, 2–4 hours, Grade 1 (Very Easy)

From the Napier i-SITE on Marine Parade, follow the coastal path north past the port and through the West Quay Wharf, where the path disappears for 200 metres. At the far end of the wharf, skirt past Ahuriri (great seaside playground) and cross a bridge to Westshore. There you will find the Rolls Royce of cycle paths. Super wide and smooth, it has great views and picnic tables with cycle racks! Just before Bay View, many locals take a 1-km diversion to Snapper Park Cafe.

After a coffee, backtrack to the main cycle path, which leads across Highway 2 and onto a lime-sand path that weaves around a hill and a wetland. It passes the airport, curves around another wetland and ducks under the highway onto an old road bridge. Just 100 metres north of the bridge turn right onto another lime-sand path back to Ahuriri and Napier. This ride is most scenic after rain.

The Puketapu Loop
18 km, 2–3 hours, Grade 2 (Easy)

On a stinking hot day, this is the best ride in Hawkes Bay. This country ride is quiet and weaves through graceful old trees. Parking is easy, and the destination involves good food and drink.

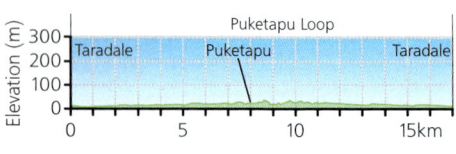

Start from Pettigrew Green Arena (Gloucester Street, Taradale). From the stopbank path beside the car park, turn right and simply follow the path all the way to Puketapu, 8 km away. Take care on two road crossings near Puketapu. After a break, follow signposts to Vicarage Bridge. At the far end, hang a sharp left and follow the lime-sand path back to Pettigrew Green Arena.

The Wineries Ride
33–47 km, 2 hours–1 day, Grade 2 (Easy)

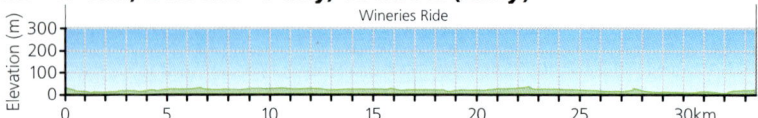

This easy ride around the Gimblett Gravels wine region is a dream for wine lovers. The wineries also serve non-alcoholic drinks and food – great for everyone!

Where to start this loop ride? Three of the wineries hire bikes (see Support Services), or you could start from Roy's Hill (near Fernhill) or the Hastings Golf Club (they welcome cyclists and have a cafe, bike racks and toilets). Triangle Cellars is another good starting point.

Roy's Hill is only 20 metres high but offers good views of the wine region. It's quite a dog-leg out to Sileni (5 km off the main loop), but they are one of the best wineries to visit with great architecture, a cellar door and a gift shop selling wine, cheese, chocolates, olive oil and kitchenware; great for those with Masterchef aspirations. Other highlights are Oak Avenue (planted in 1876) and riding the stopbank path beside the Ngaruroro River.

The Tukituki Loop
32 km, 2–3 hours, Grade 3 (Intermediate)

This is a brilliant loop for fitness seekers. Half is on road, and half is off road. There are a few good hills and a stunning 'Tuscany' landscape. The car park at Black Bridge is a popular starting point. But if you don't mind riding 4 km extra, you could also start from Havelock North.

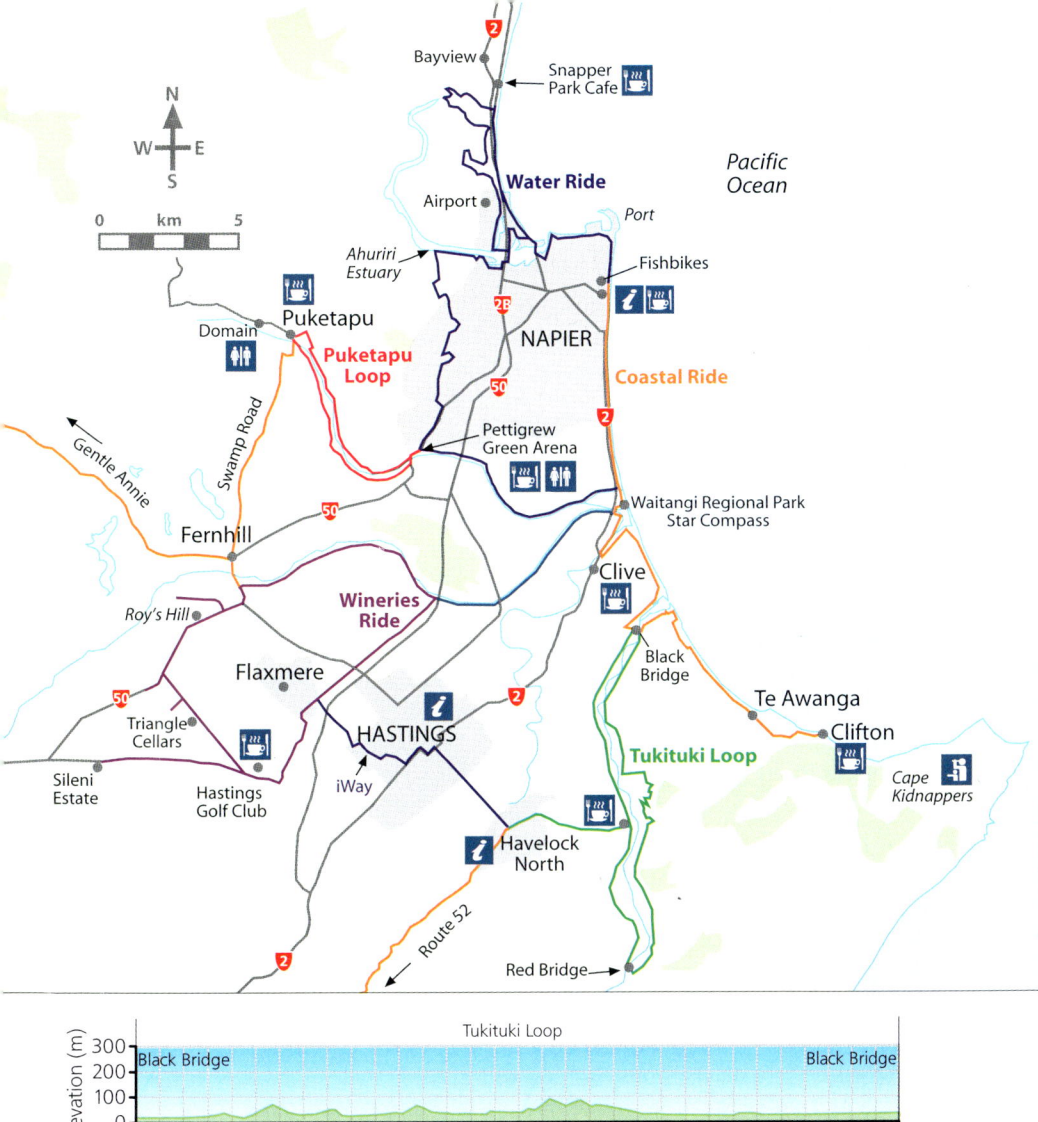

Black Bridge is on the Coastal Ride and crosses the Tukituki River, 16 km south of Napier, on the way to Clifton.

From Black Bridge, follow the wide lime-sand track underneath the bridge and onto a stopbank on the other side of the road. The trail runs along the stopbank for almost 8 km before following River Road away from the Tukituki River for 800 metres to Waimarama Road.

Turn left at the intersection to continue up valley. The trail is a mixture of on and off road from here to Red Bridge, 5 km away. Cross Red Bridge and turn

Classic New Zealand Cycle Trails

left again. Follow Tukituki Road for 9 km before turning down Moore Road for 900 metres and hooking into another lime-sand path. Follow it back to Black Bridge.

The Hawke's Bay 100
100 km, 1–2 days, Grade 3+ (Intermediate)

The Hawke's Bay 100 has been devised for cycling enthusiasts. It hits that magical 100-km mark and combines the best of the Hawke's Bay trails in one satisfying loop. It consists of five stages, each terminating at a refueling spot, and each shorter than the last.

Stage 1 (29 km): Follow the Water Ride from the Napier i-SITE north past the port, inland below Ahuriri Estuary and south through Taradale to the Pettigrew Green Arena. Then follow the Puketapu Loop to Puketapu Tavern and Store – the first pit stop.

Stage 2 (22 km): Head straight from Puketapu to Fernhill via Swamp Road. Beyond Fernhill, hook into the Wineries Ride, ignoring all side trips en route to the Golf Club Cafe.

Stage 3 (19 km): Follow the Wineries Ride to Wilson Road and turn right at Flaxmere Ave. Follow iWay cycle paths through Hastings and Havelock North to the Tandem Cafe. From Flaxmere Ave, take Maraekakaho Road, Wall Road, Southland Road, Gascoigne Street and Railway Road to the centre of Hastings. Then take the fabulous cycle path beside the main road to Havelock North. At Havelock North, turn left onto Karanema Drive and left again onto Te Mata Road, which ends at the mouthwatering Chalk and Cheese Cafe.

Stage 4 (16 km): Cross Waimarama Road and drop down River Road to hook a left onto the Tukituki River stopbank path. Cruise down to Black Bridge, and along the coast to Clive. Ride up the main street for 500 metres to a neat little cafe in a shipping container next to the petrol station.

Stage 5 (14 km): Follow the wide coastal path back to the Napier i-SITE. Then cruise into the main shopping centre for a coffee.

FACT FILE

How to get there Napier is 4 hours drive from Wellington or 5½ hours by bus (timetables: www.intercity.co.nz).

Riding surface Napier has wide concrete paths. Hastings has a mix of concrete paths, cycle lanes and lime-sand paths. Beyond the cities, you'll find mostly lime-sand paths.

History In 1769, local Maori attempted to kidnap a Tahitian crew member from Captain Cook's ship. The attempt failed, but the event lives on in the naming of Cape Kidnappers.

In 1931, Napier was destroyed by a massive earthquake and fire. It was rebuilt in the art deco style of the day and is now being proposed as a World Heritage site.

Special considerations You'll need sunglasses to deal with the glare off the Mediterranean-style lime-sand paths. The public buses in Hawke's Bay have double bike racks. There are good options for riding one way and bussing back.

Special features Some of the riverside stopbank trails are farmed, so you may meet cows and sheep.

The Puketapu Loop includes the option of a 10-minute walk to Otarara Pa for panoramic views and Maori history.

Maps Pick up a map from any local i-SITE or bike shop.

Trail websites www.nzcycletrail.com and www.iway.org.nz

SUPPORT SERVICES

Bike hire and tours Fishbike, bike hire and coffee close to the Napier i-SITE: ☎ 0800 131 600, www.fishbike.co.nz

Takaro Trails (one of the country's best cycle guiding companies, also hires bikes and offers self-guided tours of all types): ☎ 06 835 9030, www.takarotrails.co.nz

Good Fun Bike Rides: ☎ 06 650 7722/021 777 964, www.goodfunbikerides.co.nz

On Yer Bike Winery Tours: ☎ 06 650 4627, www.onyerbikehb.co.nz

Napier i-SITE Located on Marine Parade, www.napiernz.com

Hastings i-SITE Cnr Russell St Sth & Heretaunga St East: www.visithastings.co.nz

Puketapu General store and tavern with an award-winning restaurant, The Puketapu, www.thepuketapu.co.nz. Also, just 1 km off the signposted loop, is Puketapu Domain (picnic site, playground and toilets).

Pettigrew Green Arena A Subway takeaways (open 7 days), toilets.

HEARTLAND RIDE

Route 52
Hawke's Bay to Wairarapa
Distance 263 km   Time 3–4 days   Grade 3 (Intermediate)

This classic cycle tour through quintessential rural New Zealand offers quiet roads, country pubs and friendly locals.

Follow any of the Hawke's Bay Trails to get yourself to Havelock North and the start of this ride. The route takes popular cycling roads south to Waipukurau before branching off onto an abandoned highway called Route 52. This used to be State Highway 52 but due to a lack of traffic was dropped from the highway network. You can see why. Parts of it don't even have road markings. For cyclists, this is now an excellent alternative to the traffic-laden Highway 2.

There are enough well spaced country taverns and rural towns along the way to make this trip possible with a minimum of gear and food.

ITINERARY

Stage 1: Havelock North to Waipukurau
61 km, 4–5 hours

From the centre of Havelock North, head south on Middle Road for 34 km to the Patangata Tavern and turn right onto River Road. After riding down River Road for 6.8 km turn right onto Pourerere Road.

On the outskirts of Waipawa turn left onto Johnston, right at Bibby and cruise into town. Turn left at the main road to get to the shops. These roads are popular with recreational cyclists.

From Waipawa head south across the highway bridge at the edge of town. At the far end turn left onto a lime-sand path which leads to Tapairu. Follow this road left for a few kilometres where it ends at another lime-sand path which leads all the way to Waipukurau. The route is well signposted as part of the Hawke's Bay Trails.

Stage 2: Waipukurau to Wimbledon
67 km, 4–5 hours

Head south out of town on Porangahau Road. In this first leg, you will pass a stone church, the Wanstead Hotel and the Wallingford Rest Area before rolling into Porangahau at the 45-km mark. This village has a hotel and a store. There are toilets at the far end of town.

From Porangahau, backtrack for 1 km to head up Wimbledon Road to

Advanced Te Reo lessons on Route 52.

Wimbledon Tavern, 21 km away. On the way, you will pass a signpost marking the longest place name in the world. Wimbledon has a lovely pub, with accommodation. We wished we had stayed longer. You'll find the tennis courts just up the road but good luck finding the Wombles.

Stage 3: Wimbledon to Glenross Lodge
54 km, 3–4 hours

From Wimbledon, Route 52 heads west and, before long, you will have to take on the largest hill of the ride (the downhill on the other side is long and sweet). At Waione, there is a hall with a good verandah to shelter under if necessary but not much else. The next village is Pongaroa, which has a great tavern and cafe and a basic dairy that provides takeaways. About 9 km past Pongaroa is Glenross Lodge, a popular overnight destination for cyclists.

Stage 4: Glenross Lodge to Masterton
81 km, 4–5 hours

The final leg of Route 52 starts with more of the same – a farming landscape of rolling hills. After 11 km, you will reach Tiraumea Hall, which has public toilets. Then 35 km into the stage, you'll reach Alfredton. There is a school (with water fountains) at the corner where you need to turn left. Just 20 metres after passing the playground, there is a driveway on the right that leads down to the Alfredton Domain where you can find water, toilets and camping.

There is nothing much to stop for on the last 46 km to Masterton, but this is a great stretch of riding. It's mostly downhill. As you enter Masterton, Lake Henley, on the left, is a great place to relax (with public toilets and picnic tables provided). The centre of town is 2 km away.

FACT FILE

How to get there Bus or drive to Hawke's Bay or ride via the Gentle Annie from Taihape. If going from south to north, you can catch the train from Wellington to Masterton. Train timetables: www.metlink.org.nz/timetables/train/WRL

Riding surface 100% sealed road

Special considerations This is a remote area, so take at least a days food, extra tools and spare clothing. Most country pubs are closed on Mondays.

Special features New Zealand's longest place name: Taumatawhakatangihangakoauauotamateaturipukakapikimaungahoronukupokaiwhenuakitanatahu, which translates roughly as 'The summit where Tamatea, the man with the big knees, the climber of mountains, the land-swallower who travelled about, played his nose flute to his loved one'.

Maps Kiwimaps *Wellington-Wairarapa Rural Road Map* and *Napier Hastings*

SUPPORT SERVICES

Patangata Camping and food and drinks at Patangata Tavern ☎ 06 856 8030

Waipawa River's Edge Holiday Park (camping and cabins): ☎ 06 857 8976, www.riversedgeholidaypark.co.nz

Waipukurau Accommodation, restaurant, takeaways and a bike shop (in the Ford car dealership, Ruahine Motors, 85 Ruataniwha Street): Straw Stone Homestay (3km out of town): ☎ 06 858 6587, straw.atspace.com, Waipukurau Holiday Park ☎ 06 858 8184, www.waipukurauholidaypark.co.nz

Porangahau Dairy, accommodation and food: Duke of Edinburgh Hotel: ☎ 06 855 5266, Beach Road Holiday Park: ☎ 06 855 5281, www.beachrdholidaypark.co.nz

Wimbledon Tavern and accommodation: ☎ 06 374 3504

Pongaroa General store (basic) and cafe/bar: Pongaroa Hotel: ☎ 06 376 2864, www.pongaroahotel.co.nz

Glenross Backpackers: ☎ 06 376 7288, www.pongaroathewaytogo.org.nz

Alfredton Camping at the domain ($10): ☎ 06 375 8440

Masterton Restaurants, cafes, supermarkets, plenty of accommodation options: www.wairarapanz.com, check out the popular Mawley Holiday Park: ☎ 06 378 6454, www.mawleypark.co.nz

CONNECTOR RIDE

WAIRARAPA BACK ROADS
Masterton to Martinborough and Featherston
Distance 67–77 km   Time 4–6 hours
Grade 4 (Advanced) to Martinborough and 5 (Expert) to Featherston

Quiet roads and a dry climate make the Wairarapa a magnet for roadies and cycle tourists. This is one of the most common of the regularly cycled routes.

From the main street in Masterton, head east on Church Street then take a right onto Colombo Road followed by a left onto Johnstone Street to head southeast out of town. Johnstone soon becomes Te Whiti Road and heads to Martinborough via Gladstone (a small settlement with a pub, 16 km from town) and Longbush (where there is a forest restoration project). The pub is 2 km off Te Whiti road via Gladstone Road. The white Gladstone Church is also a good place to stop for a rest.

Martinborough is almost 50 km from Masterton. It is a lovely small town with great cafes, plenty of accommodation, expensive camping and several vineyards nearby. It has become a popular destination for Wellington's 'wine and diners'.

Highway 53 from Martinborough to Featherston can be busy at times, and there is a long narrow bridge across the Ruamahanga River, 2 km out of Martinborough – wait for a gap in traffic from your direction and then sprint across. Featherston has plenty of shops and accommodation.

If you are heading on to Wellington, either jump on the commuter train here or ride down Western Lake Road for 9 km to Cross Creek to join the Remutaka Cycle Trail (see page 142).

If you don't need supplies, then skirt past Featherston by taking South Featherston Road, Longwood East Road, followed by Viles Road to Western Lake Road and Cross Creek.

Notes Martinborough has several cafes and holiday homes as well as a supermarket. For camping, cabins and motel units try Top 10 Holiday Park ☎ 0800 780 909, www.mtop10.nz.

Featherston has takeaways and a supermarket on the main street. Plus Featherston Motels and Camping: 4 Fitzherbert Street, ☎ 06 308 9852. For other options see www.wairarapanz.com/featherston-accommodation

The quiet road to Martinborough.

GREAT RIDE

Remutaka Cycle Trail
Wellington to Wairarapa
Distance 25–113 km   Time 2–3 days   Grade 2–3 (Intermediate)

This trail provides over 30 kilometres of leisurely riverside cycling before diving through tunnels and weaving around forested hillsides of the Remutaka Range via a historic rail trail and finally skirting along the wild coast.

From the head of Wellington Harbour, cruise up the Hutt River Trail to Tunnel Gully and then cross the Remutaka Range on the original railway line to the Wairarapa Plains. At that point, you have a choice, to head for the country town of Featherston and catch a train back to Wellington or skirt past Lake Wairarapa to the South Coast.

All four stages listed below make great stand-alone rides, with commuter trains able to drop you at Petone, Maymorn, or Featherston stations.

ITINERARY

Stage 1: Hutt River Trail: Petone to Maymorn Station
33 km, 3–5 hours, mostly Grade 1 (Very Easy)

From the Petone Esplanade, at the head of Wellington Harbour, cross the mouth of the Hutt River on the road bridge (there is a footpath on the southern side). At the far end, ride around underneath the bridge and start following the smooth Hutt River Trail north. Stay on the eastern side of the river. After 7 km, the trail becomes smooth gravel.

At the 15-km mark, the trail ducks under the main road. At the 24-km mark the official trail becomes a bit rougher as it continues following the Hutt River.

If you stick to the official trail, you will ride to Harcourt Park and past the back of the Kiwi Holiday Park. Continue along the signposted trail to the Te Marua Dairy (30 km from Petone). This trail is a bit rough and ready. After an ice cream, say goodbye to the Hutt River Trail as you climb up Plateau Road for 300 metres before turning right and climbing Maymorn Road to Maymorn Station.

Train option If short on time, catch the Wairarapa train to Maymorn Station.

Stage 2: Remutaka Rail Trail: Maymorn Station to Cross Creek
25 km, 3–4 hours, Grade 2+ (Easy)

From Maymorn Station, go under the railway overbridge and turn left, heading for the hills. After 1 minute, you'll reach a locked gate at the trailhead. Squeeze around the gate and onto the Rail Trail. There is a short hill to tackle early on, but

Cycling around Turakirae Head on the Wild Coast.

then it is easy all the way to a tunnel that leads to a large picnic area at Tunnel Gully. Follow the road from there for 400 metres, and when it curves left, head straight, over another gate to continue following the original railway line. Just over 2 km later, at a T-intersection, turn left (the short cut to the right is horribly hilly). Hop over the next gate and turn right to coast down the old highway. At the bottom, turn right to follow signposts to the Remutaka Rail Trail car park.

From the car park, the trail is well signposted up to a great picnic area and shelter at the summit tunnel. The downhill on the far side is called the Remutaka Incline – it is steeper, and crosses the windswept Siberia Gully.

When you reach Cross Creek shelter, turn right, cross a bridge and follow a single track for 2 km to the end of Cross Creek Road. The history of the Wellington to Wairarapa railway is told in interpretation panels along the Remutaka Rail Trail.

Stage 3: Cross Creek: Lake Wairarapa to Ocean Beach
37 km, 2–3 hours, Grade 3 (Intermediate)

Ride 1 km down Cross Creek Road to Western Lake Road. Turn right and, heading southwest, cruise past Lake Wairarapa, where there is a new lakeside shelter. Near the coast (33 km from Cross Creek), climb a hill with great views (look back from the yellow letterbox). Drop down to Ocean Beach. Follow a gravel road around Ocean Beach for 4 km, to a DOC camping area set amongst low forest.

Alternative At the end of Cross Creek Road, turn left and ride 10 flat kilometres to Featherston. Featherston has cafes and a railway museum. From Featherston, catch the evening train back to Wellington.

Stage 4: The Wild Coast: Ocean Beach to Orongorongo Station
18 km, 3–5 hours, Grade 3+ (Intermediate)

From the camp site, follow the farm track southwest around the coast, over a few short hills. Crossing several streams, continue past Windy Point to Barney's Whare where there is a picnic table. From there the track hugs the Remutaka hills, past Turakirae Head. You can make a 1-km diversion to get to the actual headland. Otherwise, follow the main track to Orongorongo River. Cross the Orongorongo Bridge to a car park at the end of the trail beside Coast Road. Arrange for transport to take you back to Wellington (43 km away).

FACT FILE

How to get there From downtown Wellington, catch a train to Petone or Maymorn Station (go to www.metlink.co.nz for times and call ☎ 0800 801 700 to tell them you have bikes and to check the trains aren't replaced with buses).

Riding surface 27% sealed rd, 38% gravel path, 20% gravel road, 15% sealed path

Special considerations The summit tunnel on the Remutaka Rail Trail is almost 600 metres long. Most people take bike lights or torches to help get through it.

Reverse option Catch the train to Featherston and ride to Upper Hutt or Petone via the Remutaka Rail Trail followed by the Hutt River Trail. This option takes advantage of the prevailing wind.

Maps Pick up maps of the Hutt River Trail and the Remutuka Rail Trail at the Wellington i-SITE or from www.gw.govt.nz and there are map boards on the trails.

Trail website www.wellingtonnz.com/remutaka-cycle-trail/

SUPPORT SERVICES

Bike hire and transport Green Jersey Cycle Tour Company, offering transport, tours and bike hire in the Wairarapa: ☎ 021 074 6640, www.greenjersey.co.nz; Rimutaka Shuttles ☎ 0800 239 767, www.rimutakashuttles.com

Hutt City bike hire From Hutt City i-SITE, The Pavilion, 25 Laings Rd, Lower Hutt

Petone, Lower Hutt and Upper Hutt A range of places to stay and eat as well as several bike shops: www.huttvalleynz.com

Harcourt Park Kiwi Holiday Park is a popular destination for travelling cyclists: ☎ 04 526 7400, 43 Akatarawa Rd, http://www.wellingtonsholidaypark.co.nz/

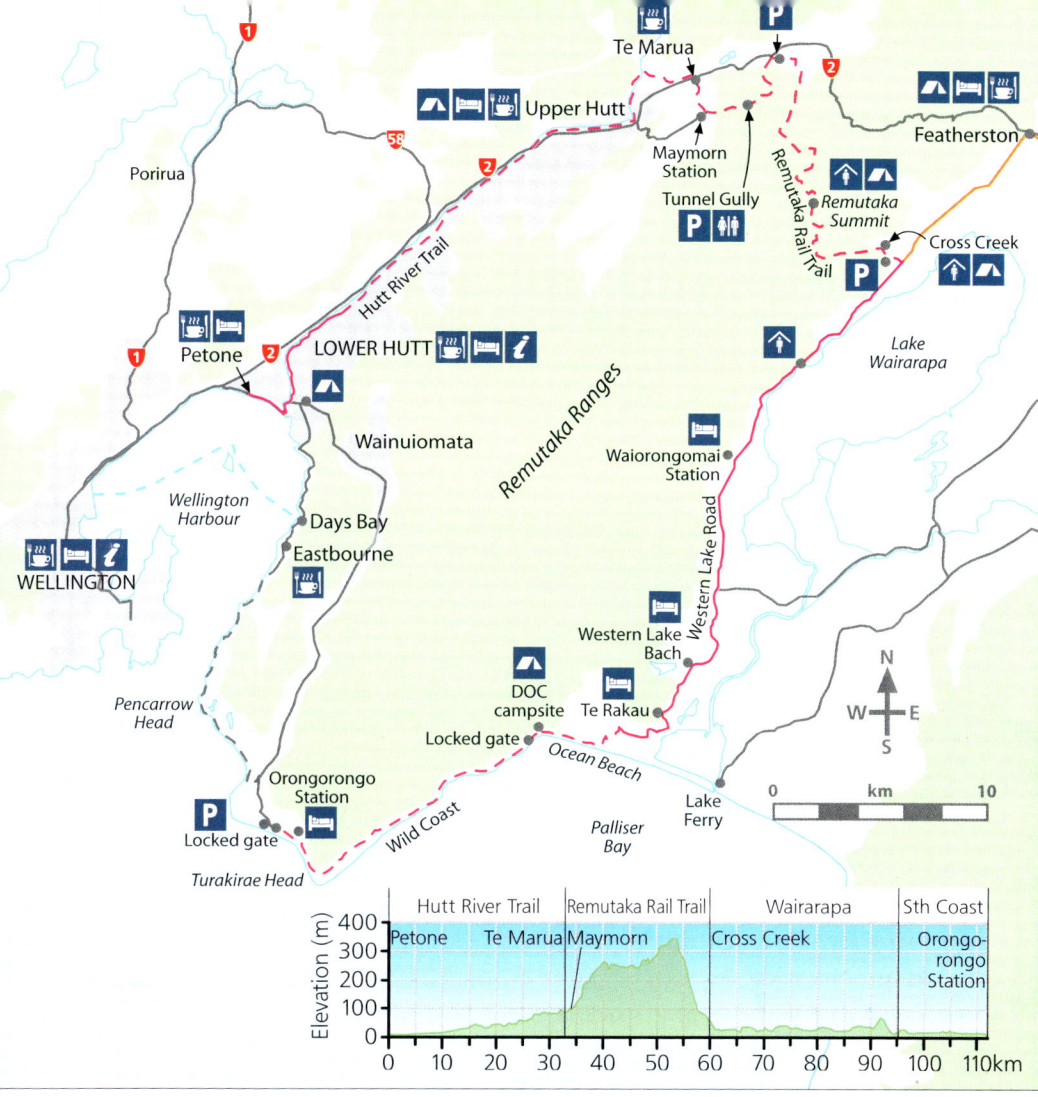

Featherston Accommodation, shops and cafes: www.wairarapanz.com

Wairarapa accommodation See www.wairarapanz.com/accommodation/

Waiorongomai Station Accommodation, ☎ 06 307 7740, www.waiorongomai.co.nz

Western Lake Bach Accommodation, ☎ 06 307 7712, email zanemiltona@hotmail.com

Ocean Beach Te Rakau Cabins, ☎ 06 307 7749, www.terakaubirding.co.nz

Orongorongo Station Accommodation, ☎ 04 568 6466/027 478 7177, www.holidayhouses.co.nz

GREAT RIDE

Queen Charlotte Track

Picton, Marlborough Sounds
Distance 72–97 km   Time 2–3 days
Grades 3–5 (Intermediate–Expert)

The Queen Charlotte experience combines adventurous mountain biking with the comforts of modern living, set among the beautiful scenery of the Marlborough Sounds.

After a scenic boat trip up Queen Charlotte Sound, the track winds through native forest, sometimes skirting the coastline, at other times traversing ridges high above the sheltered sounds. It ends with a perfect descent through mature beech forest to Anakiwa – pure biking heaven.

There are a few small resorts along the way, offering food and accommodation. Your luggage can be delivered to each night's destination, leaving you free to enjoy the track unencumbered. Water taxis service the track throughout the day, so you can also be flexible with your itinerary and choose to do as much, or as little, of the Queen Charlotte Track as you wish.

ITINERARY

Stage 1: Ship Cove to Resolution Bay
4 km, Grade 5 (Expert)

The first 2 km are steep and rough – so why do them?! Well, Captain Cook spent almost six months at Ship Cove, so it is rich in history. There are interpretation panels, a shelter, sculptures, a great lookout, and it is, after all, the start of the track. It's your choice; the boat is just as happy to drop you around the corner for an easier start at Resolution Bay. This section will be upgraded in 2018/2019.

Stage 2: Resolution Bay to Kenepuru Saddle (or Camp Bay)
23 km, Grade 3 (Intermediate)

The first climb is perfectly graded to a great lookout spot. The downhill to Endeavour Inlet was upgraded in 2014, so you'll soon be flying around the coast to Furneaux Lodge (cafe, restaurant, accommodation).

Follow the coast to Miner Camp, where you can buy snacks from a tiny trackside stall. Not far past there, veer right, away from the coast and uphill. The next significant intersection is a few kilometres later where you can go left to Camp Bay and Punga Cove for the night or right up to Kenepuru Saddle.

Just another day in paradise.

Note The track from Ship Cove to Kenepuru Saddle is closed to bikes over summer (1 December to 28 February).

Stage 3: Kenepuru Saddle to Torea Saddle and Portage
24 km, Grade 4 (Advanced), or an easy on-road alternative

From Kenepuru Saddle, the track is much hillier. Some riders choose to avoid this section and take the road from the saddle to Portage. If you stick to the track, be aware that it's exposed in places (but has breathtaking views) and drinking water is scarce, though there are water tanks at two DOC shelters along the way. Following the road will take 1–2 hours, while the track will take 3–5 hours.

On this challenging section, the track climbs to almost 500 m altitude, following the main ridge that bucks its way between Kenepuru and Queen Charlotte sounds. This section ends with a long descent to Torea Saddle, where the track pops out onto Torea Road, 500 metres from the village of Portage.

Stage 4: Torea Saddle/Portage to Te Mahia Saddle
9 km, Grade 4+ (Advanced)

From the war memorial at Torea Saddle, change into your lowest gear and sweat your way up a 300 m climb. The views make it all worthwhile. Some of the downhills are steep, and occasionally rutted, but nothing to worry about if your brakes are working well. Alternatively, take the road to Te Mahia Saddle.

Stage 5: Te Mahia Saddle to Anakiwa
12 km, Grade 3 (Intermediate)
The section to Anakiwa is biking at its best – an exhilarating single track through beautiful native forest. There are a couple of gentle climbs, but the trail mostly glides downhill.

Optional Stage 6: Anakiwa to Picton
25 km, Grade 3 (Intermediate)
There are two options for riding to Picton. The easier is to follow Anakiwa Road and Queen Charlotte Drive. This is one of the best rides in New Zealand, with great views and moderate hills.

A new option is a single track that runs from the south end of Anakiwa to Queen Charlotte Drive. And there is another new section of single track from Ngakuta Bay to Shakespeare Bay en route to Picton, called the Link Pathway.

FACT FILE

Overview The track is also very popular with walkers: be ready for them to appear at any corner. Rather than startling them, slow down and call out a friendly 'hello' as you approach.

When to ride The track is best ridden when dry, as some sections are unridable when wet. March, April, May and November are the best months. The northern section from Ship Cove to Kenepuru Saddle is closed to bikes from 1 December to 28 February every year.

Track access pass You need an $18 five-day pass to cross the private land on the Queen Charlotte Walkway. You can purchase one from the Picton i-SITE and businesses along the track, listed at www.qctlc.com

How to get there Getting to Picton: Ferries run several times a day from Wellington to Picton. Bluebridge (www.bluebridge.co.nz) and Interislander (www.interislander.co.nz).

From Picton, there are several small ferries servicing the track:

The Beachcomber, ☎ 03 573 6175, www.beachcombercruises.co.nz

Cougar Line, ☎ 0800 504 090, www.cougarline.co.nz

From Picton to Ship Cove, costs around $95-110 per person and bike.

Riding surface 96% single track, 2% gravel road, 2% unridable

Maps A pamphlet map is available at the Picton iSITE and local businesses. For more detail buy New Topo Queen Charlotte Track.

Official track website www.qctrack.co.nz

SUPPORT SERVICES

Picton Loads of shops and accommodation: www.visitpicton.co.nz

Camp Bay Punga Cove Resort: ☎ 03 579 8561, www.pungacove.co.nz, Mahana Lodge: ☎ 03 579 8373, www.mahanalodge.co.nz, Noeline's Homestay: ☎ 03 579 8375, www.thevilla.co.nz/homestay

Portage Portage Hotel: ☎ 0800 762 442, www.portage.co.nz, Treetops Backpackers: ☎ 03 573 4404, email staytreetops@xtra.co.nz

Mistletoe Bay Eco Village (with basic food supplies): ☎ 03 573 4048, www.mistletoebay.co.nz

Te Mahia Bay Resort: ☎ 03 573 4089, www.temahia.co.nz

Anakiwa Anakiwa 401 and Green Caravan Cafe: ☎ 03 574 1388, www.anakiwa401.co.nz, YHA Anakiwa Lodge: ☎ 03 574 2115, www.anakiwa.co.nz

HEARTLAND RIDE

Picton to Nelson

Distance 93 km via Maungatapu Track or 107 km via Rai Valley
Time 1–2 days   Grade 4 (Advanced)

Take a direct route to Nelson through the beautiful landscape of the Marlborough Sounds and the Bryant mountains. This unusually varied route is popular with recreational riders, sport cyclists and cycle tourers.

Starting from Picton, this tour has three distinct stages. The first is a gentle meander in and out of the tranquil bays of the Marlborough Sounds, via Queen Charlotte Drive. The second is a busier one-hour stretch along Highway 6 to Pelorus Bridge: a beautiful spot with a brilliant cafe – take the time to explore and devour.

The final stage offers a choice of continuing along the hilly highway to Nelson or branching off over a mountainous dirt road with no traffic but a few steep kilometres that require walking: the ease of a sealed road or the scenery and peace of the mountains? Either option rewards you with a long downhill into sunny Nelson.

ITINERARY

Stage 1: Picton to Havelock
35 km, 2–3 hours, Grade 3 (Intermediate)

Traffic through Picton pulses to the clamorous beat of arriving and departing ferries, so take your time heading off and you'll find that the roads will be quiet. Queen Charlotte Drive, named after the unlucky wife of mad King George III, starts from the west end of the port, next to the Bluebridge Ferry terminal. This scenic and windy road has a speed restriction, making it less palatable for motorised vehicles and an absolute dream for cyclists, roadies and tourers alike. There are three gentle hills to climb en route to the fishing village of Havelock.

There is an off-road track called Link Pathway being built in sections between Havelock and Picton – great fun for mountain bikers.

Stage 2: Havelock to Pelorus Bridge
18 km, 1 hour, Grade 5 (Expert because of traffic)

After a pit stop at Havelock, you'll ride 18 km along Highway 6 to Pelorus Bridge. This is a reasonably busy highway, and half has little or no shoulder. To avoid traffic, start early or ride late in the day. Pelorus Bridge has an excellent cafe, some pearler camping spots and cabins. The bridge itself is an ancient one-lane structure over the stunning Pelorus River (a great swimming spot).

Cruising along Queen Charlotte Drive.

Stage 3: Pelorus Bridge to Nelson
39 km via the mountains, 54 km via the highway, 4–5 hours, Grade 4 (Advanced)

From Pelorus Bridge, there are two ways to get to Nelson and, though one is 15 km shorter, they both take a similar length of time to ride. You can continue along Highway 6, through Rai Valley and over two hills totalling 600 m of climbing, then around the coast. This route can be busy, and much of it has no shoulder, but it is all sealed and suitable for road bikes. There are bike lanes and paths for the last 6 km into Nelson.

The alternative is the Maungatapu Track. This is more scenic with little traffic but involves a rough and rocky unsealed 700-metre climb over the Bryant Range. You'll need a mountain bike. To go via the Maungatapu Track, turn west off Highway 6 at Pelorus Bridge and ride up Maungatapu Road. There are two forks in the road; both are well signposted. The gravel road turns into a 4WD track 12 km from the highway and begins a relentless climb out of the Pelorus Valley. Continue straight ahead at a four-way intersection, aiming for the pylon

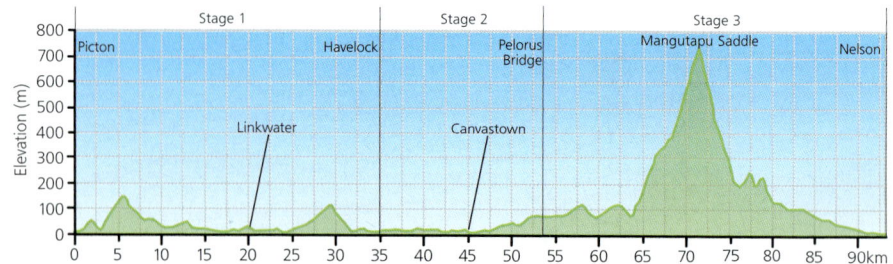

on the skyline. There is drinkable water at a stream two-thirds of the way up (about 100 metres past Murderers Rock, 4.3 km from the summit). The last few kilometres up to Maungatapu Saddle are very steep and unridable in places.

At the saddle, flex your braking fingers in preparation for a headlong descent, past the 'Water Catchment Area' sign, and into the Maitai Valley. Don't take any turn-offs to pylons – stick to the main 4WD track.

When you reach the bottom, and not far from the Maitai reservoir, the track turns right and heads up a steep 5-minute climb before diving down to a ford beside the reservoir and pitching you up a 2-minute climb on a road. This section of 4WD track down to the reservoir is closed to motorised traffic.

From the road, you will coast down into the Maitai Valley again. The gradient eases within a few minutes, and a public road leads gently down valley for 10 km past Maitai Valley Motor Camp to the edge of Nelson. When you reach town, follow the NZCT signs to the i-SITE a few minutes away.

FACT FILE

How to get there From Wellington, catch a Bluebridge or Interislander ferry to Picton. About six ferries cross the Cook Strait each day, and the scenic journey takes 3–4 hours, plus an hour's check-in time.

Riding surface 100% sealed road, unless you take the Maungatapu Track, which has 30 km of gravel and dirt.

History The Maungatapu Track is infamous for the 1866 robbery and murders of five travellers by the Burgess Gang. There is a plaque 4.3 km from the top, on the Pelorus side. The road was once the main route to Nelson but now just provides access to electricity pylons.

Special considerations Hook in with the Queen Charlotte Track or base yourself at Nelson for a few days to explore the area. The western side of the Maungatapu Track is closed to motorised vehicles.

Important contacts Nelson city council for updates on Maungatapu Track, ☎ 03 546 0200

Maps Kiwimap *Pathfinder Nelson, Picton & Districts 115*

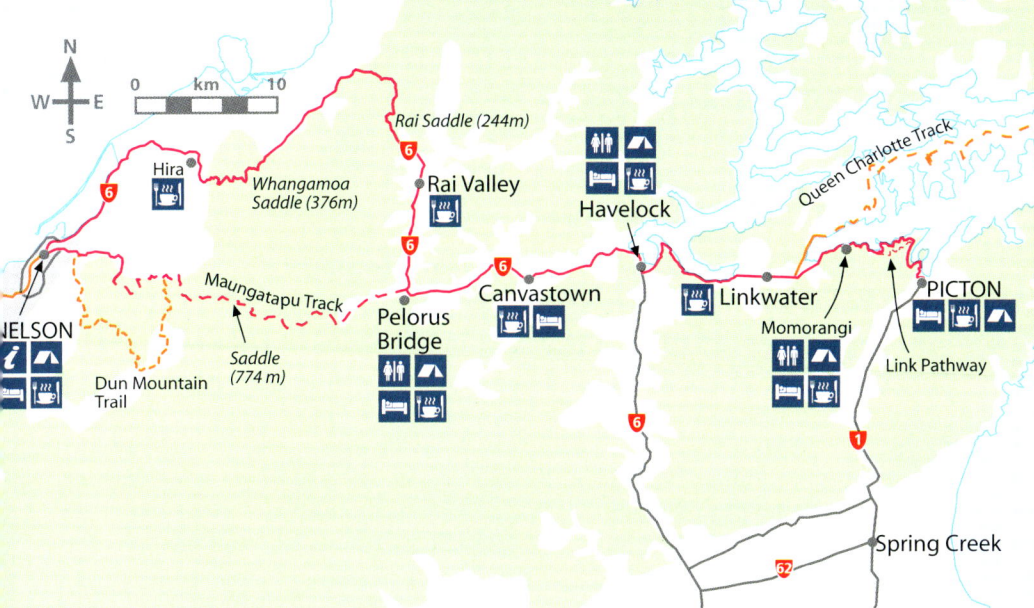

SUPPORT SERVICES

Picton Loads of shops and accommodation: www.picton.co.nz

Momorangi Bay Shop, camping, cabins: ☎ 03 573 7865 or email momorangi.camp@xtra.co.nz

Linkwater Garage, shop, accommodation: Smiths Farm Holiday Camp: Camping, cabins: ☎ 03 574 2806, www.smithsfarm.co.nz, Linkwater Motel: ☎ 03 574 2600, www.linkwatermotel.com

Havelock The green mussel capital of New Zealand: Plenty of accommodation and food: www.havelockinfocentre.co.nz

Canvastown Food, accommodation: Trout Hotel: ☎ 03 574 2888

Pelorus Bridge Great cafe (8am–4:30pm), camping: ☎ 03 571 6019, www.doc.govt.nz/parks-and-recreation/places-to-stay

Maitai Valley Motorcamp and cabins and tent sites: ☎ 03 548 7729

Nelson Waaay too many options to list. Go to www.nelsonnz.com

GREAT RIDE

Dun Mountain Trail
Nelson
Distance 45 km (full loop)   Time 4–7 hours
Grades 3–4 (Intermediate–Advanced)

The hard graft of 200 men built New Zealand's first railway in 1862. It struck out from Nelson through forested hills to the chromite mines of Dun Mountain and created one of New Zealand's best mountain bike rides.

The Dun Mountain Trail begins as a wide, well-graded climb through pine and beech forest to the pleasant clearing of Third House. Further on, the tree line morphs into a stunning alpine environment of golden tussock with dramatic views from Coppermine Saddle at the railway's end.

From Coppermine Saddle, the easiest route home is back the way you came. Alternatively, most riders take a new trail that sweeps down to the Maitai Valley. Advanced riders absolutely love this 10-km long downhill. The views are spectacular, and from the valley floor, a quiet country road drifts back to the centre of Nelson.

ITINERARY

Stage 1: Nelson to Coppermine Saddle
21 km, 2.5–4 hours, Grade 3- (Intermediate)

From the Nelson i-SITE, ride 1.5 km to just past 135 Brook Street. There you will find an interpretation board at the trail entrance. This is also a very popular mountain biking area.

The first section of the walkway is also known as Codgers Track. Follow the easy climb for 20 minutes till you pop out onto the gravel Tantragee Road. Ride up the road for 300 metres until you see another Dun Mountain Trail sign pointing to your right.

After about an hour's riding on an easy gradient, you'll come to a well-signposted four-way intersection. Follow the 'Dun Mountain' track straight ahead – it just gets sweeter and sweeter, all the way to Third House. Sitting at the top of a grassy clearing, this shelter overlooks Tasman Bay and is a rewarding goal in itself.

From Third House, you can choose between returning the way you came (the easiest option), carrying on to the alpine Coppermine Saddle and then retracing your tyre tracks (another easy option) or carrying on to complete the full loop.

Following the leader down to the Maitai River South Branch.

If going the full distance, continue up the Dun Mountain Trail, climbing above the treeline to Windy Point (signposted).

Windy Point is a good place to reassess the weather – you've got another hour of exposure above the bushline to complete this marathon. If the weather looks good, then carry on to Coppermine Saddle (878 m) a few kilometres away.

Stage 2: Coppermine Saddle to Nelson city
24 km, 2–3 hours, Grade 4 (Advanced)

With your back to the sign at Coppermine Saddle, ride straight ahead and follow the rocky trail down, down, down… for a very long way.

Eventually you'll reach, and cross, the Maitai River South Branch via an arched wooden bridge. From here, there's even more sweet riding to a T-intersection above the main Maitai River. Turn left to follow another 3 km of single track beside a pipeline down to the gravelled Maitai Road.

Finally, it's 20–40 minutes pedalling gently down a quiet country road to the centre of the sunshine capital, Nelson.

FACT FILE

Overview In bad weather, parts of the downhill are 'advanced', so it may be best to turn around at Windy Point. There is an alternative route to the end of this ride that takes you over Tantragee Saddle, but it's uphill, on a boring forestry road.

The endless descent from Coppermine Saddle.

How to get there The trail is signposted from the Nelson i-SITE.

Riding surface 50% historic rail trail, 40% single track, 5% sealed road, 5% gravel road

History The rise and fall of the Dun Mountain Railway is well explained on interpretation boards along the trail.

Special considerations This trail is popular with walkers. On the way down, control your speed and be ready to stop at any corner.

Special features The alpine zone is a mineral belt.

Important contacts Nelson City Council for updates on track conditions

Maps Pick up a trail map from the Nelson i-SITE.

Trail website Check out www.nzcycletrail.com for updates on the track.

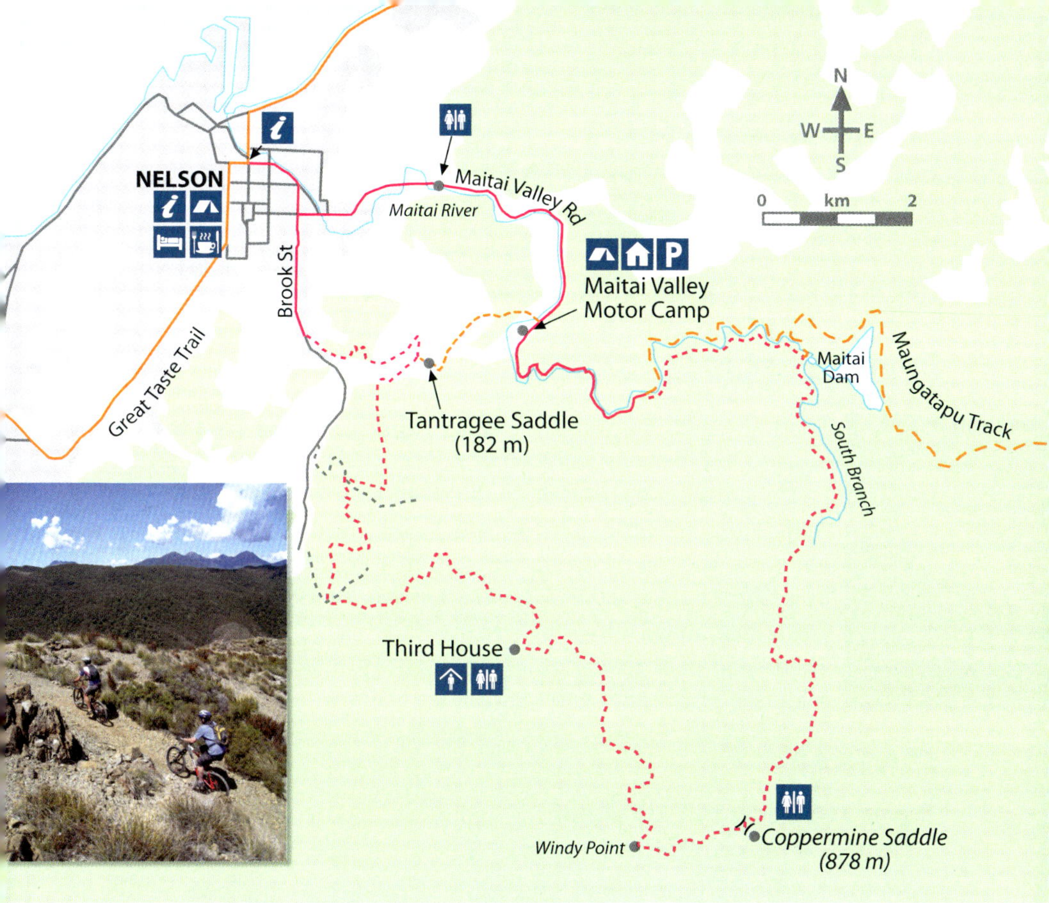

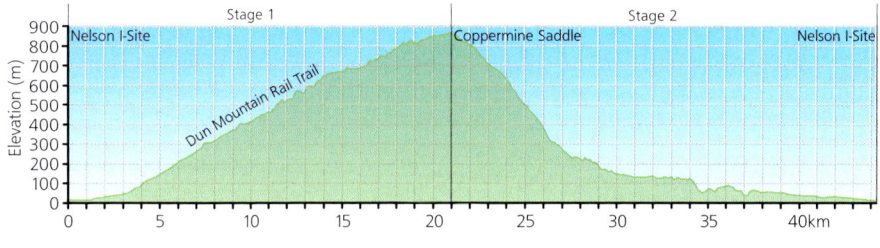

SUPPORT SERVICES

Nelson Plenty of accommodation, shops, bike rental, etc: www.nelsonnz.com

Bike hire Crank house Nelson (114 Hardy Street) ☎ 03 548 1666, www.crankhouse.co.nz, Biking Nelson, ☎ 0800 224 532, www.bikingnelson.co.nz

Maitai Valley Maitai Valley Motor Camp, ☎ 03 548 7729, www.maitaivmc.co.nz

GREAT RIDE

Great Taste Trail
A loop around Nelson and the Tasman region
Distance 165-km loop   Time Up to 5 days
Grades 2–3 (Easy–Intermediate)

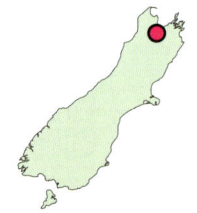

Experience the best wine, food, art and fashion on offer in Nelson and Tasman as you gently pedal from one tempting attraction to the next.

The trail heads south from Nelson along a rail trail, past the airport and around the coast to Richmond. From there, it crosses a varied rural landscape, passing through Brightwater, to Wakefield.

In future, it will extend further south, but in 2018, riders could complete the trip by taking Pigeon Valley Road to Woodstock and the quiet West Bank Road to Motueka, famous for its orchards.

From Motueka, check out the golden sands of Kaiteriteri Beach. Then head back to Nelson via the most stunning section of the trail: Mapua, Rabbit Island and the Waimea Estuary.

ITINERARY

Stage 1: Nelson to Wakefield
33 km, 3–4 hours, Grade 2 (Easy)

From the Nelson i-SITE, ride west on Halifax St, then south on St Vincent St to Totara St. Take the Railway Reserve cycle path, then ride down Beatson Road.

At the roundabout, hop onto the footpath on the right side of the road and ride down beside the highway (Whakatu Drive). This leads you to a bridge over the highway. Follow the cycle signs carefully. They direct you over a second bridge and then through an underpass. Follow the Coastal Route towards Richmond.

Just north of Richmond, the path splits in two. To the right is Waimea Estuary and Rabbit Island. Go straight ahead to Richmond and cross Queen Street at the traffic lights. Then turn right and cycle for 50 metres to the cycle path. It is signposted to Brightwater, 23 km from Nelson.

Through Brightwater, the trail weaves along a mix of streets and paths to a tunnel under Highway 6 that takes you to Lord Rutherford Road. Head south and continue along Higgins Road to Edward Street, Wakefield.

Stage 2: Wakefield to Woodstock
31 km, 2–4 hours, Grade 3 (Intermediate)

Cross Highway 6 at Edward Street and ride up Pigeon Valley Road. This climbs 300 m on a gravel road to a saddle in pine forest. A wonderful downhill run leads

A large turn-out for the opening of the Brightwater Bridge.

to Woodstock, where you will meet the other end of the Great Taste Trail. Turn right at the Motueka Valley Highway, ride north for 300 metres and turn left to cross a bridge to Motueka River West Bank Road.

Stage 3: Woodstock to Motueka
38 km, 2.5–4 hours, Grade 3 (Intermediate)

Head north down valley on a quiet, tree-lined road. Half an hour down West Bank Road there are some toilets at a local hall. Five km further down West Bank Road, you'll meet Peninsula Road on your right. Head down to Peninsula Road to a fantastic swimming hole beside the Motueka River (just behind the bowling club). There is also an icecream/coffee shop 600 metres away on the Motueka Valley Highway (head right after the bridge).

Back at West Bank Road, continue to Brooklyn (27 km from Woodstock), then turn right onto Old Mill Road. Turn left up Anderson Road and right at Umukuri Road, which leads to Highway 60. Follow the main road right to head to Motueka. An off-road trail is planned from Old Mill Road to the Motueka River bridge.

Stage 3a: Optional side trip to Kaiteriteri
14 km one way, 2 hours, Grade 3 (Intermediate)

At the Umukuri-Highway 60 intersection (4 km north of Motueka), turn left and pass through Riwaka. Alternatively, if riding from Motueka to Riwaka, follow the cycle path and cycle route signs (that's a much nicer way to go).

From Riwaka, a path leads beside the highway to Goodall Road, then down an orchard driveway and across a field to a new bridge across the Riwaka River. It then follows a new path between the road and the coast before climbing over a hill and following an easy track through Kaiteriteri Mountain Bike Park.

Stage 4: Motueka to Mapua
30 km, 1.5–2.5 hours, Grade 3 (Intermediate)
The Great Taste Trail now directs you along scenic paths beside the coast to TOAD Hall (uber popular cafe) at the south end of Motueka. From TOAD Hall follow the signs beside High Street, Wildman Road and Moutere Highway to another famous cafe at the riverside community.

From beside this cafe, the trail heads steeply up Community Road to Tasman View Road. This road rolls along the main ridge before turning left down Harley Road. Just before the bottom of Harley Road, turn right at a sign 'To Rush Lane' Follow the cycle path through a highway underpass to Tasman Park.

Now follow a trail beside Aporo Road (to be built early 2014), turn right at Marriages Road, along Pomona Road and veer left up Pine Hill Road West. At the end of this dead-end road, there is a 300-metre-long path leading to the other section of Pine Hill Road. This brings you back to the main coastal road to Mapua. Follow the signs along the coastal path to take the scenic route into Mapua.

Stage 5: Mapua to Nelson
33 km, 3–4 hours, Grade 2 (Easy)
From Mapua, catch the ferry to Rabbit Island. Follow a smooth gravel path halfway around the north side of the island and hook into a series of signs that will lead you across the island and back to the mainland. Turn left, and cut across to Cotterell Road before following an easy gravel path over farmland to a swing bridge across the Waimea River.

From here, the trail follows Lower Queen Street for a few minutes, then turns left again and heads back to the coast. It weaves around the coastline and across the Waimea Estuary on a boardwalk, a highlight of the trip. The trail reconnects with the concrete Nelson city cycle trail beside Whakatu Drive, 1 km northeast of Richmond. Turn left and follow the cycle paths back to the city centre.

Optional Stage 6: Spooners Tunnel
14 km, 1–2 hours, Grade 2 (Easy)
From Wai-iti Domain, southwest of Wakefield, follow the trail signs along a smooth path to Belgrove Tavern, 5 km away.

From Belgrove, the trail continues south for another 6 km to Spooners Tunnel (1.3 km long). This is the longest rail tunnel open to cyclists in the Southern Hemisphere. Lights are essential (seriously, we aren't kidding). Continue beyond the tunnel to Norris Gully reserve, where the trail ended in 2018. It is likely to be

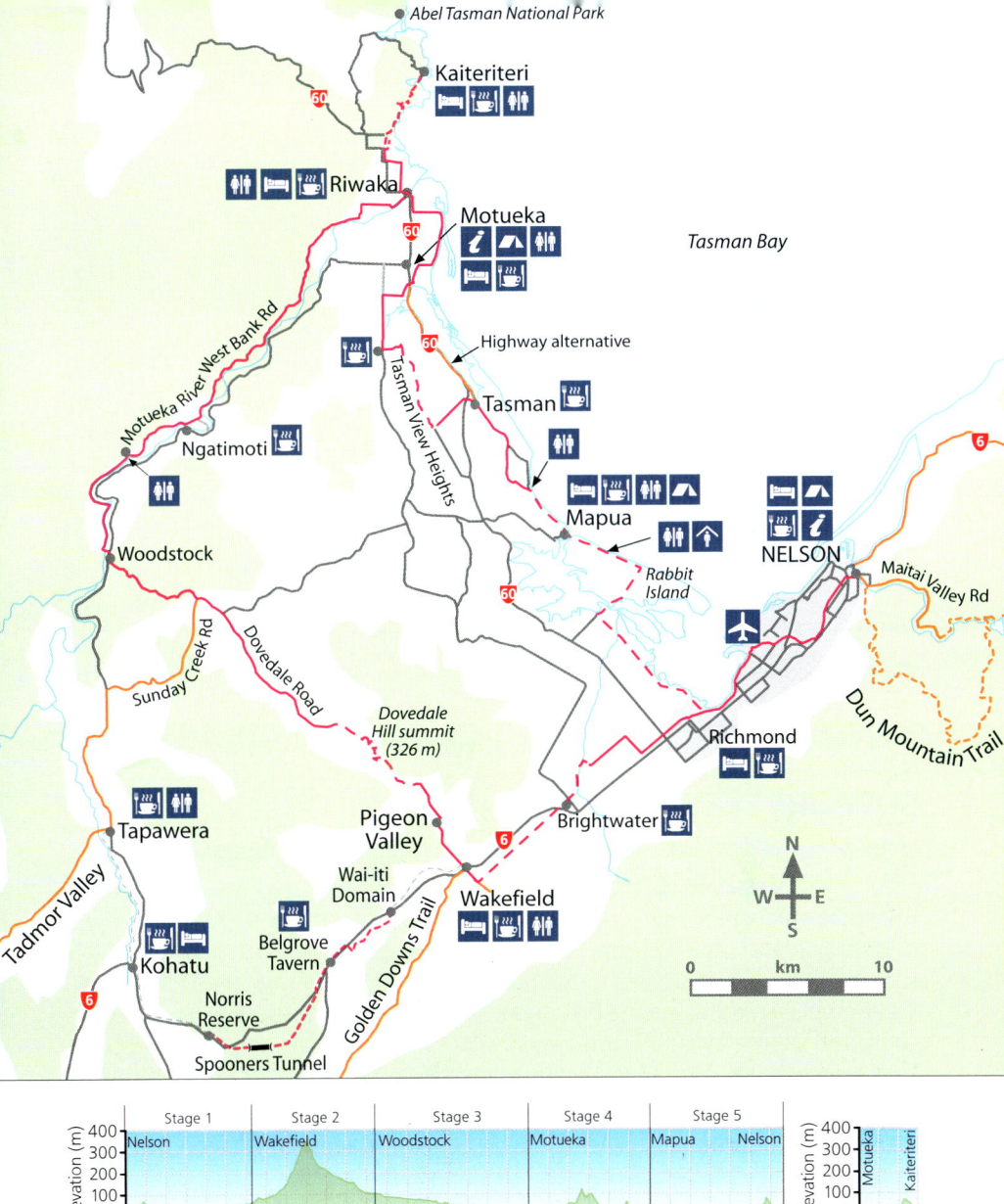

extended to Kohatu soon, where you can find a café and limited accommodation.

At the time of writing (2018), there was a 5-km gap in the trail between Wakefield and Wai-iti Domain. Only experienced riders should attempt to ride the busy State Highway 6 to bridge this trail gap. Hopefully the trail will be complete by the end of 2018.

FACT FILE

How to get there Nelson airport is right beside the trail, with a bike hire company on site, ☎ 03 539 4193, www.nelsoncyclehire.co.nz. Alternatively, catch the ferry to Picton and bus to Nelson. For keen cyclists, the ride from Picton is a treat in itself.

Riding surface A mix of smooth sealed paths and smooth gravel paths. Some sections are also along roads.

History The railway line from Nelson south operated from 1876 to 1955.

Special considerations In future, the Great Taste Trail will continue from Wakefield down to Spooners Tunnel, Kohatu and Tapawera. Until then, the short-cut link from Wakefield to Woodstock makes the Great Taste Trail a good loop trip although there is one steep hill.

Special features The region is famous for good weather, scenery and creative arts, award-winning wineries, orchards and the World Of Wearable Arts Museum and, for the blokes, the Classic Car Museum right next door.

Nelson i-SITE To book accommodation and travel, www.nelsonnz.com

Maps Kiwimap *Pathfinder Nelson, Blenheim, Picton* shows the area but not the trail. Take a photo of the cycle trail mapboard beside the Nelson i-SITE.

Trail website www.heartofbiking.org.nz and www.nzcycletrail.com

SUPPORT SERVICES

Nelson More cafes, supermarkets, cycle shops and accommodation than you could shake a stick at. Take your pick: www.nelsonnz.com

Bike hire and tours Nelson Cycle Hire (at Nelson Airport) ☎ 03 539 4193, www.nelsoncyclehire.co.nz, Wheelie Fantastic bike hire and transport ☎ 03 543 2245, www.wheeliefantastic.co.nz, Crank house Nelson (114 Hardy Street) ☎ 03 548 1666, www.crankhouse.co.nz, Biking Nelson, ☎ 0800 224 532, www.bikingnelson.co.nz, The Gentle Cycling Company, ☎ 0800 WE BIKE, www.gentlecycling.co.nz, Trail Journeys Ltd ☎ 027 473 2888, Mapua Ferry, ☎ 0800 CYCLETRAILS, www.mapuaferry.co.nz

Richmond Supermarket, cafe, takeaways, accommodation: Village Cycles: 203 Queen Street, Richmond, ☎ 03 544 7166, www.villagecycles.co.nz

Wakefield Supermarket, cafe, takeaways, accommodation: Wakefield Hotel: 48 Edward Street, ☎ 03 541 8006; Dunpuffin Railway Cottages: ☎ 03 541 8265, www.dunpuffin.co.nz, Bush Walk B&B, ☎ 027 541 9615, www.bushwalk.co.nz

Riwaka Cafe and accommodation, Eden's Edge Lodge, ☎ 03 528 4242, www.motuekabackpackers.co.nz

Cruising around the Waimea Estuary.

Motueka Shops, cafes, restaurants, accommodation: www.nelsonnz.com/i-Site/motueka-isite.html, Motueka Top 10 Holiday Park (offers bike hire and servicing): www.motuekatop10.co.nz or ☎ 0800 668 835

Kaiteriteri Cafe/restaurant, general store, accommodation and campground: www.experiencekaiteriteri.co.nz, Kaiteriteri Beach Motor Camp: Kaiteri Lodge, ☎ 03 527 8281, www.kaiterilodge.co.nz, Bethany Park Holiday Park: ☎ 03 527 8014, www.bethanypark.co.nz, Torlesse Motels: Little Kaiteriteri Beach: ☎ 03 527 8063, www.torlessemotels.co.nz

Kaiteriteri Mountain Bike Park: www.kaiteriterimtbpark.org.nz

Mapua Shops, cafes, restaurants accommodation: www.mapua.gen.nz, Cats Pjamas B&B: ☎ 03 540 3404, www.cats-pjamas.com (bike storage and workshop), Mapua Chalets: ☎ 03 540 3310, www.mapuachalets.co.nz

CONNECTOR RIDE

GOLDEN DOWNS TRAIL
Wakefield to Nelson Lakes
Distance 59 km   Time 3–6 hours   Grade 3 (Intermediate)

This trail starts in the small town of Wakefield, southwest of Nelson. It heads south through lovely countryside to Tophouse, a stone's throw from either The Rainbow trail or the lakeside village of St Arnaud. The trail is popular with recreational cyclists who head up Eighty Eight Valley Road to the top of the first or second hill, and then turn back to Wakefield for a well-deserved drink.

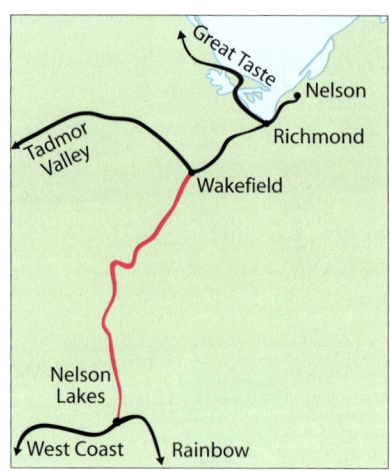

From the corner of Edward Street and Highway 6, next to the shops in Wakefield, a cycle path heads south for 500 metres onto Eighty Eight Valley Road. Continue south on Eighty Eight Valley Road, and into the countryside.

At the bottom of a fast downhill, 16 km from Wakefield, turn left onto Stock Road. This takes you over Reays Saddle (429 m) and down to Golden Downs.

From Golden Downs, continue south on Kerr Hill Road and climb over Kerr Hill (632 m). The views from a 50-metre-long 4WD track on your right at the summit are panoramic.

From the summit of Kerr Hill, a short downhill leads to Korere-Tophouse Road. Continue straight ahead, and after another 11 km, you'll reach the turn-off to Tophouse. That's 52 km from Wakefield.

Continue straight ahead to get to St Arnaud, 7 km away on Highway 63, or head left up to the historic Tophouse Hotel 700 metres away (well signposted on your left). The hotel has modern chalets out the back and also lays claim to being New Zealand's smallest pub.

If heading for the Rainbow Valley, also turn left and ride past Tophouse Hotel and along the gravel Tophouse Road out to Highway 63 further to the east. Then turn left again to head down the highway for 600 metres to the signposted Rainbow Road, the start of the Rainbow Valley Trail.

How to get there Nelson Lakes Shuttle will transport riders to either end of the trail, ☎ 03 540 2042 or 027 222 1872, www.nelsonlakesshuttles.co.nz

CONNECTOR RIDE

TADMOR VALLEY
Wakefield to Kawatiri Junction
Distance 89 km   Time 1–2 days   Grade 4 (Advanced)

For lovers of quiet back country roads, this is a fantastic way to ride from the Tasman District to the West Coast.

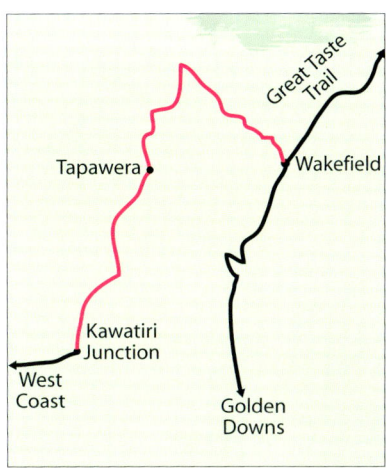

From Wakefield, follow the Great Taste Trail signs west on Pigeon Valley Road. This becomes a long gravel climb, followed by an even longer descent on Dovedale Road.

Pass through Dovedale (just a clump of houses these days), and turn left up Sunday Creek Road. It becomes a very narrow gravel road, as it climbs over to the Motueka Valley Highway.

Turn left at the highway and follow it 8 km south to the village of Tapawera, where you will find the first accommodation and shops since Wakefield (46 km away). It's a great stopover for cyclists.

From Tapawera, head southwest on Tadmor Valley Road (also known as Dry Road) for almost 40 km, where it ends at Highway 6. Turn right, and fly 7.5 km down to Kawatiri Junction. This is where you meet the Pioneer Heritage Trail (see page 194).

Notes Wakefield has public toilets, a Four Square store, a nice cafe and a highly recommended bakery (Glendenings Bakery, open 5 am to 5 pm, seven days) just 50 metres south along the highway from the Wakefield shops. Yum!

Glenhope Hu Ha Farmstay, 1 km off route on Highway 6, friendly backpackers: ☎ 03 548 2707 or 021 216 5556, http://www.huhafarmstay.co.nz/

Tapawera has a Four Square, cafe, garages, toilets, a motel and a hotel ☎ 03 522 4414 and campground ☎ 03 522 4334.

Kawatiri Junction has a shelter, toilets, camping area and a million sandflies.

The next main town, Murchison, is 47 km away.

HEARTLAND RIDE

The Rainbow
Nelson Lakes/Tophouse to Hanmer Springs
Distance 141 km   Time 2–2.5 days   Grade 3 (Intermediate)

From Nelson Lakes National Park, this trail follows a historic stock route through beautiful beech forest and high mountains to the mighty Clarence Valley and down to Hanmer Springs, a welcoming thermal resort.

Traditionally, cyclists chose either the Rainbow or the Molesworth cycle routes. Forget that! This new route combines the best of the Rainbow with the best of the Molesworth, using a new link via Lake Sedgemere. Although this ride is technically easy, it is also remote. Riders must be self-sufficient with first aid supplies and food, as there are no shops along the way. Also, a simple map-reading error could cost you the best part of a day.

The destination is Hanmer Springs, on the edge of the Canterbury Plains, where there is the chance to restock, soak in thermal pools and check out some brilliant mountain bike tracks.

ITINERARY

Stage 1: St Arnaud to Lake Sedgemere Sleepout
58 km, 1 day

From St Arnaud, ride north-east on Highway 63 for 9 km, before turning right at the Rainbow Skifield sign. From there, a narrow road dives into the Wairau Valley, crossing many side creeks en route. Some of the larger fords, especially Rough Creek, are impassable after heavy rain, so approach with caution.

Much of the lower valley is cloaked in pristine beech forest that reaches from the riverbanks up to the timberline at over 1000 m. Beyond the forest, a legion of mountains, many over 2000 m, guard the magnificent Nelson Lakes National Park on your right and the rugged Raglan Range on your left.

After breaking out of the forest, the pylon road crosses a plateau-like section of the valley before entering Wairau Gorge, where the tumbling river completes an impossible squeeze through Hells Gate, between the Turk and Mangerton ridges. Just above the gorge, you'll find Coldwater Creek, where there is an informal camping spot set in the last patch of beech forest.

Beyond Coldwater Creek, the track climbs gently into an alpine environment. After 11 km, you'll bomb down a hill and cross the Wairau River, and 500 metres later, turn left to go to Lake Sedgemere Hut. There is a public chalet (hut) and a

Sedgemere link connecting the Rainbow and Molesworth.

sleepout (shelter) a few hundred metres apart. There is nowhere else to stay or camp until Acheron Accommodation House, 60 km away, and no entry to the next stage of the trail between 7 pm and 7 am.

Stage 2: Sedgemere Sleepout to Hanmer Springs
83 km, 1–1.5 days

From the Sedgemere Chalet, follow DOC signs and orange triangle markers along a dirt 4WD track for about 24 km to the Molesworth gravel road. This track is open from 7 am to 7 pm, 5 January to mid-February. Outside this time you need to continue on the traditional Rainbow Route, which goes over Island Saddle, along the bumpy Clarence Valley, and over Jollies Pass to Hanmer Springs.

Assuming you can ride the Sedgemere link, when you reach the Molesworth Road, head south beside the Severn and Acheron rivers. You'll pass a couple of public shelters with toilets and interpretation panels. After about 33 km, you'll drop down to the historic Acheron Accommodation House, where there is water, toilets and camping. This is where the Acheron River meets the Clarence River.

From Acheron, cross the Clarence River bridge, and continue following the road south-west. After another 12 km, turn left at Jollies Pass Road and climb for 4 km to Jollies Pass (850 m). You now have a brake-burning descent to Hanmer Springs, 8 km away.

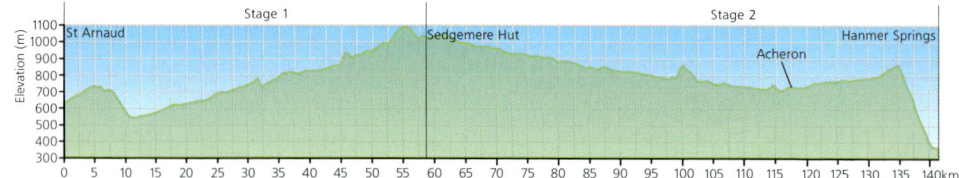

Hanmer Springs was a popular health resort for much of last century. Now it's a magnet for people who love all types of outdoor activities, especially mountain biking. There are plenty of places to eat and stay.

FACT FILE

Overview The Rainbow Trail can form one section of a week-long loop tour, which includes Lewis Pass and the Pioneer Heritage Trail.

How to get there Nelson Lakes Shuttles from Picton (www.nelsonlakesshuttles.co.nz) is an obvious option for getting to St Arnaud. Cycling from Nelson via the Great Taste Trail and Golden Downs is the best riding option.

Riding surface 70% gravel road, 18% 4WD track, 12% sealed road

Special considerations No fires are allowed in the precious remnant of native forest. Leave all farm gates as you find them. It is important to use toilet facilties where they exist. If you need to go where there is no toilet, move well away from streams and rivers and ensure you bury your waste properly. The Rainbow and Molesworth rides are sometimes overrun by 4WD use during the Christmas and Easter Holidays.

Landowners The Rainbow Road is open for a toll of $5 per rider between 26 December and Easter Monday, payable at the Rainbow Cob Homestead, near the northern end of Rainbow Road. Outside this season, permission to cross Rainbow Station must be obtained by emailling info@rainbowstation.co.nz, see www.rainbowstation.co.nz for more information.

Special features Isolation is the most outstanding feature! Followed by extremes of weather. Go well equipped.

Important contacts Department of Conservation, ☎ 03 572 9100 or see www.doc.govt.nz

Maps NZTopo250 18 Murchison is worth taking for the topographical information.

Trail websites www.nzcycletrail.com and www.doc.govt.nz

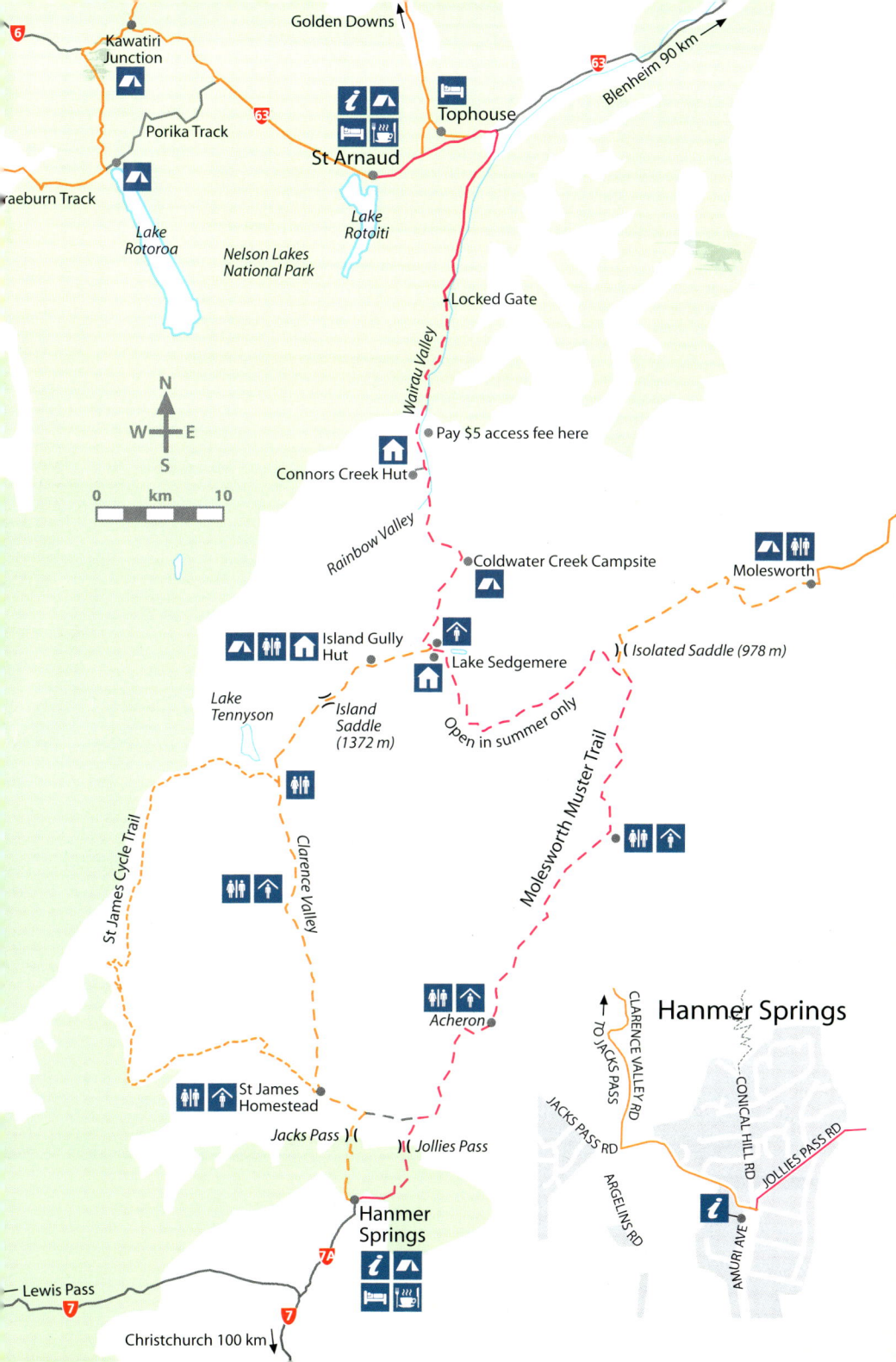

SUPPORT SERVICES

St Arnaud General store, petrol, cafe-restaurant and accommodation: www.fourcorners.co.nz/new-zealand/st-arnaud/. Alpine Lodge: ☎ 03 521 1869, Nelson Lakes Motels/Travers-Sabine Lodge: ☎ 03 521 1887, www.nelsonlakes.co.nz, Kerr Bay campsite: www.doc.govt.nz, West Bay campsite, www.doc.govt.nz

Island Gully Hut This DOC hut costs a $5 hut ticket per person per night. Water and a toilet, four bunks with mattresses, no booking system, www.doc.govt.nz

Hanmer Springs Shops, cafes, restaurants, accommodation, bike hire: www.visithanmersprings.co.nz

Bikepackers heading into the Rainbow.

> **CONNECTOR RIDE**

MOLESWORTH MUSTER TRAIL

Hanmer Springs to Blenheim
Distance 205 km   Time 2–4 days   Grade 4 (Advanced)

This ride – open to cyclists from 28 December to 3 April – passes through the country's largest farm, Molesworth Station, and runs around the base of the massive Kaikoura mountains. It is often completed in tandem with the Rainbow Valley.

The Molesworth Muster starts with a steep gravel-road climb from Hanmer Springs over Clarence Valley Road to Jacks Pass and on down to the Clarence Valley. Fit hill climbers will prefer to go over Jollies Pass instead of Jacks Pass – it is steeper but 4 km shorter.

After turning right at a Y intersection, a couple of hours steady pedalling gets you to the historic Acheron Accommodation House, which is no longer open for business but is worth a stop to study the interesting cobb construction. It's also a popular and useful camping site. Water is available from the local stream.

From Acheron, you must ride the main farm track all the way through Molesworth Station in a single day (them's the station's rules). You've got from 7 am to 7 pm to cover 50 km of dirt road. This is the most scenic section of the ride, and your destination is the old Molesworth homestead, where there are more historic cobb buildings and good camping sites.

From the homestead, you are back on a public road down the Awatere Valley for just over 100 km (it's a mix of gravel and sealed road). There are a few hills, but the route is basically making its way down to the sea, which is why we recommend doing the ride in this direction. A moderate climb over the gravel Taylor Pass rewards with a good downhill to a nice off-road path into Blenheim.

Note This is a long ride with no services: you must carry all your food, water, camping and safety equipment. For more detailed information, refer to www.doc.govt.nz/molesworth.

Easy option Learn about the history, get driven over the boring bits and have the support of a guide with The Molesworth Tour Company, ☎ 03 572 8025 or 027 435 1955, www.molesworthtours.co.nz

GREAT RIDE

St James Cycle Trail

Hanmer Springs, 130 km north of Christchurch
Distance 64 km point to point or 92-km loop
Time 1–2 days   Grade 4 (Advanced)

St James Station is a jumble of wild rivers, forest remnants and mountain ranges. With no roads, no shops and no cell phone coverage, this trail is all about the basic desire to get away from it all.

In November 2010, this tough, highland track was the first New Zealand Cycle Trail to be officially opened, providing skilled riders with an opportunity to experience the raw beauty of the retired St James Station.

Be warned, this is no easy cycle path. It is a true back-country experience for those seeking a 'tramping on wheels' type trip. The trail traverses extremely exposed areas, and the best accommodation you can hope for is the insect-proofed tent strapped to your carrier. Hanmer Springs tourist resort is the base for this ride, and it offers a fitting reward with fine restaurants and divine hot pools to pamper the weary adventurer.

ITINERARY

Optional Stage 1: St James Homestead to Maling Pass car park
26 km, 1.5 hours

We recommend starting from St James Homestead (where there is a toilet and car park) and making this a loop trip to avoid transport hassles. From the homestead, head north along Tophouse Road for 26 easy kilometres to the Maling Pass car park, (on your left just before Lake Tennyson).

Stage 2: Maling Pass car park to Lake Guyon
16.5–18.5 km, 2–4 hours

Maling Pass car park is the official start of the St James Cycle Trail. An old farm track leads from the car park, through open tussock land, up to Maling Pass, an hour away. At 1308 m, this pass marks the highest point on the trail. On the other side awaits a 30-minute downhill into the Waiau Valley.

Down in the valley, the 4WD track morphs into a cycle trail, leading through grassland valleys and matagouri scrub to a signposted intersection. Approximately 15 minutes to your left lies the picturesque Lake Guyon, where a basic 4-bunk DOC hut awaits those who wish to stay overnight. With a lot of downhill to it, Stage 1 takes only a few hours pedalling, so some riders decide to push on to Pool Hut, another 3 hours away. However, this next part of the track is challenging in places and involves some 5- to 10-minute 'foot cycling' sections.

Big climbs always reward with panoramic views.

Stage 3: Lake Guyon to Pool Hut
20–22 km, 2–4 hours

From Lake Guyon, head back to the main track and continue following the blue marker poles south to Pool Hut, 2–4 hours away. The track becomes a lot rougher now, and after crossing the Waiau River on a massive swing bridge, you will have to walk most of the way to the top of Saddle Spur. Some people get lost here as the marker poles are scarce. Keep your eyes peeled and remember: you are generally heading down valley. From the spur, it is mostly downhill or flat to Pool Hut, 5 km away.

When not staying at Lake Guyon Hut, riders tend to overnight here (another small 4-bunk hut, with mattresses but no cookers). However, Pool Hut is not insect proof, so you may prefer to tent out.

Stage 4: Pool Hut to Scotties Camp Hut
8 km, 1–2 hours

After 5 minutes cycling south of Pool Hut, you will cross another large swing bridge. The trail is often loose and rocky from here to Scotties Camp Hut with a

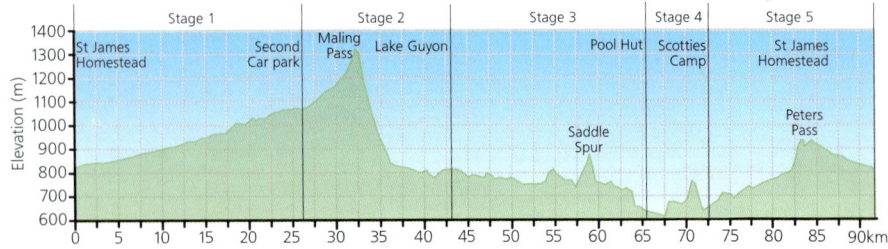

few walks required over steep bluff sections. The exception is the final downhill from Charlies Saddle to the hut, which seems to be an endless swallow dive. Allow at least 1 hour to ride from Pool Hut to Scotties Camp.

Stage 5: Scotties Camp Hut to St James Homestead
17 km, 1.5–3 hours

From Scotties Camp up to Peters Pass Junction involves lots of easy 4WD track, several rough stream crossings and a long steep hill that some people will have to walk. Give yourself at least 1 hour for this 10 km section.

There are two routes back to St James Homestead from Peters Pass Junction. You can go straight ahead on an easy 4WD track that leads out to Tophouse Road and then turn right to ride 3.5 km down the road. Or you can turn right at the junction and continue following blue marker poles onto a fantastic upgraded

Saddle Spur Bridge over the Waiau River.

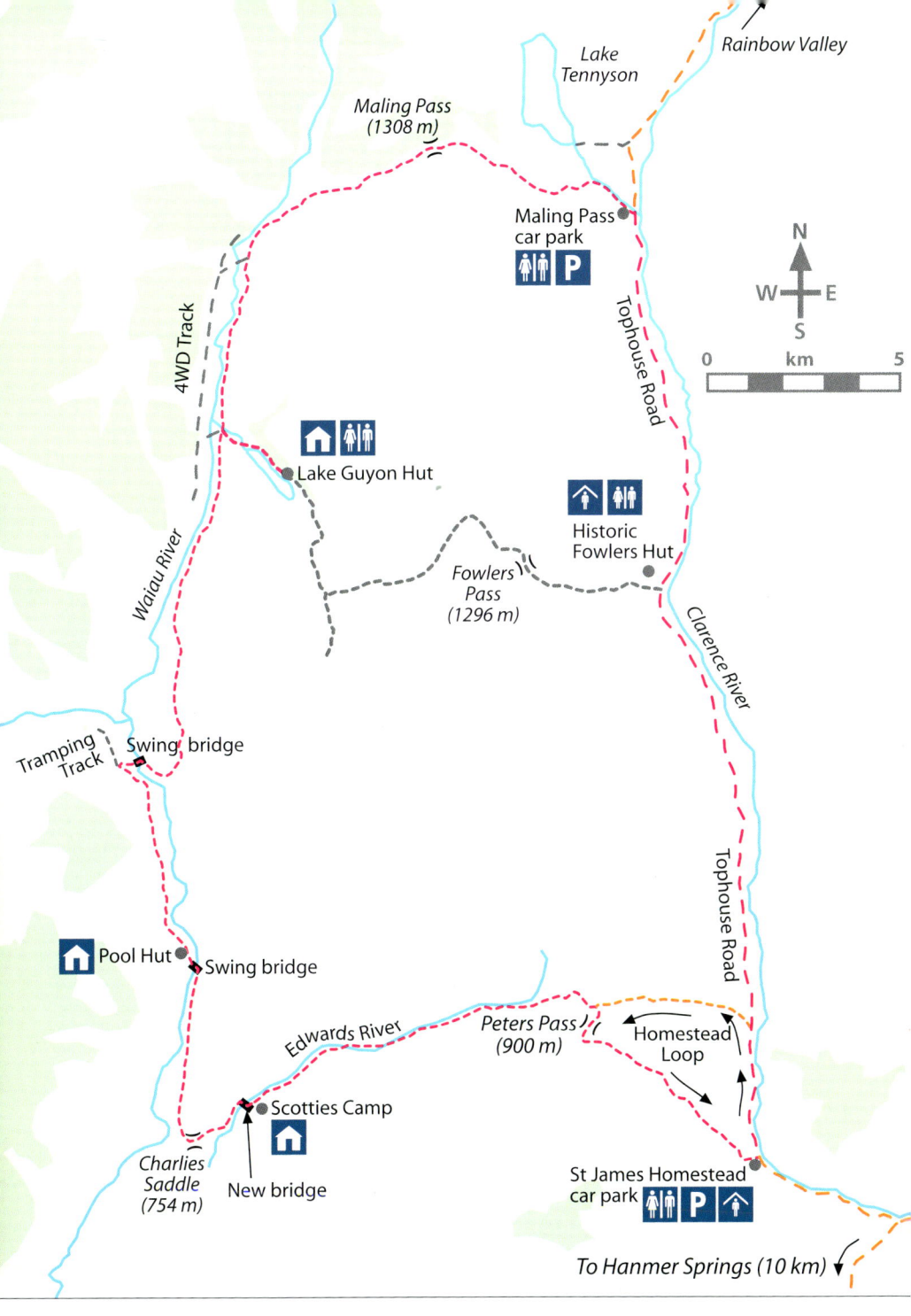

section of the track leading to the homestead. Both options take less than an hour. From St James Homestead, it is mostly downhill back to Hanmer Springs, only 13 km away.

Short & Easy Option: Homestead Loop
This 15-km, 2–3 hour ride starts and ends at St James Homestead (we recommend going anti-clockwise). Ride 2.6 km up Tophouse Road, turn left onto the trail which heads to Peters Pass. From there turn left again and follow the brilliant new track back to the homestead.

FACT FILE
Overview This track is often closed in winter due to deep snow. Be prepared for some vicious assaults from sandflies during the warmer seasons. A there-and-back day trip from Maling Pass car park to Lake Guyon is the perfect alternative for less experienced/fit riders.

How to get there From Hanmer Springs, ride or drive out of town on Jacks Pass Road and turn right onto Clarence Valley Road to start the climb proper up to the pass. After descending into the Clarence Valley, turn left at Tophouse Road. When you are 13 km from Hanmer Springs, you will see the old St James Homestead on your left, comprising a few buildings, a car park and toilets. This is the official 'end' of the St James Cycle Trail. For even more of a workout, start this ride from Hanmer Springs itself.

Transport For shuttles to and from the trail, contact St James Journeys, ☎ 03 315 5086 or 027 315 6106, www.stjamesjourneys.co.nz

Riding surface 25% gravel road, 25% 4WD track, 49% single track, 1% unridable

Special considerations There is no cell phone coverage in the St James area. Some sections of the trail are also open to 4WD vehicles and horse riders. Please respect other users.

Rivers and streams rise quickly in this area after rain: they will drop just as quickly, and if your crossing is flooded, you would do better to wait for it to go down before crossing.

Maps NZTopo50 BT24 Ada Flat. Also pick up the DOC pamphlet *St James Cycle Trail*. It includes a map of the trail and lots of useful information.

SUPPORT SERVICES
Hanmer Springs Food and accommodation: www.visithanmersprings.co.nz. Hanmer Springs Adventure Centre (bike hire), ☎ 03 315 7233 or 021 225 2292, www.hanmeradventure.co.nz

Lake Guyon Hut costs $5/night (i.e., one hut ticket).

Pool Hut and **Scotties Camp Hut** are free, but they are very basic. For more info on hut fees, go to www.doc.govt.nz/parks-and-recreation/places-to-stay

Sweating the big hill away from the Waiau.

GREAT RIDE

Heaphy Track

Kahurangi National Park: Golden Bay to the West Coast

Distance 80 km   Time 2–3 days   Grade 4- (Advanced)

The Heaphy Track is said to be the greatest mountain bike adventure in New Zealand. It crosses the magnificent Kahurangi National Park and takes in beautiful rivers, pristine forests, distant mountains and wild beaches.

From a remote road end near Collingwood in Golden Bay, the Heaphy Track climbs into the hills and crosses a large plateau called Gouland Downs. It then dives through various forest types to the Heaphy River, and follows it out to the coast. The last half day is spent following the coast south to another remote road end near Karamea at the top of the West Coast Highway.

The Heaphy is open to bicycles from 1 May to 30 November. These are the colder, wetter months, so riders must be well prepared for any conditions. Check with DOC before your ride.

ITINERARY

Stage 1: Aorere Valley Road to Perry Saddle Hut
18 km, 2–3 hours

From the car park at the end of Aorere Valley Road, ride a few minutes to Brown Hut (18 bunks). From there, the track crosses Brown River and climbs steadily for a good hour or more to Aorere Shelter, where there is water and a toilet.

From the shelter, the track continues in much the same style – good gradient and good surface – to the highest point on the Heaphy Track, Flanagans Corner at 910 m. At the Corner, there is a 3-minute side walk to a stunning lookout. Beyond Flanagans Corner, the track sidles west to Perry Saddle Hut (28 bunks, fully serviced, good views).

Stage 2: Perry Saddle Hut to James Mackay Hut
25 km, 4–5 hours

After Perry Saddle, the track is rough and rocky to Gouland Downs Hut (8 bunks, no cookers). There are fantastic views of the vast Gouland Downs, and you'll pass the famous 'boot tree' on your way.

The track is in mint condition from Gouland Downs Hut to Saxon Hut (16 bunks), which lies in the open among tussock. If the track is saturated, which it is much of the time over winter, we recommend doing an about-turn here and

Traversing the high plains of the Gouland Downs.

enjoying the fantastic riding back to Golden Bay.

From Saxon Hut to James Mackay Hut (26 bunks), DOC has done a lot of track upgrading. However there is also plenty of narrow boardwalk to keep you on your toes.

Stage 3: James Mackay Hut to Heaphy Hut
21 km, 2–4 hours

The toughest section of the track is from James Mackay Hut down a massive hill to Lewis Hut (20 bunks). The track has some rocks, ruts and roots, interspersed with long easy sections. Grade 4 riders will have a ball. Grade 3 riders should expect some walking.

From Lewis Hut down to Heaphy Hut (32 bunks), the track follows the huge Heaphy River and is virtually flat. There used to be three difficult swing bridges in this section, but they have been replaced with two nice wide ones.

Stage 4: Heaphy Hut to Karamea road end
16 km, 2–3 hours

The final 15 km stretch from Heaphy Hut out to the Karamea track end is mostly ridable, but there are a couple of walking sections along the coast where the track has been swallowed up by the sea. During high tides, these can be tricky.

About 30 minutes from the end, you'll be faced with a moderate sized hill over to Kohaihai Shelter at the road end.

From the track end, it is an easy 16 km road ride to Karamea, where there is good accommodation and food.

FACT FILE

Overview The Heaphy is not an official 'Great Ride', but it certainly is a great ride. Most riders prefer biking the Heaphy from east to west because, in that direction, they get to ride down the big hill between James Mackay and Lewis. The ride is still great in the other direction though.

Be prepared for plenty of cold wind and heavy rain.

Attempting to blast through in a day is a waste of stunning, world-class scenery. All the big huts have billies and gas cookers, so it's easy to travel light.

Stop at the character-filled Langford General Store, Bainham, 17 km southwest of Collingwood, for an ice cream and a cold drink. It's a real time warp. It's also your last chance for supplies before you hit the track, but it's closed in July and August. See their website: www.langfordstore.co.nz or ☎ 03 524 8228.

How to get there The trail ends are 453 km apart by road. It is such a long shuttle that some make the Heaphy part of a longer mountain bike tour by riding the Old Ghost Road (see page 184).

If driving, head to Collingwood in Golden Bay. 1 km before Collingwood, turn left onto Collingwood-Bainham Main Road, which becomes Aorere Valley Road just after passing Langford General Store. After another 30 km, you will reach three fords, which are unpassable after heavy rain. The track starts another 3 km up the road.

Riding surface 98% ridable tramping track, 2% unridable

History The track was surveyed by J B Saxon in 1888 and developed for use by gold prospectors. Luckily, no gold was found, and the area was left untouched. In the 1970s, proposals to turn the track into a road failed, mostly because of a boom in people tramping the track. When the area became Kahurangi National Park in 1996, cyclists were banned from riding the track. After extensive lobbying, bikes were let back in by 2011.

Special considerations Riding after dark or in groups of more than six riders is prohibited on the Heaphy. The Heaphy Track is also a Great Walk – be considerate of trampers. Control your speed and be ready to stop around any corner. Be considerate of the delicate native flora and fauna – stay on the track at all times.

Special features The scenery from start to finish is breathtaking but especially so through the Gouland Downs and along the West Coast. Wildlife to watch out for includes giant carniverous snails and great spotted kiwi.

Maps NZTopo50 BP22 Heaphy and BP23 Gouland Downs

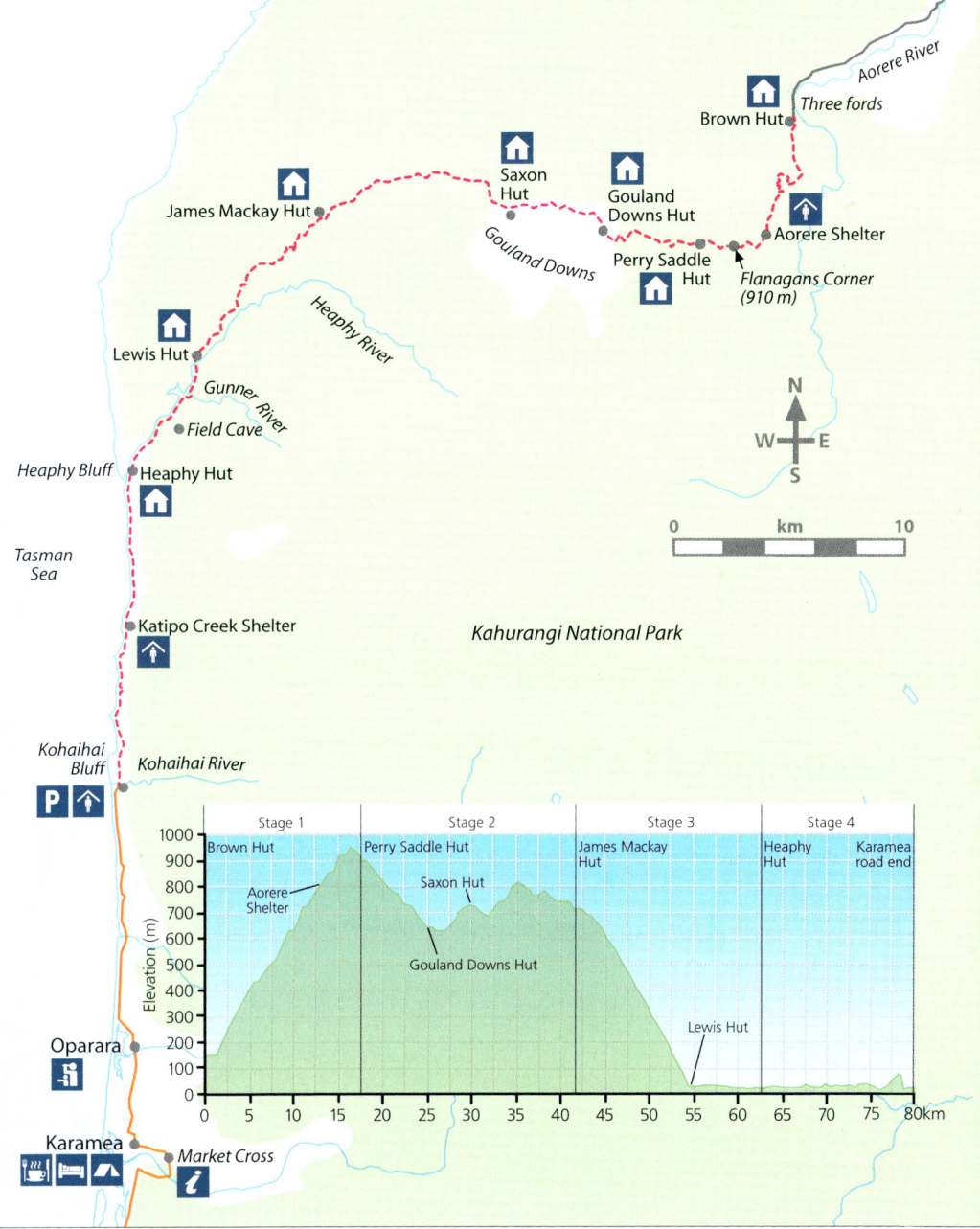

Important contacts All huts and camping sites must be booked through DOC (see www.doc.govt.nz). Contact DOC Takaka ☎ 03 525 8026 or Westport ☎ 03 788 8008 for weather and track updates.

Trail website www.doc.govt.nz/heaphytrack

Classic New Zealand Cycle Trails

The wild and wonderful Heaphy Track.

SUPPORT SERVICES

Track huts For details on all accommodation along the track, www.doc.govt.nz and book in advance.

Transport

Steve Newport in Nelson for a shuttle van, ☎ 0800 682 635, www.helibikenelson.co.nz

Trek Express for transport: ☎ 0800 128 735 or 03 540 2042, www.trekexpress.co.nz

Heaphy Track Help for car relocation: ☎ 03 525 9576, www.heaphytrackhelp.co.nz

Karamea Connections for shuttles to/from Karamea: ☎ 03 782 6767 or www.karameaconnections.co.nz

Takaka Food, accommodation and bike shop. The Quiet Revolution Cycle Shop in Takaka for last-minute bike parts: ☎ 03 525 9555, www.quietrevolution.co.nz

Karamea Food, accommodation: www.karameainfo.co.nz

CONNECTOR RIDE

HEAPHY TO OLD GHOST ROAD
Karamea to Seddonville
Distance 17 km   Time 1 hour   Grade 3 (Intermediate)

This is a beautiful road ride, but most people remember it mainly for its formidable hill – The Bluffs.

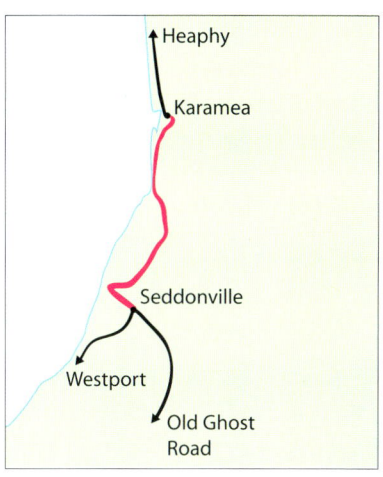

From the Karamea Information Centre at Market Cross, head south on Highway 67. After an hour of flat riding, the hill begins, almost imperceptibly. But by the time you've climbed 200 m, you will know all about it. Then there is short downhill before the main assault on The Karamea Bluffs. The road twists and turns, with lush rainforest on both sides, to the summit at View Hill Saddle (420 m). The highway then dives in spectacular fashion to the Mokihinui River bridge (45 km north of Westport).

On the southern side of the bridge, turn left and ride 2.5 km of flat to Seddonville, the launching pad for the Old Ghost Road or the Ghost Road Roundabout; both superb multi-day mountain bike adventures.

Cave Brook – a tranquil moment on the Gouland Downs.

GREAT RIDE

Old Ghost Road

Buller Gorge, 16 km northeast of Inangahua Junction
Distance 85 km   Time 2–3 days   Grade 4 (Advanced)

The Old Ghost Road is a pristine wilderness experience from the very start to the very end. It climbs through native forest, traverses spectacular alpine tops and descends the magnificent Mokihinui Valley.

The Old Ghost Road offers one of the worlds best multi-day mountain bike trips, delving deep into pristine conservation wild lands. From Lyell, a ghost town in the Buller Gorge, the trail climbs through forest for 20 km before breaking out onto the Lyell Range. There lies the spectacular Ghost Lake Hut, one of six huts along the trail.

From Ghost Lake, challenging single track has been etched out of mountainsides leading over Skyline Ridge and The Boneyard to the spectacular Mokihinui Gorge and on to the forgotten village of Seddonville, all through remote wilderness.

ITINERARY

Stage 1: Lyell car park to Lyell Saddle Hut
18 km, 2–3.5 hours, Grade 3

At the Lyell car park, you will find a new suspension bridge at the western edge of the clearing. On the far side, a historic mining track (built in the 1880s) climbs through beech forest, across a few massive slips and small streams en route to Lyell Saddle Hut. The Eight-Mile historic site is a good place for a rest stop, and the lookout at the first huge slip is good for a second rest stop. From there, the hut is about 1 hour away.

The hut is actually 5 minutes before the saddle. Look out for a branch in the track on your left that climbs to the hut 100 metres away. Sweet.

In places, the track follows a precipitous line – if you wobbled off the edge, you would have a long time to think about your last blunder as you fell hundreds of feet to certain death!

Stage 2: Lyell Saddle to Ghost Lake Hut
12 km, 2–3 hours, Grade 4

From Lyell Saddle Hut, the track climbs for 5 km to the bush edge. It then sidles south of Mt Montgomery, and north of Rocky Tor. Anyone with mountaineering inclinations should nip up Rocky Tor (1456 m) – it's truly spectacular.

Sweet singletrack along Skyline Ridge.

From there, the track leads mostly downhill to Ghost Lake Hut (grid ref 301 834), which lies in a natural alpine amphitheatre. This section of trail faces the full brunt of wind, rain and snow, so go well prepared.

Stage 3: Ghost Lake Hut to Stern Valley Hut
13 km, 2–3 hours, Grade 5
This is the toughest section of the whole trail. It was mostly hand built, so you'll find narrow grade-5 single track, tight switchbacks and even some wooden steps down a razorback ridge. Stern Valley Hut is at grid reference 334 874.

Stage 4: Stern Valley Hut to Goat Creek Hut
14 km, 2–3 hours, Grade 3
From Stern Valley Hut, the trail ascends a gentle valley to lakes Cheerful and Grim. It then climbs over Solemn Saddle and follows Goat Creek down to a turn-off to a small DOC hut called Goat Creek Hut (400 metres off the main trail).

Stage 5: Goat Creek Hut to Specimen Point Hut
11.5 km, 1–2 hours, Grade 3
Ten minutes from the hut, the trail crosses the Mokihinui River on a large bridge and then weaves along river flats and through majestic podocarp forest to Mokihinui Forks Hut. The confluence between the north and south branches of the Mokihinui is amazing and definitely worth a gander.

The trail then heads west for a few kilometres to Specimen Point Hut (another new hut built specifically for the cycle trail and offering good views of the river).

Stage 6: Specimen Point Hut to Seddonville
20 km, 2–3 hours, Grade 3+

From Specimen Point Hut, the trail is back on the historic mining track built over a century ago. Much of this track was destroyed in the 1929 Murchison earthquake, and two men died on the track, buried in a landslide triggered by the quake.

When you reach the car park, it is an easy 3-km cruise down a gravel/seal road to Seddonville, where you can hang out at the pub or the holiday park.

FACT FILE

Overview This is the wildest ride in New Zealand. Riders must be experienced in wilderness travel and go well equipped.

How to get there The ride starts from Lyell camping ground beside Highway 6 in the Buller Gorge: that's 34 km west of Murchison and 16 km northeast of Inangahua Junction. It ends at Seddonville, 50 km north of Westport. The Lyell starting point is 4 hours drive from Christchurch or 2 hours drive from Nelson.

For experienced riders, the Ghost Road Roundabout heartland ride (see page 190) solves the transport problem.

Transport For a shuttle from Westport to both trail ends contact HikenBike Shuttle, www.hikenbikeshuttle.co.nz or ☎ 027 446 7876 or Trek Express, ☎ 0800 128 735 or 03 540 2042, www.trekexpress.co.nz or Steve Newport in Nelson for a shuttle van, ☎ 0800 682 635, www.helibikenelson.co.nz

Riding surface 100% single track

Special considerations This ride climbs to well over 1300 m altitude. A storm in the alpine zone is serious business at any time of year. Standard cycling kit is *not* enough. You will need extra clothes and food. The most settled weather is over late summer–early winter (February–June).

Lyell camping ground is a magnet for sandflies, but there are very few along the trail and none up on the tops.

Important contacts Search and Rescue: consider taking an emergency locator beacon. There is virtually no cellphone coverage on the trail (the exceptions being parts of the Lyell Range between Lyell Saddle and Ghost Lake).

Maps NZTopo50-BR22 Lyell or NewTopo The Old Ghost Road

Trail website www.oldghostroad.org.nz

SUPPORT SERVICES

Huts Accommodation for 1–4 nights on the track costs $140. For booking go to www.oldghostroad.org.nz – booking is essential.

Seddonville Seddonville Hotel, ☎ 03 782 1828, Seddonville Holiday Park: ☎ 03 782 1314, www.seddonvillepark.co.nz, Rough and Tumble Lodge: ☎ 03 782 1337, www.roughandtumble.co.nz

Granity Miners on Sea Ltd (food and accommodation), ☎ 03 782 8664, www.minersonsea.co.nz

Westport Lots of food and accommodation, www.westport.nz.com

Murchison Accommodation and food: www.newzealand.com/int/murchison

The historic mining trail beside Mokihinui Gorge.

CONNECTOR RIDE

WESTPORT TO GHOST ROAD ROUNDABOUT

Westport to Waimangaroa
Distance 17 km   Time 1 hour   Grade 3 (Intermediate)

This is a boring but useful link between the main transport hub, Westport, and the Old Ghost Road Roundabout. It's not much fun, so if you get offered a lift – take it!

From Westport, head northeast on Brougham Street, which is Highway 67. After crossing a long bridge just north of town, take the next left down Utopia Road and then right down Garveys Road. It rejoins the highway a few kilometres later. Continue northwest to Waimangaroa, 16.8 km from the Westport i-SITE (on Brougham Street).

Waimangaroa is on the Ghost Road Roundabout ride (see page 190), at the base of the big climb to Denniston. Waimangaroa to Lyell, at the start of the Old Ghost Road, is 41 km of mostly gravel road.

Note If you decide to get a shuttle to Waimangaroa, you may as well take it all the way up to Denniston to save yourself a big hill climb.

> **HEARTLAND RIDE**

Ghost Road Roundabout
Seddonville to Lyell
Distance 173 km   Time 3–5 days   Grade 4 (Advanced)

For die-hard mountain bikers, this will be one of the best multi-day loop trips on the planet. The Roundabout delivers spectacular scenery and fantastic wilderness riding to create a must-do adventure – for those who dare!

This ride starts with the Old Ghost Road, from Lyell to Seddonville (see page 184). That's 2–3 amazing days' riding in itself. After a pit stop at Seddonville, the next treat is the Charming Creek Walkway, a long-standing mountain bikers' favourite. This section includes tunnels, bridges and forest, and leads through to the small settlements of Ngakawau and, 2 km down the road, Granity. There you will find food, internet access and blissfully hot showers.

From Granity, the final day starts with an easy 1-hour spin down the West Coast highway to the Waimangaroa dairy, and the turn-off to the climb to Denniston (a not-so-easy 1-hour gutbuster). Then the remote Denniston Shortcut leads through more impressive wilderness for half a day, back to Lyell car park. It's a fabulous grand loop but not one for the faint-hearted.

ITINERARY

Stages 1–6: Lyell to Seddonville (see Old Ghost Road)
88 km, 2–3 days

Start by riding the Old Ghost Road (see page 184).

Stage 7: Seddonville to Granity
20 km, 2–3 hours

Heading southeast from Seddonville, follow Charming Creek Road for 10 km of mostly gravel road over some small hills to the start of Charming Creek Walkway.

From there, the well-signposted walkway runs mostly flat or downhill past various mining relics (some are under shelters), along beech-tree boulevards, over swing bridges and through tunnels. It's a feature-packed track and, in 2012, DOC upgraded it, making it a comfortable grade-3 riding experience. The track pops out at the back of Ngakawau, a few hundred metres from a store and hotel. From the hotel, ride south down Highway 67 for 2 km to Granity. This is home to the famous Miners on Sea (see services on page 192).

Dropping off the northern end of the Mount William Range.

Stage 8: Granity to Lyell
65 km, 7–10 hours

Ride down the highway for another 12 km, to Waimangaroa. It has a small store where you can stock up on food to get you over the final leg of the big loop. Their pies are famous.

From the store, ride straight up Stewart Street, left along Neighbours Street and then right up Denniston Road. What follows is a stiff 8-km climb, but it's all sealed. You are about to ride the Denniston Shortcut, a route pioneered by hardcore cycle tourers in the 1970s.

When you reach a T-intersection near the top of the hill, turn right to the 'Friends of the Hill'. At the top, there is a big building on your right (with toilets). From that 'Friends of the Hill' building, follow the Mackley Route sign east and ignore any minor turn-offs. After 40 minutes, you will reach a fork (it is 200 metres after crossing a bridge – grid ref. 044 774). Turn right and climb steeply onto the Mount William Range. Near the top, turn left at a 4-way intersection. You'll then get some great views for the next kilometre.

Now follow the main road down to Stevenson Stream and then Mount William Stream. At grid ref. 086 738, swing left, uphill. Before long, you will dive down to the Orikaka/Mackley River. This is a big river and should be treated with respect. If it is swollen and brown, then wait for it to drop. In low flows, it is just ridable.

On the far side of the Orikaka/Mackley River, a steep climb awaits. At the top of that 15-minute climb, ignore the first two left-hand turns, then ignore a right turn and drop down to the pylon where the wires fork and turn left to follow the main gravel road down. After that tricky bit, navigation is straightforward. Continue along the main road that follows the pylons.

At Pensini Road, turn left and then 1 km later veer right and 1 km later you'll reach Highway 6 at the Iron Bridge. Cycle left along the highway for 2.5 km and you will reach the Lyell car park and camping ground. The 'Roundabout' is complete.

FACT FILE

How to get there Drive to Lyell in the Buller Gorge. It is 34 km west of Murchison, on Highway 6, and 63 km east of Westport. There is an airport in Westport with daily flights.

Transport For shuttle from Westport to both trail ends contact HikenBike Shuttle, www.hikenbikeshuttle.co.nz or ☎ 027 446 7876.

Riding surface Mostly sweet single track, but also a small amount of gravel and sealed road

History Pockets of this part of the West Coast have been mined and logged. There are lots of mining relics to be seen.

Special considerations Do not attempt the Denniston section (stage 7) if it has been raining heavily. The Orikaka/Mackley River will be uncrossable.

Important contacts Department of Conservation, Westport, ☎ 0800 222 33

Maps NZTopo50 – BR21 Granity and NZTopo50-BR22 Lyell are essential.

Trail website www.oldghostroad.org.nz

SUPPORT SERVICES

Seddonville Seddonville Hotel, 03 782 1828, Seddonville Holiday Park: ☎ 03 782 1314, www.seddonvillepark.co.nz, Rough and Tumble Lodge: ☎ 03 782 1337, www.roughandtumble.co.nz

Ngakawau Store: 03 782 8026; Ngakawa Tavern: ☎ 03 782 8035, www.charmingcreektavern.co.nz

Granity Miners on Sea Ltd (food and accommodation), ☎ 03 782 8664, www.minersonsea.co.nz

Westport All services, including a bike shop: www.westport.nz.com

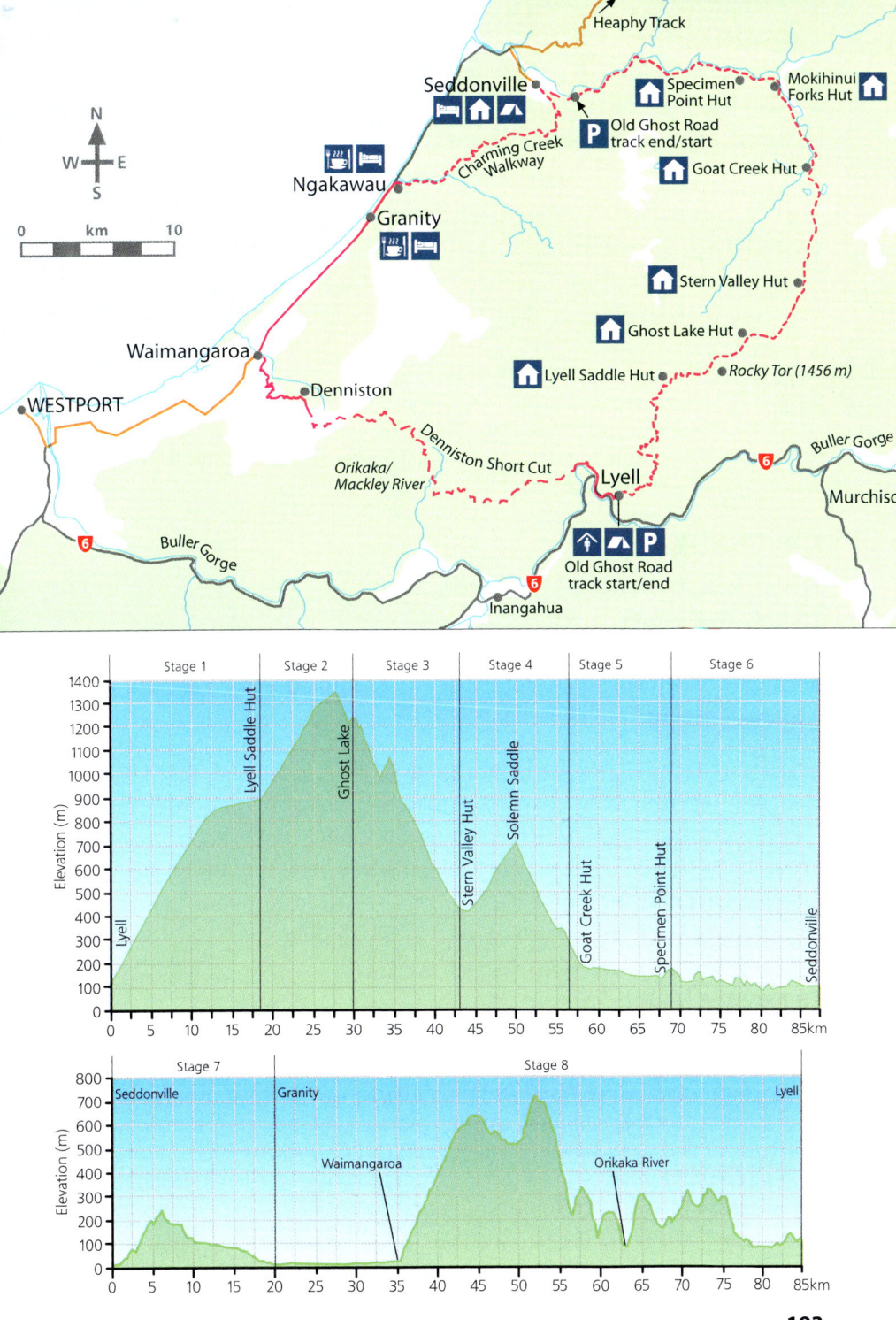

HEARTLAND RIDE

Pioneer Heritage Trail
Nelson Lakes to the West Coast
Distance 278 km   Time 3–4 days   Grade 3 (Intermediate)

This is one of our favourite South Island tours, travelling along bush-clad roads and quiet highways. Discover the real West Coast as you journey from Nelson Lakes to Greymouth via Springs Junction.

Leave the busy Tasman district behind as you head to the wild West Coast. The towns are smaller, the traffic is lighter, the bush grows thicker and, in summer, the sandflies are hungrier. Keep moving, dip into a river or seek refuge in a small town pub to meet some locals and confirm why the Coast is a region like no other.

ITINERARY

Stage 1: St Arnaud to Murchison
75 km, 4–6 hours

From St Arnaud, head west on scenic Highway 63 for an easy 25 km to Kawatiri Junction, where there is a shelter, toilets and a camping area.

At the junction, turn left and follow Highway 6 for 6 km before turning left down Gowan Valley Road. 11 km down this road you'll reach a T intersection just before the lake. Turn left to go to the lake and campground, or right to head over Braeburn Track. This is an 11 km gravel road climbing over a large hill.

When you reach Tutaki Road turn left, and at Mangles Valley Road turn right. At the Highway, turn left and cruise in to Murchison, a great spot to stop for a night.

Alternative route   The Porika Track (Grade 4+) is an adventurous alternative for fit riders. The downhill to Lake Rotoroa is a brake burner.

Stage 2: Murchison to Springs Junction
78 km, 4–6 hours

From Murchison, ride south along Fairfax Street. This soon turns into Matakitaki Road. Follow it for 28 km to a concrete bridge over the Matakitaki Gorge. Then head west on Matakitaki Road and then Maruia Saddle Road over the Glenroy River (a great spot for a swim), 30 km from Murchison. Continue through stunning beech forest and over the Maruia Saddle on a 4WD track. Turn left when you hit Highway 65 and, when you are 60 km from Murchison, you will reach the tiny settlement of Maruia, with some motels and a small cafe.

Just over 2 km down the highway, turn right onto West Bank Road to take a break from the traffic again. This is part gravel/part seal, and 14 km later, you'll

Flying down the Braeburn Track.

rejoin the highway and turn right to cruise into Springs Junction, 2 km away, which boasts a utilitarian cafe and motel.

Stage 3: Springs Junction to Reefton
44 km, 2 hours

This stage through Victoria State Forest is one of the most beautiful sections of road riding on the planet. We loved it. It's uphill for about 9 km to Rahu Saddle and then down, down, down for 35 km through beech forest with babbling streams beside the road all the way to Reefton.

Stage 4: Reefton to the Blackball Hilton
57 km, 3–4 hours

From Reefton you have two choices; the easy way and the hard way. We've described the easy way below, but if you love mountain biking, take a look at the Big River option on page 198.

For the easy option, head south on Highway 7 to Ikamatua, 26 km away. You may want to do this early in the morning as it can be a busy section of road.

At the south end of Ikamatua, turn right onto Atarau Road. This quiet and scenic back route leads to Blackball, famous for its salami and the 'Formerly the Blackball Hilton' heritage hotel. Blackball is 1.6 km off Atarau Road.

Stage 5: Blackball Hilton to Greymouth
24 km 1–2 hours

From Blackball, head back out to Taylorville-Blackball Road and ride south, staying on the north side of the Grey River all the way to the large Highway 6 bridge leading to the centre of Greymouth.

FACT FILE

How to get there Nelson Lakes Shuttle from Picton (☎ 03 540 2042 or www.nelsonlakesshuttles.co.nz) is an easy option for getting to St Arnaud. Cycling from Nelson via the Great Taste Trail and Golden Downs is the best riding option.

Riding surface 90% sealed road, 10% gravel road

History The coal mining town of Blackball was the birthplace of the New Zealand Labour Party. The hotel is over 100 years old and is in close to original condition.

Special considerations Murchison locals sometimes complain about the condition of the road over Maruia Saddle. We have always found it to be in good condition for cycling.

SUPPORT SERVICES

St Arnaud General store, cafe-restaurant, accommodation: www.nelsonlakes.co.nz. Kerr Bay/West Bay campsites: www.doc.govt.nz

Lake Rotoroa Gowan Bank Backpackers (incl. small cafe), 700 m north of lake, ☎ 03 523 9962. DOC camping area, ☎ 03 521 1806 or www.doc.govt.nz

Murchison Many shops, food and accommodation options: www.newzealand.com/int/murchison/

Maruia Motels: ☎ 03 523 8898 or 021 0266 9979, www.maruiamotels.co.nz

Springs Junction Alpine Motor Inn and Cafe, ☎ 03 523 8813 (they seldom answer); Marble Hill Campsite (4 km east of the Junction), www.doc.govt.nz

Reefton Plenty of accommodation and food options: www.reefton.co.nz Bike shop: Reefton Sports Centre, 56 Broadway, ☎ 03 732 8593

Ikamatua Store, garage, accommodation: Ikamatua Hotel: ☎ 03 732 3555 or 027 385 8430, www.ikamatuahotel.co.nz, Ahaura Hotel: ☎ 03 732 3876 or 027 322 4700; Ahaura Domain Camping Ground, ☎ 03 732 3876

Blackball Formerly the Blackball Hilton: food and budget hotel, ☎ 03 732 4705, www.blackballhilton.co.nz

Greymouth Accommodation and food: www.greydistrict.co.nz

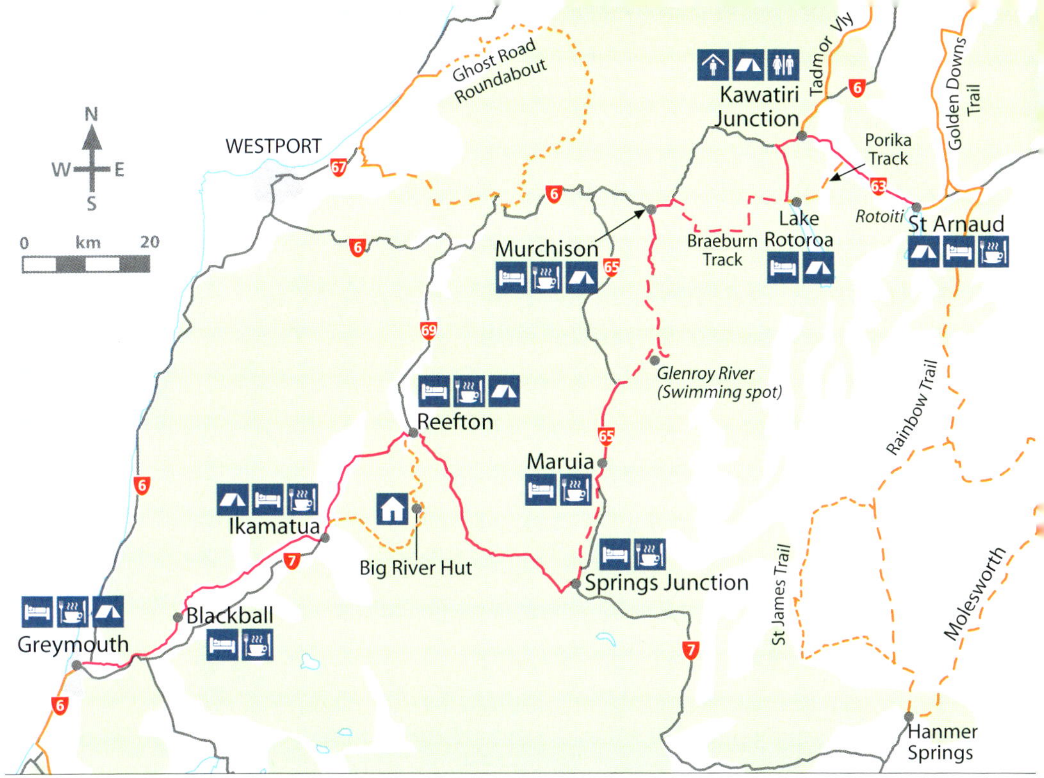

Ghost Road Roundabout
WESTPORT
N
W
E
S
0
km
20
Kawatiri Junction
Tadmor Vly
Golden Downs Trail
Porika Track
Lake Rotoroa
Rotoiti
St Arnaud
Murchison
Braeburn Track
Glenroy River (Swimming spot)
Reefton
Rainbow Trail
Maruia
Ikamatua
Big River Hut
Springs Junction
St James Trail
Molesworth
Blackball
Greymouth
Hanmer Springs

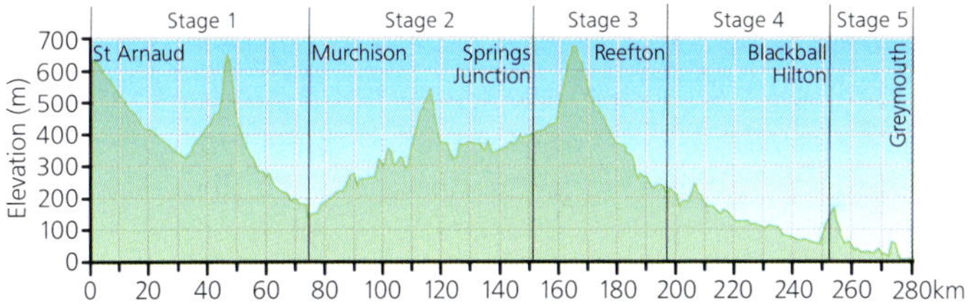

Stage 1
Stage 2
Stage 3
Stage 4
Stage 5
St Arnaud
Murchison
Springs Junction
Reefton
Blackball Hilton
Greymouth
Elevation (m)
0
100
200
300
400
500
600
700
0
20
40
60
80
100
120
140
160
180
200
220
240
260
280km

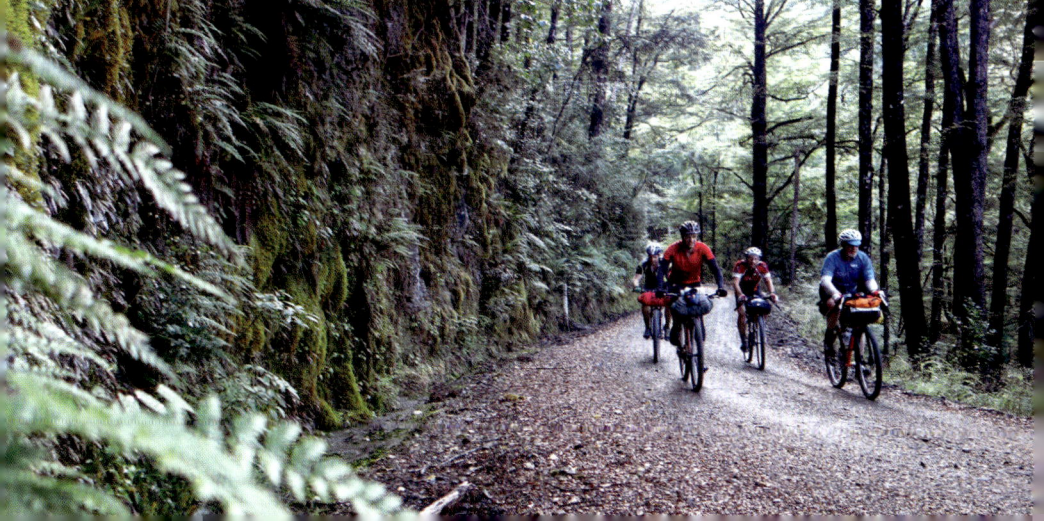

`HEARTLAND RIDE`

Big River
Reefton
Distance 51 km   Time 4–7 hours   Grade 4 (Advanced)

Historic mining road + native bush scenery + rocks and fords likely to destroy numerous bike parts = a classic old-school ride.

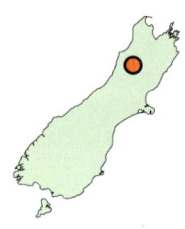

ITINERARY

Stage 1: Reefton to Big River Hut
26 km, 2–3 hours

From Reefton, ride south on Highway 7 for 1 km, then turn left onto Soldiers Road. This soon turns to gravel and climbs up Devils Creek Valley for 9 km to the Alborn Coal Mine car park. One hundred metres further on Big River Road veers off to the left.

The ride continues for another 2–3 hours through native bush, on a rocky but ridable 4WD track to Big River (impassable in flood). Soon after the Drake Mine sign, go straight ahead at a fork in the track (don't turn right). Close to the hut, you'll cross Big River on a new bridge and then you'll see the hut perched on top of a hill ahead of you. Various sites in this area were extensively mined for gold in the 1800s. Some old machinery remains, and the new signs saying 'DANGER: DO NOT Drink Water or Touch Soil in This Area' stand as testimony to the long term environmental effects of mining.

The spacious Big River Hut ($10 per night) overlooks the Big River township site and surrounding countryside.

Stage 2: Waiuta Track to Highway
25 km, 2–4 hours

The walking track from Big River to Waiuta, another mining ghost town, is now open to cyclists! DOC has done some major upgrades over the last few years. It's now 13 km of grade-4 riding along sections of dream-like single track. A few walking sections remain, but in dry conditions, it is 99% ridable.

Waiuta has several buildings and mining remains to investigate. From Waiuta, a 14 km-long, narrow gravel road glides down through the beautiful Blackwater Valley to the highway.

FACT FILE

Riding surface A mix of gravel road and 4WD tracks
Maps Refer to NZTopo50 BS21 Reefton and BT21 Waiuta.
Special considerations There are no support services and no cell phone coverage on this ride.

Bikepacking from Reefton to Greymouth via the Waiuta Track.

CONNECTOR RIDE

ARTHUR'S PASS TO WEST COAST

Arthur's Pass to Kumara
Distance 71 km   Time 3-4 hours   Grade 3 (Intermediate)

Arthur's Pass is the highest road pass in the Southern Alps and has the most beautiful alpine village in New Zealand. Catch a train or bus from Christchurch to Arthur's Pass village and glide down to the West Coast Wilderness Trail.

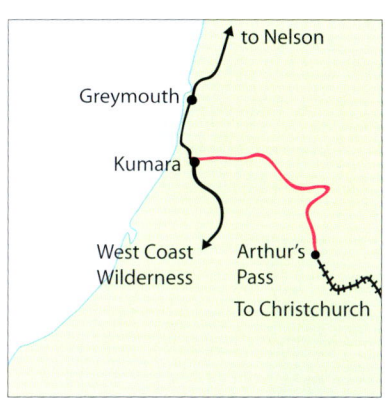

From Christchurch, one train (TranzAlpine) and two buses (West Coast Shuttles and Atomic Shuttles) travel daily to Arthur's Pass. The train is more scenic but more expensive. Cycling the road to Arthur's Pass is not a good option unless you are a hardened road rider – much of the road from Christchurch to Arthur's Pass has no shoulder and is reasonably busy.

Arthur's Pass village has a store, three cafes and several accommodation options, including an excellent youth hostel. Stay an extra night and spend a day checking out the nearby walks.

From the village, ride 4 km uphill to Arthur's Pass, right on the spine of the Southern Alps. There is a monument just before the pass and of course spectacular scenery the whole way over. On the way down the other side, you'll soon be coasting at 50 kph. We were chased by kea all the way to a massive viaduct 6 km from the pass.

At Otira, 9 km from the pass, you can stop off at the Otira Hotel. Next stop is Jacksons Hotel, another watering hole in the middle of nowhere. Jacksons is a fast 28 km down from the pass.

The small town of Kumara is 70 km from Arthur's Pass village if you go straight along the main highway, but we recommend you take the much quieter and more scenic route via Lake Brunner – it's 1 km longer and has 20 km of gravel.

From Jacksons, ride 1 km and then turn right at the Lake Brunner sign and cross the Taramakau River. Just 5 km on from the river, go straight onto the Kumara-Inchbonnie Road. After another 5 km, the road enters forest and becomes gravel. Skirt around Lake Brunner, through more forest and then down beside the Greenstone River to cross the Taramakau once again, just before Kumara.

Kumara has a store, a hotel and other accommodation. It is on the West Coast Wilderness Trail.

GREAT RIDE

West Coast Wilderness Trail
Greymouth to Ross
Distance 137 km   Time 2–4 days   Grade 2 (Easy)

Rugged coastlines, wild forests and hypnotic views of the Southern Alps are matched pedal stroke for pedal stroke against fascinating slices of pioneering life and West Coast hospitality, making this an unforgettable experience.

From Greymouth, the track traces the pounding Tasman Sea south to the Taramakau River before ducking inland to Kumara, a historic mining town. From there, you enter ancient rainforest en route to Cowboy Paradise, a replica western town, complete with saloon, boardwalks and a shooting range.

The third day is mostly downhill, travelling beside the mighty Arahura River and then the more intimate Lake Kaniere water race, heading for the wild food capital of New Zealand, Hokitika.

Those hankering for more can ride the fourth day, which continues south, following old tramlines to the village of Ross, with the chance to get high on the Tree Tops Walkway in Lake Mahinapua forest, one of New Zealand's oldest scenic reserves.

ITINERARY

Stage 1: Greymouth to Kumara
30 km, 3–5 hours

From the Greymouth Railway Station, on Mackay Street, head to the Grey River stopbank just across the road. On top is a smooth cycle trail heading out to the coast via a lagoon and the famous Greymouth Bar – a 400-metre stretch of reclaimed land from where you can watch fishing boats come and go.

Backtrack to the start of the bar and head south along the coast. After 7 km, you will pass the Seaside Holiday Park, where you can stop in for a snack if need be. Carry on south, enjoying the stunning coastal vistas, and when you are almost 13 km from town, turn left to the Paroa Tavern. From the back of the tavern, the trail follows beside the highway, weaving through patches of forest before heading inland again and crossing the historic Taramakau River road and rail bridge. From there, an old tramline leads to the small town of Kumara, an ideal place to stop for the night and learn about the area's history.

Exploring the wilderness doesn't get much better than this.

Stage 2: Kumara to Cowboy Paradise
35 km, 4–6 hours

From Kumara's Theatre Royal Hotel follow trail signs towards the hills on Tui Street and at the end turn right and follow the road onto a trail. You will later climb a cool single track to the Kapitea Reservoir, with a mountain backdrop.

Ride down to the far end of the reservoir and between Kapitea and Kumara reservoirs and along a sweeping boardwalk. The trail then follows Loopline Road and Old Christchurch Road before taking a minor road to Kawhaka Reservoir. Cross and head into the real wilderness. You will follow a historic pack track up the Kawhaka Valley to Kawhaka Pass at 317 m. From there, the trail turns right and runs beside a water race for a couple of kilometres and descends to cross the Wainihinihi Gorge. The stage finishes at a replica western town called Cowboy Paradise.

Stage 3: Cowboy Paradise to Hokitika
36 km, 3–5 hours

The third stage starts with a swooping but gentle downill to the Arahura River. This downhill is so sweet you might feel like riding back up and doing it again!

Follow a gravel road down beside the Arahura River. It has special significance to Maori as a source of quality pounamu. There is a tough 1-km climb out of the valley, through native forest, followed by a descent along Milltown Road to Lake Kaniere. It's a beautiful lake with good swimming for hardy souls. As soon as the road leaves the lake, turn right onto the old Kaniere Water Race

Classic New Zealand Cycle Trails

track. After a couple of kilometres, the trail leaves the water race and weaves through regenerating forest on the way towards Kaniere (a suburb of Hokitika). Part of this section of trail runs on and beside Lake Kaniere Road. The final few kilometres into Hokitika are on the 'Old Kaniere Tram', right beside the river with awesome views. Straight after passing under the highway bridge, turn right and ride into the centre of town, 100 metres away.

Stage 4, Hokitika to Ross
36 km, 3–5 hours

From Hokitika, take the cycle path beside the highway bridge south and turn right on Golf Links Road. Where the end of this road meets the highway, follow signs to Mahinapua Track 7 km from town. It is an old tramline leading to Woodstock-Rimu Road. Turn right at the road, and a few minutes later you'll pass the signposted turn-off to the treetop walkway and cafe.

When you reach Highway 6, 18 km from town, turn right and after another 2 km, turn left onto Paiere Road. This is the old railway line. The road soon peters out and becomes a rail trail leading south for 11 km. There are more camera-worthy views, this time of a lagoon and wetlands and the coast (from the old Totara River bridge).

When you reach a T-intersection with Ross Beach Road, turn left and ride to Ross township, a cool little spot with lots of history and a few places to eat.

FACT FILE

Overview This is the West Coast's answer to the Otago Central Rail Trail. The scenery is wonderful, and the riding is very engaging, but you can't buy a latte every 10 km, and you should take a good raincoat.

How to get there Highway 6 stretches from Nelson to the West Coast and on through to Queenstown. Highway 73, through Arthur's Pass, provides an east/west route through the Southern Alps. By road, it is just 3 hours from Christchurch Airport to Greymouth. KiwiRail operate the world famous TranzAlpine Express train to Christchurch. Air, bus and rental car transport are also widely available.

Riding surface A bit of everything! The sections of track on Stage 2 stand out as being particularly awesome.

Special considerations In 2018, a 2.5 km section of trail south of Hokitika was still being built. You'll need to ride beside Highway 6 until it's finished.

Special features Attractions and experiences along the trail include gold panning; a paddle-boat cruise; rafting; dolphin watching; jade, wood and bone carving, pottery, glass, sculpture and ruby rock art studios.

Maps and trail website www.westcoastwildernesstrail.co.nz

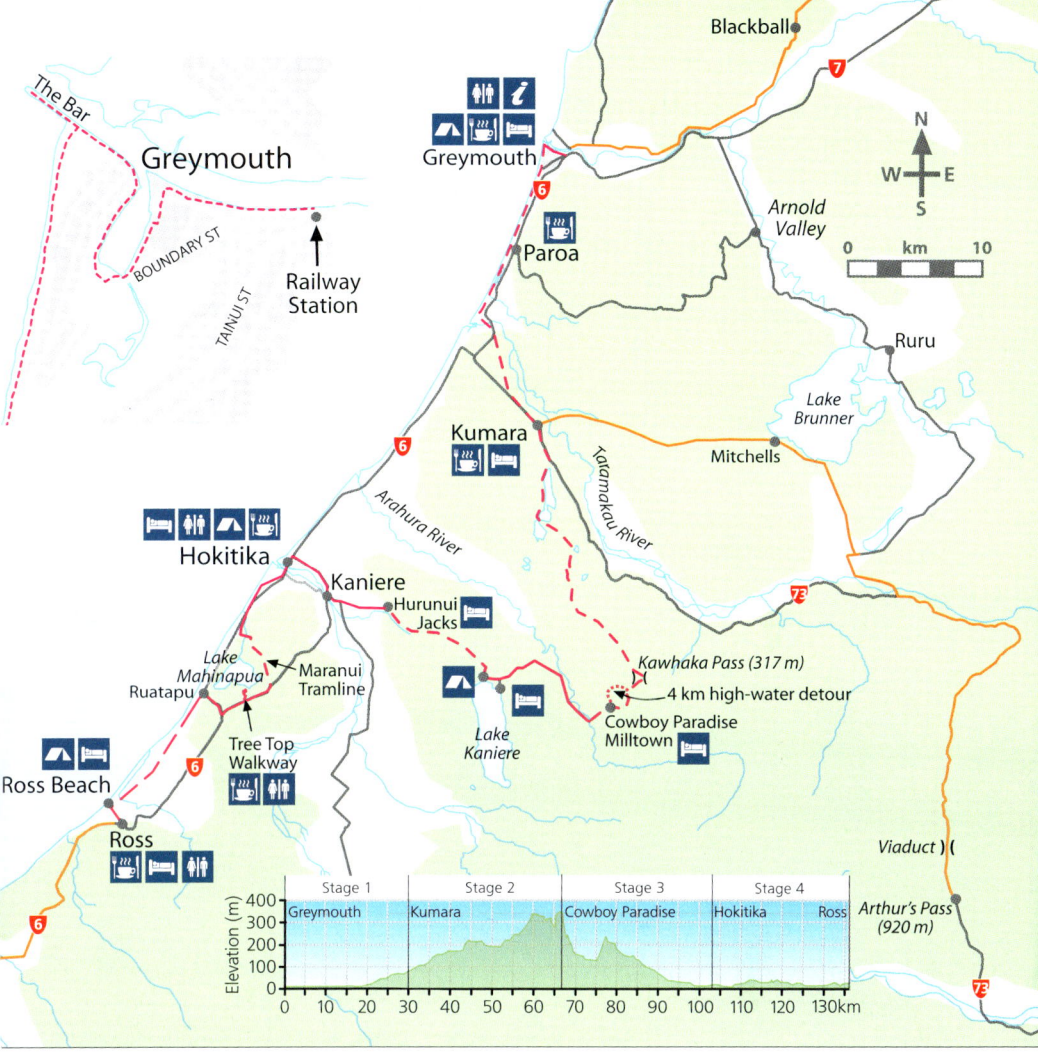

SUPPORT SERVICES

Trail transport Wilderness Trail Shuttle www.wildernesstrailshuttle.co.nz or ☎ 03 755 5042; West Side Rides ☎ 021 260 9233, www.westsiderides.co.nz; Cycle Journeys in Twizel, ☎ 03 377 2060, www.cyclejourneys.co.nz

Greymouth Restaurants, cafes and accommodation: www.greydistrict.co.nz; Bike Shop, Colls Sportsworld ☎ 03 768 4060, Mann Cycles ☎ 03 768 0255

Kumara Tearooms, pub, accommodation: www.kumarawestcoast.org. Theatre Royal Hotel (awesome!): ☎ 03 736 9277, www.theatreroyalhotel.co.nz. Route 73 Motels, ☎ 03 736 9717

Kawhaka (50.3 km from Greymouth) Paul Sinclair offers basic camping and genuine West Coast hospitality: ☎ 027 246 0266

Classic New Zealand Cycle Trails

Milltown Cowboy Paradise has accommodation, booze and pub food, www.cowboyparadise.co.nz, ☏ 03 280 9559 (for a taste of the gun crazy American South)

Lake Kaniere Holiday homes: www.holidayhouses.co.nz/Lake-Kaniere.asp or phone the Hokitika i-SITE on 03 755 6166. Kaniere Glamping/House Truck ☏ Kim Judd 03 755 6073 or 021 177 6093

Hurunui Jacks Accommodation at Lake Kaniere Road ☏ 03 755 8683, www.hurunuijacks.co.nz

Hokitika Shops, supermarkets, cafes, accommodation and bike shop: www.hokitika.org, Hokitika Cycles and Sports World has hire bikes, ☏ 03 755 8662, www.hokitikasportsworld.co.nz

Ross Groceries, cafe and accommodation. Ross Motels: ☏ 03 755 4153, www.rossmotels.co.nz; The Empire Hotel (with camping facilities): ☏ 03 755 4005; Ross Beach Top 10 Holiday Park: ☏ 03 429 8277, www.rossbeachtop10.co.nz

Sweeping boardwalk across the Kapitea Wetlands, south of Kumara.

Greymouth Coastal Path section of the West Coast Wilderness Trail.

HEARTLAND RIDE

Touring the Wild West

Ross to Wanaka
Distance 402 km   Time 4–7 days   Grade 4 (Advanced)

The West Coast dishes up a veritable feast of glaciers, rain forests and wild coastlines and includes some breathtaking lakes in the mix, all against the backdrop of the Southern Alps.

This trip forms a natural extension to the West Coast Wilderness Trail and has been a popular tour for over 50 years. We recommend riding from north to south for one simple reason – the sun will be behind you most of the way, so you won't have to squint to appreciate the beauty that surrounds you. And surround you it does!

From the small town of Ross, 30 km south of Hokitika, the ride passes lakes and national parks on its way to Wanaka. You will be cycling close enough to hear, smell and touch the flora and fauna that make up some of our most ancient forests.

ITINERARY

Stage 1: Ross to Whataroa
75 km, 4–6 hours

From Ross, head south on Highway 6 for 5 km before turning right down Bold Head Road. This provides a quiet alternative to the highway and follows the coast for a few kilometres. It is gravel, so if you have skinny tyres, stick to the highway. Take a left onto Beach Road, 16 km from Ross, and you'll pop back onto the highway 5 minutes later.

Head south on the highway to tranquil Lake Ianthe (26 km from Ross and a good spot for a break). Then roll on down the highway to Harihari (at 44 km).

Heading south, the scenery just gets better. About 75 km from Ross is a small town called Whataroa, which makes a good stopping place for the first night.

Stage 2: Whataroa to Fox Township
53 km, 4–5 hours

Continue south, past Lake Wahapo, to the turn-off to Okarito. Okarito is a popular 10-km side trip because its lagoon offers fantastic kayaking, as well as dramatic beach and walking tracks. The one downside is that accommodation is limited in this backwater, so book ahead.

Lake Wanaka: the destination.

Assuming you aren't going to Okarito, continue south on Highway 6, past Lake Mapourika to Franz Josef township (30 km from Whataroa). This vibrant tourist town has all the services you need, and of course you can visit the glacier.

You can take the back route in to Franz Josef by turning left opposite Franz Josef School onto the Gibb Trail for 1 km, then right at Cron Street.

Franz or Fox Glacier? Which is the better one to choose? Well, if you plan to take a guided walk, then Franz Josef is the glacier to visit. But if you plan to cycle to just one glacier, then head for Fox (see page 214).

From Franz Josef township, the 23-km journey south to Fox crosses three tough hills. Fox township is a little smaller than Franz, and a bit less touristy. The DOC visitor centre in Franz is worth checking out.

Stage 3: Fox Township to Pine Grove
35 km, 2–3 hours

Accommodation between Fox and Haast is sparse, but Pine Grove, in the middle of nowhere, is one option. It's basic, the people are helpful, and the price is right.

The first 26 km from Fox is mostly downhill and leads to a small shelter and toilets at the start of the Copland Track.

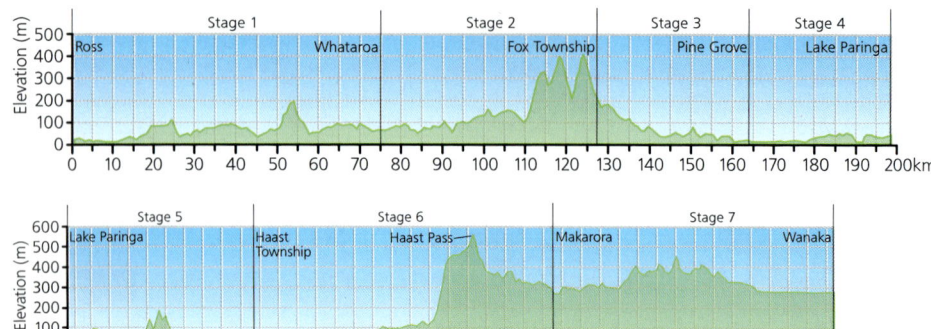

Stage 4: Pine Grove to Lake Paringa
34 km, 2–3 hours

From Pine Grove, the highway passes through impressive stands of forest, with trees that tower up to 50 metres. Cross glacial-fed rivers and, after 34 km, you'll reach Lake Paringa Recreation Area. This is an attractive spot and well worth taking time to explore. You can hire kayaks at the lake.

Stage 5: Lake Paringa to Haast Township
51 km, 3–5 hours (including a walk at Ship Creek)

From Lake Paringa, head south through more stunning forest, past Lake Moeraki (16 km) and on to a recreation area at Ship Creek, with toilets and a shelter. This is 37 km from Lake Paringa and has pleasant short walks; one along the beach, another into a swamp forest.

One of our best DOC visitor centres lies 10 km on from Ship Creek: you could spend a great afternoon there learning about the land you're riding through.

Haast township, 3 km further along the highway, has a general store, takeaways and good accommodation options.

Stage 6: Haast to Makarora
80 km, 5–8 hours

From Haast township, the highway follows the broad Haast River for 45 km to Pleasant Flat Recreational Area, a convenient spot for a rest. From there, you will cross the Haast River and start climbing seriously. The pass is 564 metres high, and the 2 km beyond the Gates of Haast Bridge are very steep. The road passes waterfalls, straddles a canyon and is an exhilarating to ride. The pass itself, 59 km from Haast township, lies nestled in the forest of Mt Aspiring National Park. Well done – you have crossed the Southern Alps and are now entering Otago.

From the top, freewheel for ages! Almost 20 km from the pass lies Makarora Tourist Centre, a great spot to stop for the night.

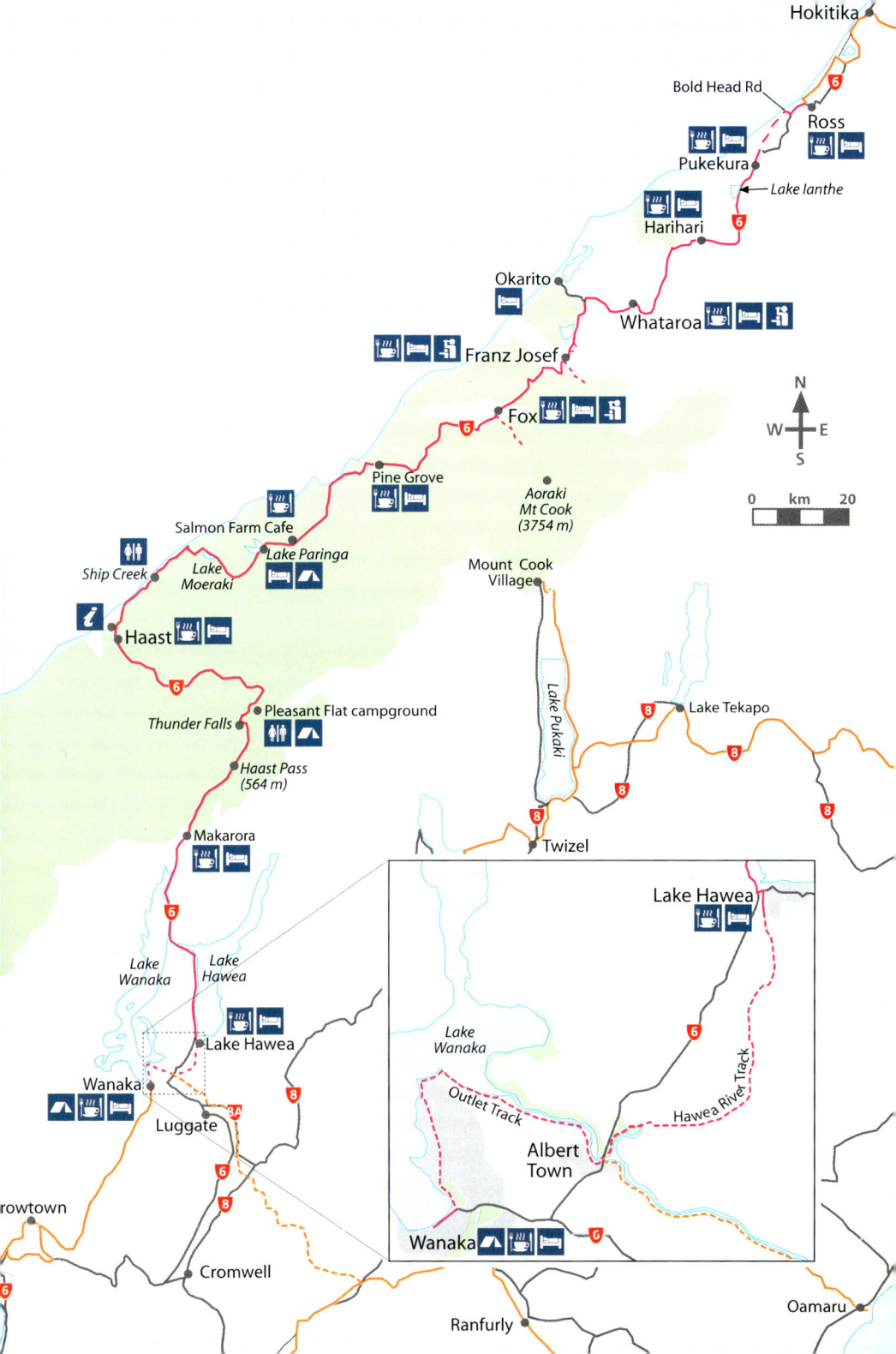

Stage 7: Makarora to Wanaka
74 km, 4–6 hours

From Makarora, the road soon meets the northern tip of Lake Wanaka, follows the lake, then nips over a hill to Lake Hawea. After 48 km, you can turn left to ride into Lake Hawea township, where you'll find all the services your stomach desires.

Now, from Lake Hawea township you can continue following Highway 6 to Wanaka, but there is a more enjoyable alternative, if you have fat tyres. An easy gravel path leads from Lake Hawea to Wanaka. From Lake Hawea, ride 1 km south on Domain Road to Cemetery Road. On your right, take the signposted Hawea River Track. The track ends at the highway, just north of a narrow bridge across the Clutha River. Cross the road carefully and take a pedestrian path over the bridge. Then head right, on a gravel path (the Outlet Track) beside the river, which leads around the lake to Wanaka. Near the town, if the path is too busy, you can hop off to follow the quiet Lakeside Road instead.

Wanaka is a lake-side tourist town, full of shops, cafes and accommodation options. It is well worth spending a few days here as you recover from your West Coast adventure.

FACT FILE

Overview Although not a lot of the trip is on the coastline, you pass many attractive lakes, and there are opportunities for short walks/rides out to the Tasman Sea.

We recommend doing this trip as a 'credit-card tour'. Just pack a few spare clothes and your credit card. Riding light means riding fast, and you can cover this amazing route in just a few fantastic days of pedalling.

Haast Pass itself is enveloped in dense forest and provides no views. It is often raining on one side of the pass and fine on the other – pick your timing with care.

This trip is a regular offering on the cycle tour operators circuit.

How to get there The best way to get to Ross is to ride the West Coast Wilderness Trail. If travelling from Christchurch, catch the TranzAlpine train (or bus) to Arthur's Pass township, then after a 4-km, 80-m climb to the pass summit (920 m), cross the Main Divide and descend to Kumara. That is an incredible 1-day ride in itself. From Kumara, follow the West Coast Wilderness Trail south.

Riding surface Mostly sealed highway. There is an option to do 24 km off road on the last day.

History The first person to cycle down the West Coast and over Haast Pass was explorer A P Harper in 1900. He had to carry his bike for a few days. The road was completed in 1965.

Special considerations This is a popular route for tourist campervans. Traffic volumes peak in January and February. It is quieter in March and April. Go well prepared for torrential rain – the coast is known for deluges any time of year.

Special features This trip is all about the natural beauty of forests, glaciers, mountains and sea.

Maps Kiwimap *South Westland Rural Road Map*

SUPPORT SERVICES

Ross Groceries, cafe and accommodation. Ross Motels: ☎ 03 755 4153, www.rossmotels.co.nz; The Empire Hotel (with camping facilities): ☎ 03 755 4005; Ross Beach Top 10 Holiday Park: ☎ 03 429 8277, www.rossbeachtop10.co.nz

Pukekura Food and accommodation: ☎ 03 755 4144, www.pukekura.co.nz

Harihari General store, food, accommodation: Hotel Hari Hari: ☎ 03 753 3026 or 0800 833 026, www.hotelharihari.com, Flaxbush Motel: ☎ 03 753 3116, www.flaxbushmotels.co.nz

Whataroa Dairy, pub, accommodation: Whataroa Hotel: ☎ 03 753 4076. Guided tours to see the rare kotuku (white heron): ☎ 0800 523 456, www.whiteherontours.co.nz

Okarito Accommodation: www.okarito.net. Okarito Beach House ☎ 03 753 4080, okaritobeachhouse.com. Kayak hire: www.okarito.co.nz

Franz Josef and Fox Glacier Food, petrol, shops, accommodation, scenic flights and guided walks: www.glaciercountry.co.nz

Highway 6 north of Jacobs River Pine Grove Motel: budget accommodation, ☎ 03 751 0898, www.pinegrovemotel.co.nz

Salmon Farm Cafe (8 km north of Paringa): ☎ 03 751 0837

Lake Paringa Accommodation: Lake Paringa Lodge: ☎ 03 751 0894, www.lakeparingalodge.co.nz, Lake Paringa Campsite (no booking required): www.doc.govt.nz

Haast Village General store, petrol, cafes, restaurants and accommodation: www.haastnz.com

Makarora Accommodation, food, Makarora Tourist Centre, www.makarora.co.nz, Makarora Mountain View Accommodation, ☎ 0800 800 443 or 03 443 1532, www.makarora.co.nz

Lake Hawea Food, accommodation: Lake Hawea Holiday Park ☎ 03 443 1767, www.haweaholidaypark.co.nz

Wanaka Food, accommodation and bike shops: www.lakewanaka.co.nz

> **CONNECTOR RIDE**

THE GLACIER TRACKS

Fox and Franz Josef glaciers
Distance 10 km return each   Time 1 hour each way   Grade 2 (Easy)

The massive Fox and Franz Josef glaciers originate from the highest flanks of the Southern Alps and flow down to rain forest, almost at sea level. They are the most awe-inspiring attractions in New Zealand.

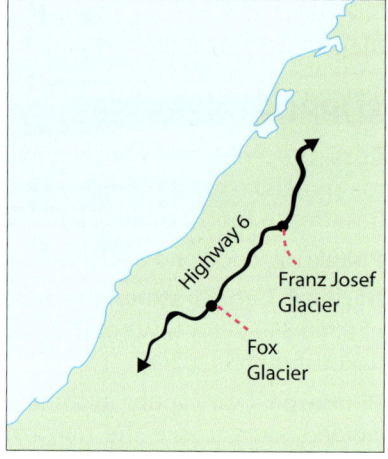

There are bike tracks leading from both Franz Josef and Fox townships to the glaciers. The better of the two trails is the Fox as it takes you closer to the glacier.

From just beyond the south end of Fox township, on the main road, turn left and follow a gravel path into the lush native forest. The last kilometre to the car park is along the glacier road. You will have to leave your bike at the car park as the glacier is now 1.6 km away via a walking-only track. Take a lock with you.

After checking out the glacier, head back the same way. It's a lot of fun.

Note To fully appreciate the enormity of the glaciers, take a walk up to them. The Glacier Tracks were built in 2011 and have since won awards for their design and construction.

CONNECTOR RIDE

CROWN RANGE
Wanaka to Arrowtown
Distance 51 km   Time 1 day   Grade 5 (Expert because of traffic)

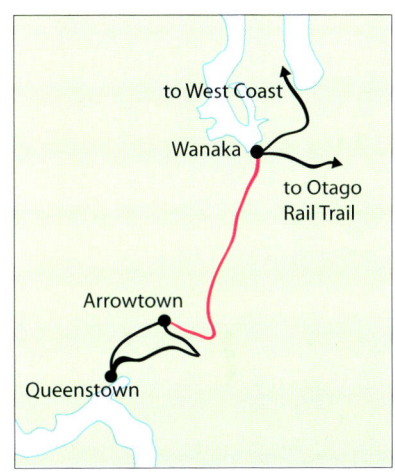

The road over the Crown Range is a significant challenge for cyclists, but it also opens the door to a stunning landscape and is an excellent route through to Queenstown. From the Wanaka end, the road makes a very long but gentle climb up the Cardrona Valley.

From downtown Wanaka, head southwest along Ardmore Street for 600 metres and turn left up McDougall Street. This becomes Cardrona Valley Road and climbs steadily to the iconic Cardrona Hotel (25 km from Wanaka).

From Cardrona, the scenery just gets better and better, and after another 15 km, you'll reach the car parking area at the top of the Crown Range Road, where there are breathtaking views across to Queenstown and The Remarkables. You have now gained 800 m elevation over a distance of 39 km.

Five kilometres down the hill, turn right into Glencoe Road (gravel) and, 3 km later, veer left down Tobins Track (dirt 4WD track). At the bottom, you'll cross a footbridge and ride up onto a sealed road, which is at the back of Arrowtown (where you'll find food and accommodation). This is a great short cut to Arrowtown, where you can hook into the Queenstown Trails and ride off road to Queenstown.

Notes This road has become significantly busier over the last 10 years, although large trucks are still not allowed to use it.

The historic Cardrona Hotel is still open for business, ☎ 03 443 8153 or www.cardronahotel.co.nz

Arrowtown has plenty of food and accommodation available.

CONNECTOR RIDE

WANAKA TO OTAGO CENTRAL RAIL TRAIL
Wanaka to Omakau via Thomsons Saddle
Distance 82 km   Time 1–2 days   Grade 5 (Expert)

This adventurous link uses a combination of the Upper Clutha River Track, some sealed road riding and a gravel road over the Dunstan Mountains to form a cunning connection with the Otago Central Rail Trail.

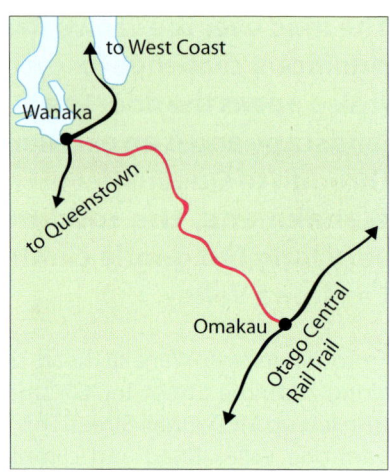

From Wanaka, head 5 km northeast to Albert Town. There is a cycle path beside the main road as far as Puzzle World, then cross the highway and take a gravel path around Mt Iron to Old Racecourse Road. Turn left and take the path beside Aubury Road and down Gunn Road to a DOC car park next to the Outlet Track.

Turn left and take the Outlet Track to Albert Town bridge. Go straight under the bridge, down a short dead end road and you will find sign posts for the Upper Clutha Track. Follow them to a car parking area.

At the car parking area, check out the signs, and then ride up to a large foot bridge. On the other side, turn left and climb up the gravel track. It is easy to follow for 14.5 km to Shortcut Road (Highway 8A).

Turn left and ride down to and across the Clutha River bridge, then take the next right along the Luggate-Tarras Road towards Tarras. After another 20 km, veer right down Maori Point Road, to Highway 8. Then head right down the highway for a few hundred metres, and just after crossing a bridge, turn left onto Ardgour Road. This sealed road leads to Thomson Gorge Road, which is gravel and climbs over Thomsons Saddle (980 m), through Thomsons Gorge and on to Highway 85 at Omakau. Like most of Central Otago, this trip offers expansive views but is exposed to the elements.

From Omakau, you can follow the Otago Central Rail Trail south to Alexandra (28 km away), or head north to Lauder and on to Ranfurly.

The Upper Clutha River Track, between Albert Town and Luggate.

HEARTLAND RIDE

Hurunui Heartland Ride
Kaikoura to Christchurch
Distance 239–259 km   Time 2–4 days   Grade 3 (Intermediate)

This classic cycle touring route, has a few special twists and turns recommended by locals and tested by us. From the coastal resort of Kaikoura to the farming centre of Amberley, this ride follows scenic back-country roads.

South of Amberley, the trail was under construction. It should be mostly off-road to Christchurch by 2020.

This new Heartland Ride skirts the base of the Kaikoura mountains, then heads to the open plains of the Hurunui district, hopping from one small town to the next on seldom-used roads. It's not as direct as Highway 1 but a lot safer, more enjoyable and interesting. This is rural New Zealand at its best.

This ride passes through the region hardest hit by the November 2016, magnitude 7.8 earthquake. The effects of the earthquake can still be seen in several rerouted sections of road and a scattering of older buildings abandoned as a result of shake damage.

The last 60 km into Christchurch wasn't finished at the time of writing but is the focus of millions of dollars of urban cycleway construction and will be very cool when completed.

ITINERARY

Stage 1: Kaikoura to Mt Lyford village
60 km, 4–7 hours

From the Kaikoura shops, head west out of town on Ludstone Road for 2.6 km before turning right down Red Swamp Road. After another 2 km, turn left down Kowhai Ford Road. Unsurprisingly, this leads to a ford across Kowhai River (6 km from town). The ford changes all the time, and after heavy rain, it is not crossable. On the far side, continue down the road for another 1 km, then turn right at the Inland Kaikoura Road. This is the scenic route to Hanmer Springs.

Follow the Inland Kaikoura Road up several hills. The biggest climb is 200 m elevation, about 27 km from Kaikoura. And the highest point of the day is the last climb over the Whales Back (518 m), just before a final descent to Mt Lyford.

Mount Lyford Lodge is right beside the road and has good food and accommodation. The village, which lies a few kilometres up Mount Lyford Forest Drive, is one of those sleepy holiday-home settlements with no shops but options to rent a night's accommodation and have a meal catered with advanced bookings.

Stage 2: Mt Lyford to Culverden
50 km, 2–4 hours
This stage is either downhill or flat. From Mt Lyford, continue following the Inland Kaikoura Road to Waiau, a small village with a hotel, campground, general store and park. After leaving town, you'll soon cross the Waiau River, then turn left onto Inverachs Road. From the end, follow Mount Palm Road, Constitution Road, Isolated Hill Road and finally turn right at St Leonards Road to reach Culverden.

As you approach Culverden, turn left down Montrose Ave and right at St Leonards Street for the quietest route to the shops.

Meeting the alpaca on the Inland Kaikoura Road.

Stage 3: Culverden to Amberley
92 km, 5–9 hours
From the centre of Culverden, ride west on School Road, turning right after 1 km to stay on School Road, which becomes Top Pahau Ford Road. This takes you away from the highway, and after 13 km, you should turn left at Balmoral Station Road.

After 24 km, just before rejoining Highway 7, you'll pass Balmoral Recreation Reserve on your right, which is a huge camping area beside the Hurunui River. At the highway, turn right and ride across the 350-metre-long Hurunui Bridge (wait for a gap in traffic as this is a narrow bridge). Hurunui village is 1 km past the bridge. It has toilets and a camping area, and after earthquake strengthening, there may once again be food available here.

From Hurunui, ride down the highway for another kilometre before turning right onto Medbury Road to take the back route to Amberley.

Follow Medbury Road to the end, then turn left onto Horsley Down Road. From there, you can either take the sealed road route via Hawarden (which has public toilets, a picnic area and a general store) and Pyramid Valley or you can take Christians Road (gravel) through Masons Flat, and then Dalmeny Road. It's 4 km shorter. Your choice. Either way, you're aiming for Broxton Road, followed by Macdonald Downs Road then Ram Paddock Road. Expect several honest hill climbs!

Ram Paddock Road leads most of the way to Amberley. Turn right at Mount Brown Road (83 km from Culverden), then veer left at Douglas Road, which leads right into town.

Stage 4: Amberley to Kaiapoi
37 km, 2–3 hours

There are several new sections of off-road trail yet to be built between Amberley and Christchurch. We will describe the route as best we can for now.

A volunteer group is building a shared path from Amberley down to Grays Road (1.3 km from town). Until the path has been built you'll have to ride south on Highway 1, for 1.5 km, to Grays Road. Follow Grays Road west for 1 km and turn left down Stockdills Road. When you are 4.9 km from town, turn right (there are little cycle trail signs to help you) and go to Kowai Stream. Walk down the stream for 200 metres (it is usually dry), then exit south onto Terrace Road (there will be an alternative flood route signposted in 2018).

Turn right at Leithfield Road and follow it west. Cross first the railway line, then the Inland Scenic Highway to continue straight onto Western Terrace Road (where the seal soon ends). At Marshmans Road, turn left and follow it all the way down to Fawcetts Road (near Ashley). Turn right, and look for a cycle path beside the road, which runs 3 km to the town of Rangiora, 26 km from Amberley.

From Rangiora, a cycle path has just been built beside Lineside Road (Highway 71) to Kaiapoi (37 km from Amberley). In 2018, we recommend taking a shuttle from Kaiapoi to Christchurch.

Stage 5 (under construction): Kaiapoi to Christchurch
20 km, 1 hour

If you want to ride from Kaiapoi, you can follow back streets and stopbank tracks to the Waimakariri River Bridge. This is a very busy, narrow bridge. The New Zealand Transport Agency has plans to add a cycle path to it in 2020, but until then, it's not safe. There are also plans to build a cycle path from the bridge to connect with the Railway Cycleway, which leads to Hagley Park near the centre of Christchurch.

Now what have I forgotten?

FACT FILE

Overview Since the 2016 earthquake that shook this region, local cyclists and businesses have joined forces to develop this new Heartland Ride. The long-term plan is to extend it all the way north to Picton.

How to get there Catch one of the Intercity buses from Picton to Kaikoura if heading south. From Rangiora or Kaiapoi, you can catch a commuter bus, which can take up to two bikes into Christchurch, see www.metroinfo.co.nz

Riding surface 85% sealed road, 15% gravel road

Special considerations If you want to find out how the cycleways between Rangiora and Christchurch are progressing, just ask on the Kennett Brothers Facebook page or check out the Hurunui Trails website.

Website www.hurunuitrails.org.nz

Maps Kiwimap Rural Road Maps, *Marlborough-Kaikoura* and *Canterbury*

SUPPORT SERVICES

Kaikoura Large town with food and accommodation. Famous for swimming with seals and whale watching: www.kaikoura.co.nz

Mt Lyford Small holiday settlement. Mount Lyford Lodge beside the main road provides basic accommodation and food. There is also lovely accommodation beside a small lake 2 km up the road, and food can be provided there (book in advance through Mt Lyford Holiday Homes, www.lyfordholidayhomes.co.nz, phone 03 315 6523). Check out the alpaca shop a few kilometres south of the lodge on the Inland Kaikoura Road.

Waiau Small scenic town, with a park at its centre and a holiday park, hotel, general store and cafe: www.visithurunui.co.nz/the-region/waiau-rotherham

Rotherham (6-km diversion) Small town with food and accommodation: www.visithurunui.co.nz/the-region/waiau-rotherham

Culverden Large town with toilets, food and accommodation (we recommend the Red Post Café): www.visithurunui.co.nz/the-region/culverden-hurunui/

Balmoral Reserve Huge camping site with basic facilities. No shops.

Hurunui village Small settlement with camping ground. The café and hotel closed after the 2016 earthquake but may reopen in the near future.

Hawarden: Small town. Public toilets at the park and a Four-Square store. The pub has closed down. There is accommodation at Bently Country Stay a few kilometres north of town.

Waikari (4.5-km diversion): Small town with food, accommodation and campground: www.visithurunui.co.nz/the-region/hawarden-waikari/

Ram Paddock Road Luxury accommodation at Claremont Country Estate and Karetu Downs Homestay: www.karetudowns.co.nz

Amberley Large town with food (including a supermarket) and accommodation: www.visithurunui.co.nz/the-region/amberley-leithfield/

Rangiora Large town with food and accommodation: www.visitwaimakariri.co.nz

Kaiapoi Large town with food and accommodation: www.visitwaimakariri.co.nz

Christchurch: Major city with everything!

HEARTLAND RIDE

Little River Rail Trail
Christchurch to Little River
Distance 60 km   Time 4–8 hours   Grade 2 (Easy)

Built in the 1870s, and largely disused by the 1960s, this abandoned rail trail has been transformed into the most popular cycling route in Canterbury, attracting over 45,000 riders a year.

The history of the railway line has been brought to life with fascinating interpretation panels along the trail, and Little River, tucked into the base of Banks Peninsula, complements the ride with its exquisite cafe, art gallery and gift shop in the old station.

The ride is completely flat and easy, although there are a few on-road sections that require traffic sense. The most scenic section is the last 24 kilometres from Motukarara to Little River via lakes Ellesmere and Forsyth.

Bird spotters are also in for a treat. Lake Ellesmere has the most diverse bird population anywhere in New Zealand. Up to 150 different species can be seen from the trail. Don't forget sun block, binoculars and your favourite ornithology field guide!

ITINERARY

Stage 1: Christchurch to Motukarara
36 km, 2–4 hours

From Cathedral Square, in the heart of Christchurch, ride down to the end of Worcester Boulevard and around the south side of Hagley Park. Cross Moorehouse Avenue into Grove Road. The trail now leads through suburban streets to Brougham Street. Cross at the lights and head west following the cycle path. It will take you to a motorway underpass, after which you keep heading west to Springs Road.

Head down Springs Road for 900 metres, then turn right down Marshes Road for 400 metres before turning left onto a cycle path that leads to Prebbleton, a picturesque village with shops, toilets and a water fountain.

The trail jumps on and off the road as it passes through Prebbleton and is then back onto a cycle path beside Birchs Road to Lincoln. Cycle lanes lead down East Belt and Edward Street, just missing the shops (and toilets) and taking you out of town to a new subdivision. A cycle path leads down Liffey Springs Drive to

The trail skirts Lake Ellesmere, an internationally significant wildlife area.

Moirs Lane. From there, the cycle trail cuts across country for 10 minutes to link up with Collins Road East for 100 metres. It then turns right onto River Road for a few kilometres. At one point, turn left to stay on River Road.

When River Road turns right and leaves the river, you should go straight ahead on a path beside the river. Follow the river, cross a wooden bridge and then follow Park Road. Pass Waihora Park, which has casual camping and a DOC nursery, to reach Motukarara Railway Station (picnic area with toilets).

There is a great cafe (Blue Duck Cafe) 900 metres off the rail trail, but you have to ride down Highway 75 to reach it (see map on page 227).

Stage 2: Motukarara to Little River
24 km, 2–4 hours
From Motukarara Railway Station, the trail is completely off road and skirts lakes Ellesmere and Forsyth. Parts of the trail pass through farms with gates and cattle stops. The birdlife is amazing; we saw thousands, including the rare kotuku (white heron) and spoonbills within 100 metres of the trail!

The trail ends just past the head of Lake Forsyth at Wairewa Pa Road. Head left down the road for 50 metres, then right up Highway 75 for 300 metres to reach Little River; it's a welcome destination with cafes and art galleries.

FACT FILE

How to get there Christchruch is 5 hours drive from Picton or you can cycle the Hurunui Heartland Ride from Kaikoura.

From Little River, catch the Akaroa Shuttle back to Christchurch. It leaves several times a day and costs $37 per person, including bikes, ☎ 0800 500 929.

Riding surface 50% gravel, 50% sealed – mostly dedicated cycle paths but also some cycle lanes and a few road sections

History Trains ran to Little River from the 1880s to the 1960s. In 1899 a local newspaper reported 'Cyclists, both men and women, boast of having beaten the train from Station to Station… '. In 1999, plans were formulated to turn the route into a rail trail as a millenium project.

Special features Restored railway stations, birdlife and great cafes.

Important contacts You can buy a small guidebook about the trail from the Little River info centre. Written by noted author Fiona Farrell, the book focuses on natural and cultural heritage. There is also a free pamphlet with a map available.

Trail website Check out www.littleriverrailtrail.co.nz for maps and updates.

SUPPORT SERVICES

Christchurch Natural High for bike hire, transport and tours: ☎ 0800 444 144, www.naturalhigh.co.nz. City Cycle Hire for bike hire and transport: ☎ 0800 343 848, www.cyclehire-tours.co.nz

Prebbleton A cafe and dairy right beside the trail.

Lincoln Plenty of places to buy food a few hundred metres off the trail.

Motukarara The Blue Duck Cafe, 900 metres from Motukarara Station: ☎ 03 329 7800, camping available at Waihora Park, 500 km before Motukarakara Station ($10 per night) ☎ 03 329 7818

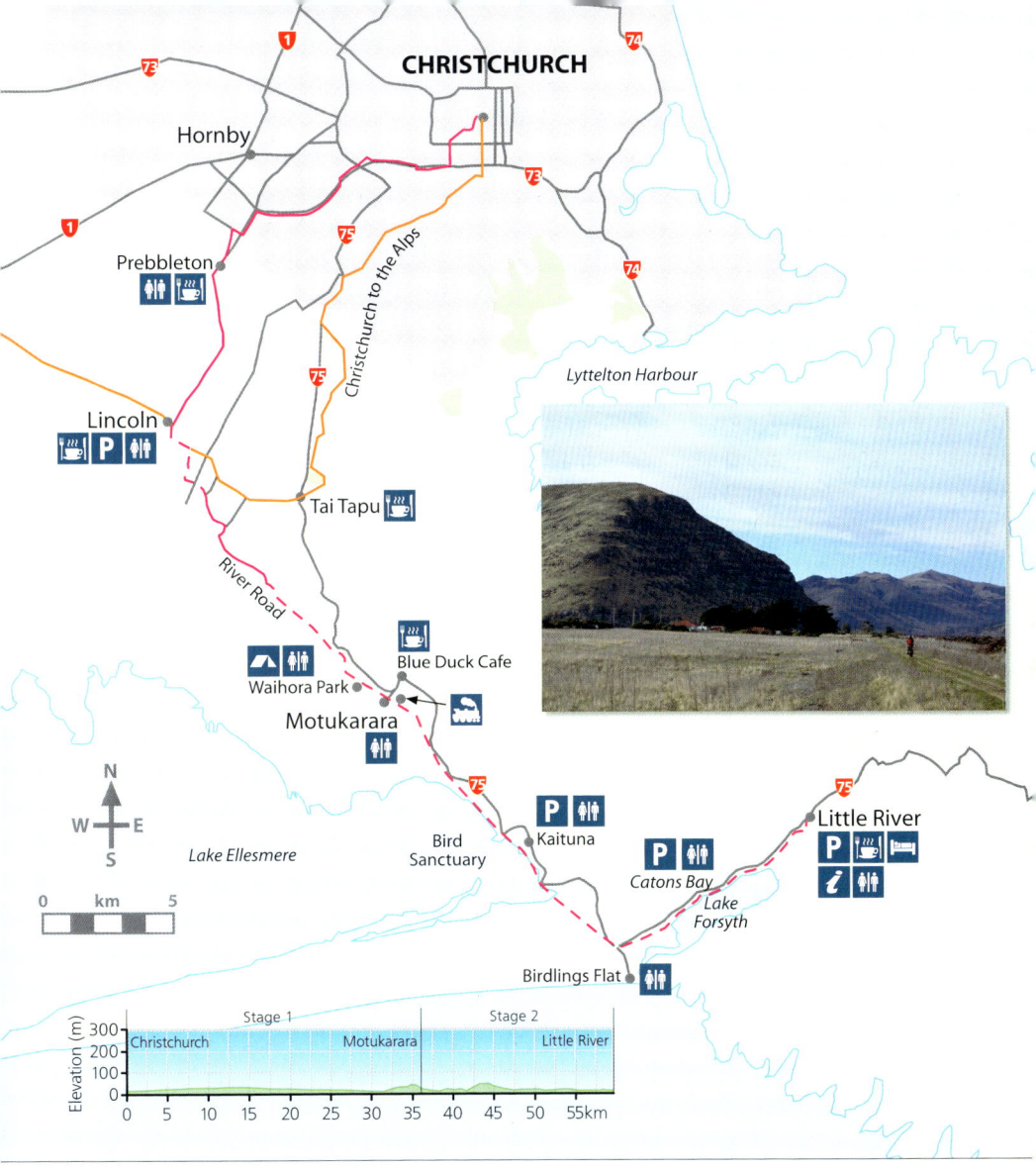

Little River Cafes, general store and accommodation: www.littleriver.org.nz for general information; Little River Hotel ☎ 03 325 1007, www.littleriverhotel.co.nz; Silo Stay Accommodation, ☎ 03 325 1977, www.silostay.kiwi.nz

HEARTLAND RIDE

Christchurch to the Alps
Canterbury Plains and the Southern Alps foothills
Distance 308 km   Time 4–5 days   Grade 5 Expert (bad traffic)

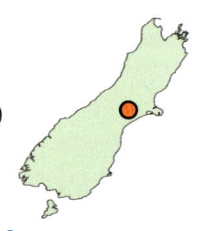

Great weather and relatively flat terrain make the quiet roads of Canterbury simply perfect for cycling. There are also lovely small towns and friendly locals to make cyclists feel welcome.

From Christchurch, the cycling city, this tour starts by following a well-beaten cycling route out to a popular cyclists' cafe before cutting across the vast Canterbury Plains to the Rakaia Gorge. From there, the route hugs the foothills of the Southern Alps, crossing several glacially fed rivers and hopping from one small town to another before crossing the foothills via Burkes Pass, just over 700 m above sea level.

From the pass, the whole landscape suddenly changes. You will cross the famous Mackenzie Basin, a barren land of low tussocks with expansive views of the mountains that grow larger by the hour as you cruise to the emerald Lake Tekapo where you meet the start of the Alps 2 Ocean Great Ride.

ITINERARY

Stage 1: Christchurch to Tai Tapu
20 km, 1–2 hours

From the Port Hills end of Colombo Street, swing right and follow Cashmere Road around the base of the hills. After 4 km, turn left to stay on Cashmere Road (don't go onto Hendersons Road). A little later, turn right to stay on Cashmere Road (just follow the road signs).

Cashmere Road ends at a T-intersection, where you turn right onto Kennedys Bush Road, and then a minute later, left onto Glovers Road.

Glovers Road soon leads to Halswell Road, where you turn left and put up with lots of traffic for 2 km before turning left again onto Old Tai Tapu Road, a quiet country road ending at a great cafe in Tai Tapu settlement.

Alternative If you prefer off-road cycle paths, then follow the Little RIver Rail Trail from Hagley Park to Lincoln (page 224).

Stage 2: Tai Tapu to Hororata
54 km, 3–4 hours

Ride 7 km to Lincoln, but use the Little River Rail Trail to avoid the very centre of

Easy pedalling across the plains with NZ Cycle Tours.

town and take the 9-km cycle path beside Boundary Road and Lincoln Rolleston Road to get to Rolleston, which is 17 km from Tai Tapu and has shops.

From Rolleston, cross Highway 1 via Rolleston Drive and turn left at Hoskyns Road and left again at Jones Road to take Wards Road to Charing Cross, an eight-road intersection on the Canterbury Plains. Take Bealey Road from there to Hororata, which has various bed and breakfast options close by.

Stage 3: Hororata to Mount Somers
61 km, 4–6 hours

The next day, continue along Bealey Road to the intersection with Cordys Road, turn left and then a little later left again onto Milnes Road, then right onto Leaches Road. Follow this all the way through to Rakaia Gorge Road (Highway 77) and on to the gorge, 28 km away. This is a popular picnic and camping area (there are well-signposted spots on both sides of the bridge).

After crossing the bridge, there is a steep climb up to a turn-off on the left to Mount Hutt Station Road. Methven is 14 km away down this road and has lots of services, but if you don't need to go there, just continue straight ahead on the Arundel Rakaia Gorge Road (Highway 77). Just over 60 km from Hororata, turn

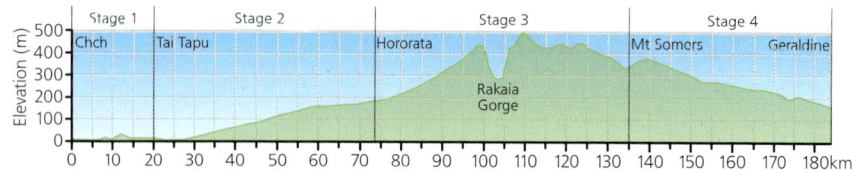

right down Pattons Road. The centre of Mount Somers is 1 km away.

Stage 4: Mount Somers to Geraldine
49 km, 3–5 hours

From Mount Somers, head south out of town on Hoods Road and turn right at the Arundel Rakaia Gorge Road (aka Scenic Highway) 1 km away. Now follow the highway for almost 4 km before turning right down Peters Road (which becomes Anama Settlement Road) and follow this to a five-way intersection. Veer left and take Mayfield Klondyke Road to Mayfield (14 km from Mount Somers). Mayfield has a few shops, including a cafe.

From there, stay on the main road south for 20 km. Just after crossing the Rangitata River bridge, turn left and go to the Arundel Bridge Reserve.

After a rest, head up Bridge Street, left at North Boundary Road and left again at Peel Forest Road. This leads via lovely country lanes back to the main highway, which you then follow to Geraldine. It is gently downhill the whole way, and Geraldine is a lovely large town.

Stage 5: Geraldine to Fairlie, via the Seven Sisters
80 km (or 46 km via Highway 79), 1 day

There are a couple of options for this stage. The bold and fearless will ride the most direct route, along Highway 79 to Fairlie. But due to high traffic volumes and sections of road that are too narrow to be safe, experienced cycle tour operators are taking a longer more enjoyable route, which we describe below.

Head out of Geraldine on Highway 79 for 4 km then turn left down Earl Road, right at Goodwin Road and left onto Seven Sisters Road. At the end of this road, turn right onto Waitohi Temuka Road, and then left down Waitohi Pleasant Point Road, which leads to the town of Pleasant Point, 26 km from Geraldine.

From Pleasant Point, follow Highway 8 west to Cave (50 km from Geraldine), which has a picnic area, and then a further 30 km on to the lovely small town of Fairlie.

Stage 6: Fairlie to Lake Tekapo
44 km, 3–5 hours

Continue following Highway 8, over Burkes Pass and down to the brilliant holiday town of Lake Tekapo. There are plenty of places to stay here, and we recommend

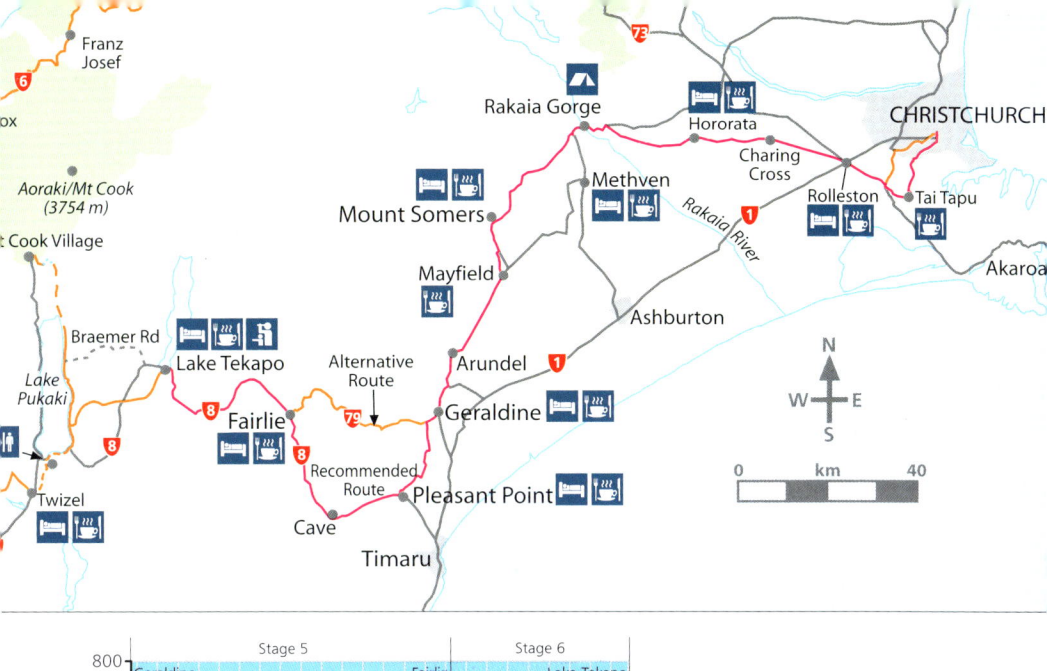

checking out the hot pools 1.5 km from town. Head down Lakeside Drive, past the Holiday Park to Tekapo Springs. A walk up to Mt John Observatory is also good value. Most people like to visit the Church of the Good Shepherd on the lake front.

From Lake Tekapo, people can follow the Alps 2 Ocean Cycle Trail along Canal roads to Lake Pukaki and beyond (see page 234).

FACT FILE

Overview As part of a stand-alone week-long tour, you might consider doing this from the Southern Alps to Christchurch as you would have more downhill.

How to get there Bus, fly or drive to Christchurch.

Riding surface 100% sealed road

History The first bridge across the Rakaia River was built in 1882.

Special considerations In winter, the roads from Christchurch to Methven are busy with ski traffic. And in the height of summer, they are busy with general tourist traffic.

Answering the call of the open road.

Special features This ride leads across the largest plains in New Zealand to the largest mountains in New Zealand.

Maps Kiwimap *Canterbury Rural Road Map*

SUPPORT SERVICES

Christchurch Lots of shops and accommodation, and several bike shops: www.christchurchnz.com

Natural High (bike hire and tours): ☎ 0800 444 144, www.naturalhigh.co.nz

Rolleston Supermarket, cafes, restaurants

Hororata Cafe, accommodation (see Google): Hororata Cafe and Wine Bar (they also do takeaways): 2 Hobbs Street, ☎ 03 318 7059

Mt Somers General store, accommodation, restaurant, bar: Mt Somers Tavern, Mt Somers Holiday Park: ☎ 03 303 9719, www.mountsomers.co.nz, Stronechrubie High Country Cuisine & Chalets: ☎ 03 303 9814, www.stronechrubie.co.nz

Geraldine Supermarket, restaurants, bars, cafe, takeaways, accommodation: www.geraldine.nz

Fairlie Food, shops, accommodation: www.fairlienz.com

Lake Tekapo Supermarket, general store, shops, accommodation: www.tekapotourism.co.nz

Enjoying the grand scenery and deserted roads of the Mackenzie Basin.

GREAT RIDE

Alps 2 Ocean Cycle Trail
Mount Cook village to Oamaru
Distance 282–306 km   Time 4–6 days
Grades 2–3 (Easy to Intermediate)

The Alps 2 Ocean Cycle Trail leads riders on an unforgettable journey, from the base of the Southern Alps, through a landscape steeped in fascinating natural and cultural heritage to the shores of the Pacific Ocean.

The full trail has eight stages from Aoraki/Mount Cook to Oamaru. It is mostly downhill or flat, and the prevailing nor'wester is usually a welcome tail wind.

Highlights include excellent panoramas of New Zealand's highest mountain range, riding around the edge of lakes Pukaki and Ohau and sidling across the base of the Ohau mountain ranges, all with breathtaking views. Lower down, you skirt around lakes Benmore, Aviemore and Waitaki before passing the Elephant Rocks and Vanished World limestone wonderland en route to the Pacific Ocean.

If you don't have time to do the whole trail, cherry-pick stages 2, 3 and 4 – they have the best scenery, the least traffic and lots of purpose-built cycle path.

ITINERARY

Stage 1: Tekapo or Mount Cook Village to Highway 8.
37 or 55 km, 4–8 hours, Grade 3 (Intermediate)

Tekapo start The easiest place to start this ride is Tekapo village. From the shops, follow the A2O signs south on Aorangi Crescent and Andrew Don Drive to the Tekapo Canal road, which is closed to public vehicles but open for walking and cycling. As you approach Lake Pukaki, you'll be treated to a panorama of the Southern Alps.

You will usually find lots of people fishing at the end of the canal. There is a great place for a break, 100 metres off the road, at the canal outflow.

From the canal, coast down the road to a T-intersection and turn left along Hayman Road. The turquoise Lake Pukaki will be on your right. After 6 km, and only 1 km before Highway 8, there is a signpost pointing right where the trail heads onto a cycle path.

Mount Cook start The official start used to be Mount Cook village. It's a cool place to hang out, with great short walks, a climbers' museum and five-star accommodation at the Hermitage. But you have to take a helicopter trip to

Glacier blue Lake Pukaki with a backdrop of mountains, including Aoraki/Mt Cook and Mt Tasman.

get across the Tasman River, which is expensive (at least $100 per person) and weather dependant, not to mention the carbon emissions, so most people are starting from Tekapo now.

Stage 2: Lake Pukaki to Twizel
21 km (or 26 km from alternative start), 2–3 hours, Grade 2 (Easy)

Lake Pukaki is a great place to start the A2O Cycle Trail if you don't have time to do the full ride. Either start 1 km up Hayman Road or from Tekapo B power station (5 km further up Hayman Road).

If driving Highway 8 from Lake Tekapo, get ready to turn right onto Hayman Road just after Lake Pukaki comes into view. Only 1 km up Hayman Road is a small car park at the point where Alps 2 Ocean becomes an off-road path. This purpose-built trail is fantastic! You will skirt around the bottom of the lake, and across the dam to a rest area with toilets and a cafe that specialises in salmon.

From the rest area, cross the highway and follow signs to another section of trail that crosses Pukaki Flats to Twizel. It is 21 km from the start of the single track around Lake Pukaki, to Twizel – all off road.

Stage 3: Twizel to Lake Ohau Lodge
39 km, 3–5 hours, Grade 2 (Easy)

From Twizel, ride to the right of the shopping centre and take Nuns Veil Road out to Glen Lyon Road, turn left and cruise down to the Pukaki Canal. Cross the canal and follow the road beside it to Lake Ohau. That's 20 km.

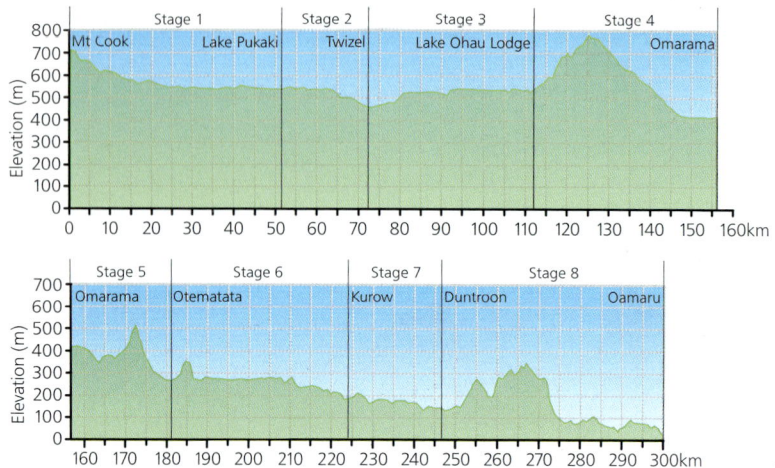

At the lake, turn left, cross the dam and then turn right onto a 4WD track that leads to a weir. About 20 metres past the weir, turn hard right to follow a new single track around the lake edge to Lake Ohau Road. This is another brilliant section.

At Lake Ohau Road, turn right and ride 9 km to Lake Ohau Lodge. You will pass a beautiful council camp ground about halfway down this road, but the lodge is even more stunning, and a darn sight more comfortable.

The hydro lakes occasionally spill over the Ohau River weir (a few weeks a year). The alternative flood route takes you south of Lake Ruataniwha. From Twizel, ride south on a path beside Highway 8. After crossing the bridge at Lake Ruataniwha, turn right and follow a gravel road around the lake and beside Ohau River to the A2O cycle path at the edge of Lake Ohau.

Stage 4: Lake Ohau Lodge to Omarama
42 km, 4–6 hours, Grade 3 (Intermediate)

From the lodge, the trail heads around the base of the Ohau Range and up a long climb, offering excellent views and fun cycling down the other side. After 18 km, you will meet Quailburn Road. Turn left and change into a big gear! The road is slightly downhill, and there is usually a tailwind. It's gravel for several kilometres and leads most of the way to Omarama.

When you reach the highway, look to your right, and you'll see the new cycle trail heading towards some willows. This fun section leads to a picnic area with toilets just before the Omarama bridge. Make sure there is no traffic on the highway before nipping across the bridge and after 100–200 metres picking up another cycle path that leads right into Omarama.

Omarama has some amazing hot pools. You'd be mad not to check them out.

Classic New Zealand Cycle Trails

Stage 5: Omarama to Otematata
24 km, 1.5–2 hours, Grade 3 (Intermediate)

From the small settlement of Omarama, the trail runs beside Highway 83 to a camping reserve at Sailors Cutting, beside Lake Benmore. From there, it was on the highway to Otematata in 2018, although there are plans to take it off-road.

Stage 6: Otematata to Kurow
44 km, 3–5 hours, Grade 3 (Intermediate)

Beyond Otematata, you will leave the highway on Loach Laird Road and skirt Lake Aviemore from Benmore Dam to Aviemore Dam. In 2018, you had to rejoin the highway and follow it towards Kurow. The last 4 km is off-road. (There are plans to take more of the trail off-road.) Riding around the lakes is peaceful and easy, apart from one short steep climb.

Stage 7: Kurow to Duntroon
23 km, 2–3 hours, Grade 3 (Intermediate)

From Kurow, the trail goes alongside the Waitaki River, through the Kurow Winery and back to the river en route to Duntroon. This welcoming village is notable for cosy accommodation and the Vanished World museum.

Stage 8: Duntroon to Oamaru
53 km, 4–6 hours, Grade 3 (Intermediate)

From Duntroon to Oamaru, the trail follows a fine selection of quiet country roads that are complemented by sections of off-road cycle path. Keep your eyes peeled and follow the A2O signs to keep on the trail.

Check out the Vanished World (pick up a pamphlet from Duntroon), and Elephant Rocks (popular for rock climbing). With huge granite rocks and fossils aplenty, you may want to take your time exploring this fascinating area.

The last 5 km run along a rail trail, through the Oamaru Gardens and past the famous Victorian Precinct. The trail finishes at the long pier at the end of Wansbeck Street, where you can relax at The Galley cafe (☎ 03 434 0475) beside the Pacific Ocean.

Oamaru is famous for its historic quarter, where a group of entertaining neo-Luddites shun most modern inventions and even choose penny farthings as their preferred mode of cycling.

FACT FILE

Overview This 300-km trail begins in the Southern Alps at Aoraki/Mt Cook National Park and descends 780 m through the Mackenzie Basin down the Waitaki Valley to Oamaru and the Pacific Ocean.

How to get there Although the main start point is Aoraki/Mount Cook village, you can obviously start wherever you wish. Most people start from Lake Tekapo.

For transport along the trail contact Cycle Journeys in Twizel, ☎ 03 377 2060, www.cyclejourneys.co.nz or Trail Adventures in Oamaru ☎ 027 937 4473, www.trailadventures.co.nz

Riding surface The first half, to Omarama, is mostly on a new gravelled cycle path. From Omarama the second half is a mix of on- and off-road (sealed and gravel).

Special considerations The helicopter can only fly in reasonably good weather.

Maps Go to the trail websites below and take Kiwimap *Otago-South Canterbury Rural Road Map.*

Trail website www.alps2ocean.com

SUPPORT SERVICES

Refer to www.alps2ocean.com for a full list of services on this trail.

Mt Cook village Cafes, restaurants, accommodation: www.mackenzienz.com

Braemar Station Accommodation: Pine Cottage or Shearers Lodge available: ☎ 03 680 6844 or 027 254 4206

Lake Pukaki Mt Cook Alpine Salmon Shop & Lake Pukaki Information Centre : ☎ 03 435 0427, www.alpinesalmon.co.nz

Twizel Supermarket, cafes, restaurants and a range of accommodation: www.twizel.info, Jake's Hardware for limited bike parts and basic repairs: 24 Market Place, ☎ 03 435 0881 or 022 525 3767

Lake Middleton Camping Ground (late Sep to early May) www.doc.govt.nz

Lake Ohau Accommodation and meals (bookings recommended): Lake Ohau Lodge: ☎ 03 438 9885, www.ohau.co.nz

Omarama General store, restaurants, cafes and a range of accommodation options: www.discoveromarama.co.nz

Otematata General store, cafe, dairy, bike hire and tours, accommodation: Otematata Holiday Park: ☎ 03 438 7826 or www.otematata.kiwi.nz; Otematata Lakes Hotel: ☎ 03 438 7899, www.bestdampub.co.nz, Pedal and Paddle Aoraki: ☎ 021 395 221, www.pedalandpaddleaoraki.co.nz

Kurow Food, petrol, a small range of accommodation and a museum: www.kurow.org.nz

Duntroon Food, camping and accommodation: Duntroon Recreational Reserve: ☎ 03 431 2850; Vanished World natural history centre and trail: www.vanishedworld.co.nz; Kowhai Cottage B&B, ☎ 027 423 9711. Duntroon Railway Accommodation, ☎ 027 418 1435

Oamaru Supermarkets, cafes, restaurants, accommodation and bike shops: www.waitakinz.com

> **CONNECTOR RIDE**

OMARAMA SADDLE
Omarama to Otago Central Rail Trail
Distance 80 km   Time 6–8 hours   Grade 5 (Expert)

This remote short cut between the Alps 2 Ocean and the Otago Central Rail Trail will appeal to fit adventurers. It follows gravel roads and 4WD tracks (with several fords) through a Department of Conservation reserve. Stopping at the historic Vulcan Hotel in St Bathans is a popular option.

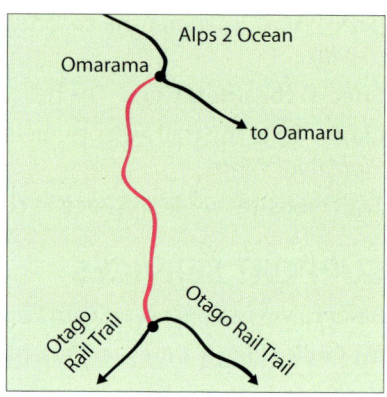

Head southwest from Omarama on Highway 8 for 1 km before turning left onto Broken Hut Road. Go past Twin Peaks and, 17 km from Omarama, veer left at the 'Access to Oteake Conservation Park' sign. Almost 2 km further on, you'll reach a parking area with a DOC sign. This is the start of a 31-km 4WD track.

Head through the gate behind the sign and follow orange marker poles along a good 4WD track on the West Manuherikia Track. After 4 km, veer left and settle into an hour-long, 8-km climb to Omarama Saddle. This is a steep grade, and you may wish to walk it.

At Omarama Saddle, the track forks. Drop straight down the other side to go to St Bathans. A fast downhill leads quickly to Top Hut (8 bunks). After 30–45 minutes of downhill, you will reach Boundary Hut (8 bunks). These identical DOC huts are open to the public.

From Boundary Hut, there are several stream crossings and, after 7 km, you will see a signposted track to your right. We thought this track looked unridable, so we carried straight ahead to a gravel road and a DOC signboard. Once there, turn right and ride 1.5 km to the Homestead campsite among the trees. St Bathans' historic Vulcan Hotel is 15 km away: take a left down the gravelly Hawkdun Runs Road followed by a right turn up Loop Road.

From St Bathans, continue down Loop Road for 6 km, then turn left to ride down Highway 85 for 2 km before turning right down Hills Creek Road. After 7 km, at the end of the road, turn right again, and you will soon find yourself at the small town of Oturehua, right beside the Otago Central Rail Trail.

Trail Map   NZTopo50 CA15 Omarama and CB15 Idaburn

Satisfaction on the top of Omarama Saddle.

GREAT RIDE

Otago Central Rail Trail
Clyde to Middlemarch
Distance 151 km   Time 3–5 days   Grade 1+ (Very Easy)

The disused railway line from Alexandra to Middlemarch has been transformed over the years and is now a world-class cycling trail. Out-there scenery, zero traffic and genuine Otago hospitality makes this one of New Zealand's most popular cycling holidays.

This is the 'flagship' of New Zealand Cycle Trails. It was officially opened in 2000 and has developed into one of the most popular cycling holidays in the country. The trail can be ridden in either direction. You are more likely to get a tail wind riding from west to east, but really the weather is generally settled in Central Otago, so it's not a big deal which way you go. Easter is the most popular riding time, when the colours of the deciduous trees are stunning.

Now that the Roxburgh Gorge and Clutha Gold trails have been built, it is very tempting to do a big anti-clockwise tour, starting with a train trip from Dunedin to Middlemarch, then pedalling the Otago Central Rail Trail to Alexandra and continuing on with the Roxburgh Gorge and Clutha Gold trails to Lawrence. However, for the sake of tradition, we will describe this trail from Clyde to Middlemarch.

ITINERARY

Stage 1: Clyde to Alexandra
8 km, 1 hour

The rail trail officially starts/ends at Clyde with an 8 km straight line section to Alexandra. A better alternative to this boring bit is the Alexandra Anniversary Track on the other side of the river (cross the bridge at Clyde and turn right to ride around and under the bridge then down the valley). It is much more scenic and fun but a grade or two harder.

Stage 2: Alexandra to Omakau
29 km, 2–4 hours

From Alexandra, the ride starts with a gentle climb up the huge Manuherikia Valley. On your right is the Raggedy Range, which the trail soon climbs over. The rustic Chatto Creek restaurant (on the left 17 km from Alexandra) is a hugely popular stopping point. Omakau has food and accommodation and is close to Ophir, which is well worth a visit and has New Zealand's oldest post office.

One of several massive viaducts along the trail.

Stage 3: Omakau to Oturehua
29 km, 2–4 hours

The middle of this section is famous for its rocky tunnels and the Poolburn Viaduct. Make sure your camera battery is charged and take your time. Closer to the end of this section is Hayes Engineering (book ahead for a fascinating tour), and at Oturehua itself is Gilchrist's Store, New Zealand's longest running store, trading since 1898. Don't miss it.

Stage 4: Oturehua to Ranfurly
25.5 km, 2–3 hours

After another 12 km of gentle climbing, you will reach the summit of the rail trail at 618 m. Check out the Red Barn info centre on the way to Ranfurly. Ranfurly has great accommodation options and some interesting small shops.

Stage 5: Ranfurly to Hyde
32 km, 2–3 hours

The section from Ranfurly to Daisybank includes a 96-metre-long steel truss bridge at Waipiata across the Taieri River, where there is a picnic and camping area. From Daisybank, at the 109-km mark, there are three bridges, a tunnel and good views of the river and trees en route to Hyde.

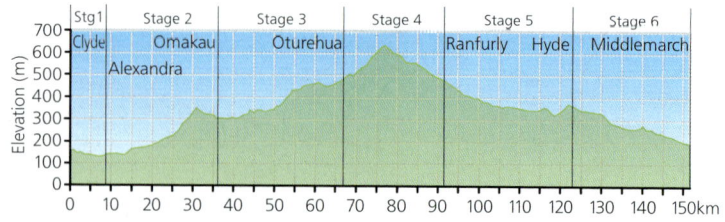

Stage 6: Hyde to Middlemarch
27.5 km, 1.5–2.5 hours

The trail has a slight downhill slope most of the way from Hyde to Middlemarch – the end of the line, so to speak. The historic Hyde Station is just a few kilometres south of Hyde.

From Middlemarch, the most fitting end to your trip is to catch the Taieri Gorge train to Dunedin (see Fact File). Most days, it leaves from Pukerangi (25 km south of Middlemarch). On Fridays and Sundays over summer it leaves Middlemarch at 1 pm. Alternatively, for very fit riders, Dunedin is 75 km away via Highway 87.

FACT FILE

How to get there Start from either Clyde or Middlemarch. From Dunedin, you can start in style by catching a historic train to Middlemarch or Pukerangi and the trail start.

Riding surface 100% gravel, some rough in places

History The railway line was completed around 1900, and the section from Clyde to Middlemarch was closed in 1990. DOC proposed turning it into a rail trail in 1993, and it was officially opened in 2000. The section of railway from Dunedin to Middlemarch is still open and makes a fantastic start/end to your trip.

Special considerations Winters and summers can be extreme in Cental Otago. Autumn is really the best time to ride.

Special features For $10 you can buy a special Rail Trail Passport and have it stamped at towns along the ride to prove you did the whole trail.

Important contacts For details about the train from Dunedin to Pukerangi (or Middlemarch), contact Dunedin Railways, ☎ 03 477 4449, www.dunedinrailways.co.nz

Maps Pick up the free Otago Central Rail Trail pamphlet, which includes a good map, from any local information centre.

Official trail website www.otagocentralrailtrail.co.nz

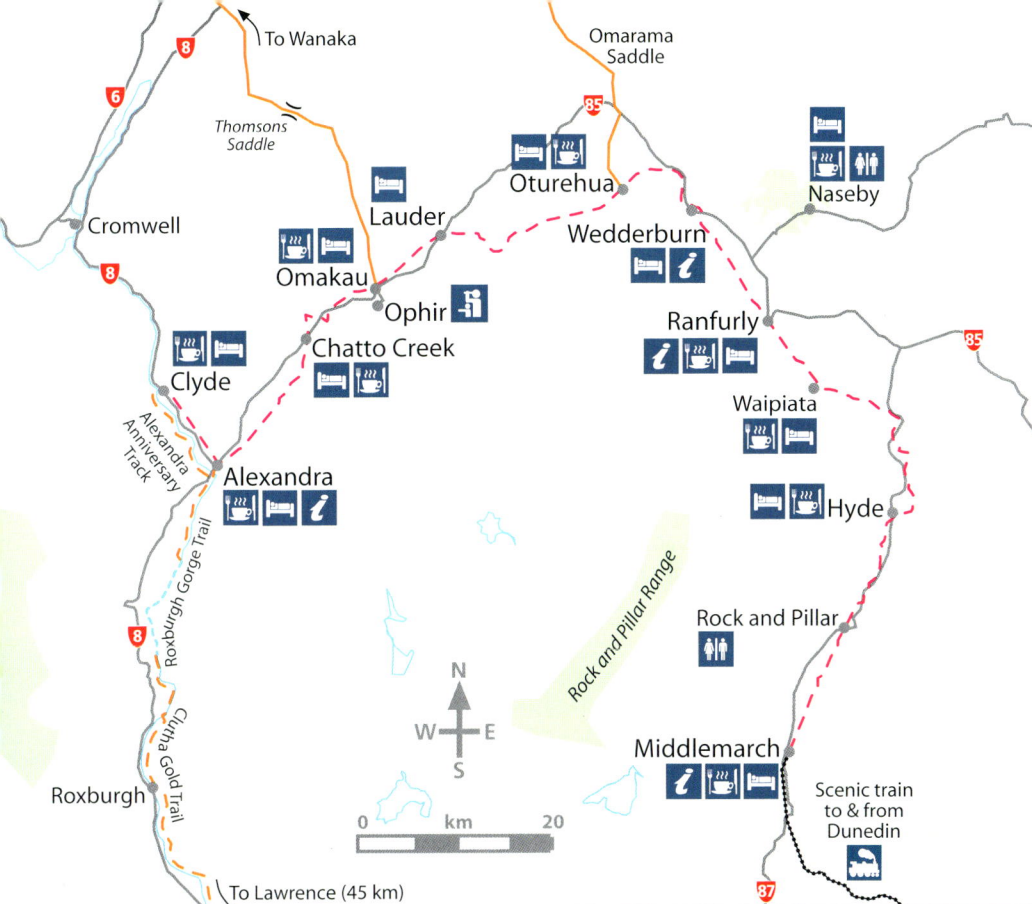

SUPPORT SERVICES

The locals along the trail have had over 10 years to develop food and accommodation services, and they have done a superb job of it, so much so that eating, drinking, shopping and socialising are what the trail is about for many riders.

The services are very well listed on the trail website, so there is no point in repeating them here.

If you want someone to organise your trip along the Rail Trail, contact Trail Journeys in Clyde. They have over 500 hire bikes and also organise accommodation, meals and transport: ☎ 0800 030 381, www.trailjourneys.co.nz

Altitude Bikes in Alexandra offers a similar service: ☎ 03 448 8917 or 021 456 918, www.altitudebikes.co.nz

Shebikeshebikes in Clyde and Omakau also offer bike hire and tours, ☎ 03 447 3271 or www.shebikeshebikes.co.nz

GREAT RIDE

Roxburgh Gorge Trail
Alexandra to Roxburgh Dam
Distance up to 34 km   Time 2–3 hours for each section
Grade 2 (Easy)

The Roxburgh Gorge is a stunning landscape of steep hillsides strewn with giant boulders leading down to a willow-lined river and lake. Over summer, this is one of the hottest places in the country, but the lake is never far away for a swim.

This trail consists of two sections connected by a boat trip, or you can do two there-and-back trips. The trail starts in Alexandra and follows the Clutha Mata-au River through the Roxburgh Gorge to the Roxburgh Dam, linking with the Clutha Gold Trail.

Use this trail to make one of the finest connectors between the Otago Central Rail Trail and the Clutha Gold Trail.

ITINERARY

Stage 1: Alexandra to jetty opposite Doctors Point
10 km one way, 1 hour each way

The trail starts from Alexandra. If you are riding from the shopping centre, then cross the road bridge heading south on Highway 8. The bridge is narrow, but it has a pedestrian path on the western side. At the far end, turn right down a gravel path that leads to the Clutha Mata-au River, then turn right again to head down river on the Roxburgh Gorge Trail.

If you are driving to the trail, also head across the bridge and take the first road on your right - Earnscleugh Road – for 350 metres before turning right again down a short steep driveway that leads to the Anniversary Track. This ends at a car park beside the river. Just follow the obvious track down river and onto the Roxburgh Gorge Trail.

Whichever start you choose, simply follow the wide smooth trail beside the river, past huge rocks and tiny Chinese rock bivvies, until you reach a jetty and a toilet, which are opposite Doctors Point.

Stage 2: Doctors Point Jetty to Shingle Creek (Boat)
12 km, 1–1.5 hours one way

A trail has not yet been built along this section because of land access issues. Instead, there is a boat service that can take you down the river. For many this

Easy riding beside the tranquil Lake Roxburgh.

is a highlight because the views from the river offers a new perspective on the scenery, with sights such as historical cottages, water races and rusting relics. Your captain should be able to fill you in on the history of the area.

Stage 3: Shingle Creek to Roxburgh Dam
12 km one way, 1–2 hours one way

There is a tin shack next to the jetty at Shingle Creek should you need to shelter from the rain. From the shack, follow the trail south, uphill to Elbow Creek. It gets quite close to the highway before turning towards Lake Roxburgh and weaving almost down to the water's edge.

In the last kilometre of the trail, there is a series of switchbacks climbing to a broad saddle. Just past the top, you'll sqeeze through a cattle stop and reach a small car park with signboards. A steep track then leads down to a major lookout over the dam. The Clutha Gold Trail starts 1 km away at the far side of the Roxburgh Dam.

FACT FILE

Overview The Roxburgh Gorge Trail leads from the Otago Central Rail Trail in Alexandra to the Clutha Gold Trail, 8 km north of Roxburgh township. You can ride across the dam to get to the start of the Clutha Gold Trail.

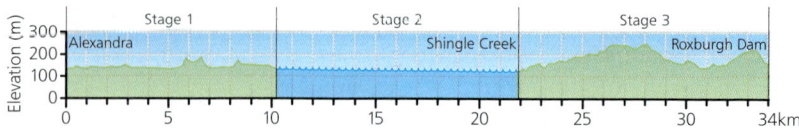

How to get there Drive to either end of the trail if riding it in stages. Otherwise, ride the Otago Central Rail Trail to the start. And from the end of the trail, ride the Clutha Gold Trail, which leads to Lawrence.

Riding surface 100% wide smooth gravel

History In the 1860s, Roxburgh Gorge was crawling with gold miners, many of them from China. The Roxburgh Gorge Dam was built between 1949 and 1957 and flooded 30 km of the gorge, creating Lake Roxburgh.

Special considerations A maintenance contribution of $10 for a day, or $25 per adult for a season or $50 per family for a season covers the cost of trail maintenance for both the Roxburgh Gorge and Clutha Gold trails.

Mobile phone coverage in the Roxburgh Gorge is patchy at best.

Special features You can still find the remains of tiny schist huts built into the rock by Chinese miners. One of them has a tunnel leading under the trail to another hut. These huts are on the shady side of the gorge, and it is hard to imagine how the miners survived through the winters.

Maps There are maps on the trail website.

Trail website www.cluthagold.co.nz

SUPPORT SERVICES

Boat Drop into the Alexandra I-Site (☎ 03 448 9515) for an update on boating options down the gorge or pre-book a trip with Clutha River Cruises in Alexandra ☎ 022 068 3302, www.clutharivercruises.co.nz, or Beaumont Jet, ☎ 027 784 5649, www.beaumontjet.co.nz

Alexandra Lots of cafes, restaurants, bike hire, shops and accommodation: www.alexandra.co.nz, Altitude Bikes ☎ 03 448 8917, www.altitudebikes.co.nz

Roxburgh Dam Lake Roxburgh Lodge, restaurant, bike and kayak hire (highly recommended): ☎ 03 446 8220, www.lakeroxburghlodge.co.nz

Roxburgh A few cafes, shops, and accommodation: Information Centre: ☎ 03 446 8920; Riders Rest accommodation: ☎ 03 446 8988, www.ridersrestroxburgh.com, Roxburgh Teviot Country Motels and Backpackers: ☎ 03 446 8364; Roxburgh Motels: ☎ 03 446 8093 or 027 546 8093, www.roxburghmotels.co.nz, The Commercial Hotel/Backpackers: ☎ 03 446 8160, www.centralotagonz.com

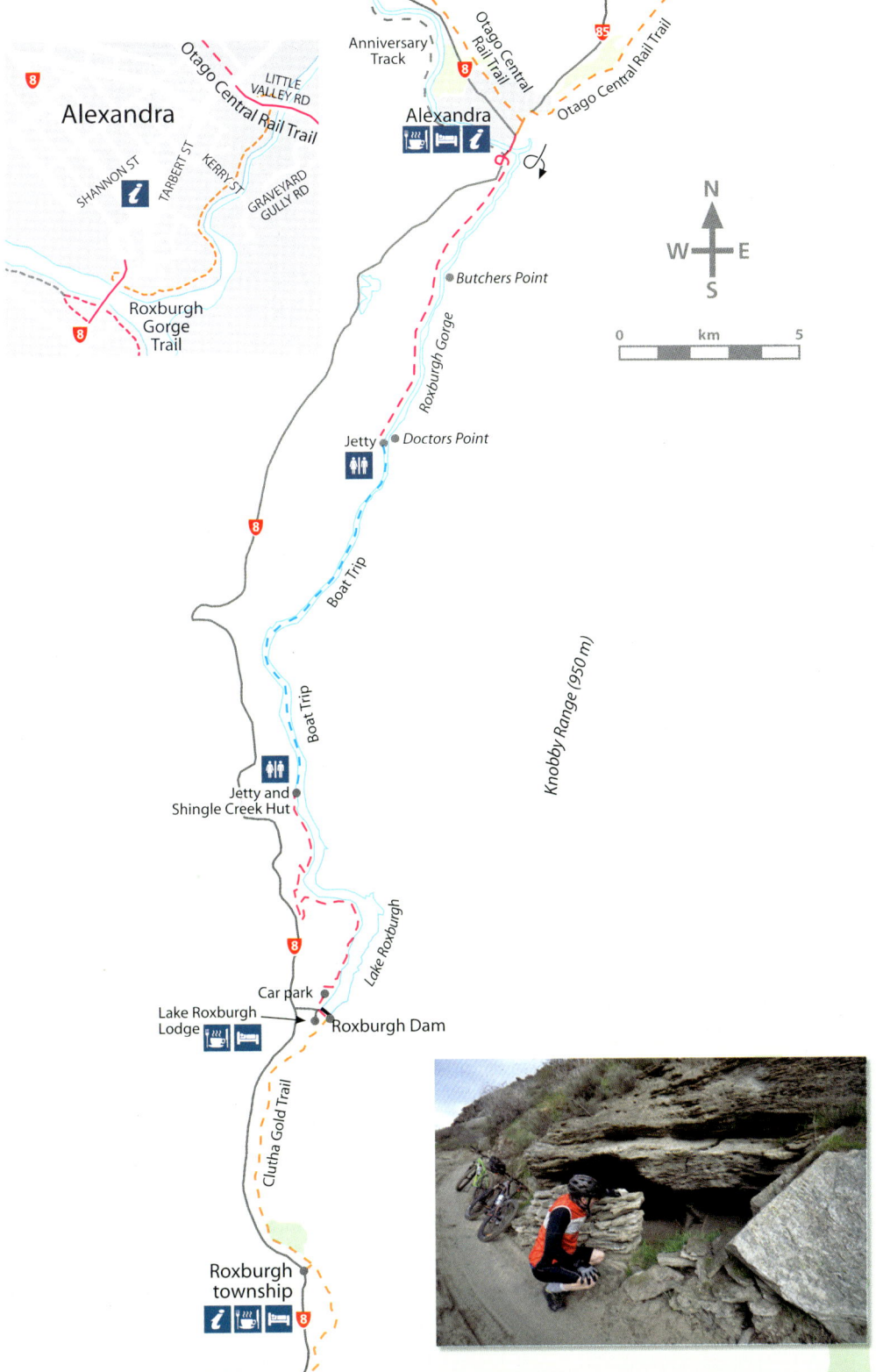

GREAT RIDE

Clutha Gold Trail
Roxburgh Dam to Lawrence
Distance 78 km   Time Up to 2 days   Grade 2 (Easy)

Explore New Zealand's largest river on this brilliantly designed trail, where every twist and turn reveals new views and the history of one of the world's biggest gold rushes is brought to life.

From the end of the Roxburgh Gorge Trail, the trail weaves through riverside forest to Roxburgh township. Then from Roxburgh, it continues down valley, passing lovely picnic spots such as Pinders Pond – a great place for a swim in summer. Beyond the small settlement of Millers Flat, the trail follows a mix of old railway line and equally old road.

After just over 50 km, the trail reaches Beaumont, where you can rest for a night. From here, you will leave the river and roughly follow the old railway line to Lawrence, passing a major historical Chinese settlement on the way.

The scenery is absolutely stunning and the trail easy and wide. This will suit anyone who enjoyed the Otago Central Rail Trail.

ITINERARY

Stage 1: Roxburgh Dam to Roxburgh township
10 km, 1 hour

The trail starts on Roxburgh East Road, just a few hundred metres down from the dam. It follows the edge of the Clutha Mata-au River, weaving through forest and past little bays, in a way that engages you with the environment and makes you lose track of time – just as all great cycle trails do.

When you reach the first bridge across the Clutha, cross it to ride into Roxburgh township, where you will find shops, galleries and accommodation.

Stage 2: Roxburgh township to Millers Flat
21 km, 2 hours

Head back across the Clutha Mata-au River on the road bridge and continue following the trail, right, beside the road to start with and then branching away to follow the river again. After half an hour, you'll reach Pinders Pond, a popular picnic and swimming spot. Next, the trail and road squeeze past Dumbarton Rock, which once stretched all the way across the river. About 6 km later, the trail crosses the road and uses the old railway formation for the first time but not for

Looking for the mother lode on the Clutha Gold.

long. You will rejoin the river again for a few kilometres before jumping back up onto the road and rolling into Millers Flat, a small settlement with a general store, a park and a few places to stay.

Stage 3: Millers Flat to Beaumont
25 km, 2–3 hours

The section of track between Millers Flat and Beaumont is partly on a separate cycle path beside the river, and partly on the old railway formation from Roxburgh to Lawrence. There are also a few short sections on a quiet road called The Millenium Track. You will pass many interesting features, the most significant being the beautiful tree-lined Clutha Mata-au River. This is a popular stretch of the river for kayaking, and there are several short tracks leading down to the river's edge.

Beaumont is a very small settlement with a hotel and an Icelandic chef!

Stage 4: Beaumont to Lawrence
22 km, 2 hours

This varied stage branches away from the Clutha Mata-au River to swap between following the old railway formation and running beside the highway. You will be climbing almost imperceptibly away from Beaumont before descending gently to Lawrence. There are several points of interest, including an old railway

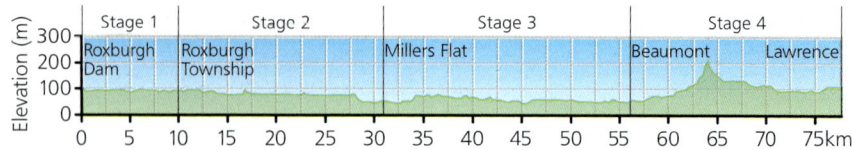

tunnel, the remains of New Zealand's largest Chinese settlement and the final destination, Lawrence, an old gold mining town, with fascinating history and great cafes. Make sure you take the time to check out the historic Empire Hotel, 1.4 km before Lawrence.

FACT FILE

Overview This trail has it all – history, scenery, interesting communities and a great riding experience on a well-designed track. We happily recommend it as one of the top three easy trails in the country.

How to get there Roxburgh Dam, at the start of the trail, is 2 hours' drive from Dunedin via highways 1 and 8 and 1.5 hours drive from Queenstown. Lawrence, at the end of the trail, is 1 hour's drive from Dunedin.

The Grand Tour Riders can complete an 8-day circuit of Otago as follows. Leave Dunedin via the Taieri Gorge Excursion Train, then bike 140 km of the Otago Central Rail Trail to Alexandra. Next, ride and boat through the Roxburgh Gorge to the start of the Clutha Gold Trail. This leads to Lawrence, 1 hour's shuttle from Dunedin. Alternatively, the fit and fearless may prefer to ride via the Lawrence to Dunedin Connector (see page 255).

Riding surface Mostly smooth wide gravelled trail.

History Lawrence was the centre of a gold mining boom in the 1860s that saw its population swell to over 11,000. The Lawrence information centre and museum, and nearby Gabriels Gully mining area are well worth investigating. The railway line reached Lawrence in 1877, where it stalled for 30 years. In 1928, it finally reached Roxburgh. It was used to carry materials for the construction of the Roxburgh Dam, and in 1968, it closed for good.

Special considerations The Clutha Mata-au River is not generally considered safe for swimming as there are many undercurrents and eddies. However, some of the bays are OK, and Pinders Pond is a popular swimming location.

Special features The powerful Clutha Mata-au River is the largest by volume in New Zealand, flowing 338 km from Lake Wanaka to the Pacific Ocean. Its swift blue waters make a striking contrast to the greenery of the tree-lined banks that this trail explores.

Important contacts Information centres at Roxburgh and Lawrence.

Maps There is an official trail map available from local I-Sites and businesses.

Trail website www.cluthagold.co.nz

SUPPORT SERVICES

Trail Transport and Bike Hire from Altitude Bikes in Alexandra: ☎ 03 448 8917 or 021 456 918, www.altitudebikes.co.nz, Trail Journeys in Clyde: ☎ 03 449 2150; Dunedin Bike Hire: ☎ 021 175 0832, www.ibikehire.co.nz

Alexandra Cafes, restaurants, shops, accommodation: www.alexandra.co.nz

Roxburgh Dam trail head Lake Roxburgh Lodge and Restaurant: www.lakeroxburghlodge.co.nz

Roxburgh Cafes, shops, information centre, accommodation: Information Centre: ☎ 03 446 8920; Clutha Gold Cottages: ☎ 03 446 8364 or www.cluthagoldcottages.co.nz; Roxburgh Motels: ☎ 03 446 8093; The Commercial Hotel/Backpackers: ☎ 03 446 8160, www.centralotagonz.com/Roxburgh, Riders Rest accommodation: ☎ 03 446 8988, www.ridersrestroxburgh.com

Millers Flat Food, accommodation: Arcadia Bed & Breakfast: ☎ 03 446 6881; Millers Flat Holiday Park: ☎ 03 446 6877; Faigans Cafe Store: ☎ 021 206 4997

Beaumont Accommodation and food: Beaumont Hotel: ☎ 03 485 9431. Beaumont School Holiday Home: ☎ 021 488 709

Lawrence Supermarket, cafes, shops, accommodation: www.lawrence.co.nz

Grade 2 trails don't get any better than this.

CONNECTOR RIDE

LAWRENCE TO DUNEDIN
Clutha Gold to Dunedin via Lake Waihola
Distance 100 km   Time 1–2 days   Grade 5 (Expert)

For those who want to ride all the way to Dunedin, here is the best route that we could find. There is a fair bit of traffic on some sections but also some fantastic scenery and a couple of cycle paths on the way into the city.

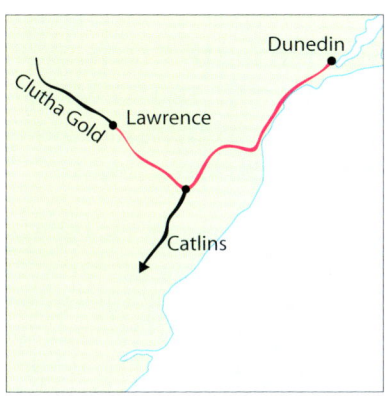

From Lawrence, follow the main road out of town and all the way to Milton. This has virtually no shoulder for half of it, so you want to be wary of traffic. Stuart Reserve, 25 km from Lawrence, has toilets, a shelter and picnic tables. Milton is 37 km from Lawrence and has plenty of shops.

Highway 1 from Milton to Lake Waihola has much more traffic but an excellent shoulder. Waihola (52 km from Lawrence) has a public park, a holiday park, motel, cafe and store.

From Waihola, head up North Foreland Street for 200 metres, then turn right into Goodwin Street and left up Finlayson Road. Change into bottom gear – this road climbs a tough 300-m hill over to Taieri Mouth. If the climb doesn't take your breath away, the views from the top will.

From Taieri Mouth (64 km from Lawrence), head left past the boat yard, cross a bridge and then follow the coast for 17 km to Brighton. That's a cruisy ride, as flat as a pancake. Brighton has the Bluegum Bed and Breakfast, a dairy with takeaways and a big park at the beach, with toilets and picnic tables.

From Brighton (81 km from Lawrence), take the following roads into the centre of Dunedin (this is the official recommended route): Brighton Road, past the Green Island shops, along Main South Road to a signed cycle path on your left (it is 100 metres past Emerson Street). Follow the cycle path uphill to the end of South Road (beside the motorway). Follow South Road all the way to Princes Street, which leads right to the Octagon in the centre of Dunedin. South Road does a couple of odd turns, so stick to the street signs.

Note Try to ride the section from Lawrence to Milton in the weekend to avoid trucks in the narrow Manuka Gorge.

Bikepackers may prefer taking the remote and hilly route via Irvine Road, Waipori Road and Waipori Falls Road instead.

> **GREAT RIDE**

Queenstown Trails
Queenstown and Arrowtown
Distance up to 100 km   Time 1 hour to 4 days
Grades 2 (Easy) and 3 (Intermediate)

Surrounded by Queenstown's stunning mountain ranges, this 100-kilometre trail network covers a variety of terrain, taking in lakes, rivers and the Gibbston wine producing region.

There are several options in the Queenstown Trail network, and they are quite diverse. Choose carefully. The main ride is a 70-km loop from Queenstown (New Zealand's adventure capital) to the charming heritage town of Arrowtown, then down to the world-famous bungy jumping Kawarau Bridge and back to Queenstown. That is a fabulous two-day journey.

In addition to that loop, there are three other trails – two challenging there-and-back trips, with one heading out to Jacks Point and the other out to Gibbston, and then there is jewel in the crown, an easy loop around Lake Hayes.

ITINERARY

Stage 1: Queenstown to Arrowtown
26–35 km, 3–5 hours, Grade 3 (Intermediate)

Coast down to the waterfront at Queenstown and turn left, following an easy cycle path around the edge of the lake to Frankton. At the head of Frankton Arm, you have two choices. The shorter option climbs up to the golf course, past 'Hendis Hole' (an infamous developer's folly), down Grant Road and through an industrial area to the Shotover River. To take this option, turn left to follow the trail under the new Shotover River Bridge and up to the old Shotover Bridge.

Alternatively, you can get to the same bridge by riding up to Kawarau Road, and along to Southberg Ave. At the corner, a track links to the end of Robertson Road, and about 100 metres up that road, you can ride up past a kindergarten to a trail that leads for 7 km around the water's edge of the Kawarau and Shotover rivers to the old Shotover Bridge.

Cross the bridge and loop around underneath it to continue up river. Now carefully follow signs along a mix of trail and road to Arrowtown. Be prepared to tackle a couple of steep hills on the way (making this option a grade 3) plus some tricky navigation through Millbrook Resort.

Queenstown offers remarkable all-year-round riding.

The trail leads though the west end of Arrowtown to the Chinese huts. Then just nip up to the main street 50 metres away. It is one of those movie-set type streets that radiates character. Only it's the real thing!

Stage 2: Arrowtown to the historic Kawarau River bridge
14 km, 1.5–2 hours, Grade 2 (Easy)

Once again, you have a couple of options, but the choice is quite simple really – if you don't want to be bored out of your tree, don't follow the path beside the road heading south; it has no redeeming features.

The best option is to drop back down to the Chinese huts beside the Arrow River and follow the path down river, crossing five bridges on the way to the historic Kawarau Bridge. After crossing a cyclist's bridge tucked under the highway bridge, you will turn left and follow Arrow Junction Road for a while before the trail begins again on your left and leads to an impressive suspension bridge and then an impressive underpass. No expense has been spared. The trail then leaves the river and follows the original highway to the Kawarau Bridge. If bungy jumping is happening, hop off your bike and walk past the action.

There is a cafe at the bridge, and starting from the car park, the Gibbston River Trail leads to a few renowned wineries.

Stage 3: Kawarau River bridge to Queenstown
32 km, 2–4 hours, Grade 3 (Intermediate)

The final leg of this ride does involve a few hills. Don't say we didn't warn you! Ride back towards Arrowtown on the track you rode in on for just over 4 km. When you reach Morven Ferry Road, look for a turn-off 30 metres away to your right. From there, a new trail crosses farmland and drops down beside the Kawarau River. This is a really enjoyable section with stunning views. It takes you back to the old bridge across the Shotover River.

Cross the bridge and take the track down river, under the highway bridge, left past the quarry and down to the river again, following a series of 'Frankton Flats' signs. This track will bring you out to Robertson Road, where you can nip out to the Kawarau Road. Go down to the traffic lights and use the pedestrian crossing on this busy road, then follow cycle paths down to the lake edge. Turn right at the lake, and you'll be back in Queenstown before you know it.

Optional Stage: Lake Hayes Loop
9 km, 1 hour, Grade 2 (Easy)

Lake Hayes offers an easy, single-track spin around a beautiful lake – ideal for a family outing.

From Queenstown, head northeast on Highway 6. A couple of kilometres past the new Shotover River bridge, turn into the signposted car park on the left. Ride down to the lake and complete a lap in either direction. Apart from a couple of stiff wee climbs, this ride is easy peasy lemon squeezy.

Optional Stage: Kelvin Peninsula and Jacks Point Track
14 km one way, 2–3 hours, Grade 2 and 4 (Easy and Advanced)

This ride comprises some brilliant single track, with awesome lakeside vistas.

From the southern end of the Kawarau River Bridge (cross on the pedestrian path) just out of Frankton, you'll see a 'Kelvin Peninsula Track' sign. Turn sharp right and drop down to the water's edge to follow a single track and a short section of road around the lake. After about 20 minutes, you'll reach the Wakatipu Yacht Club near the end of the peninsula. It's a great place for a picnic before heading back the same way or carrying on around the lake to Jacks Point.

From the yacht club, continue southwest around the peninsula, passing beside the golf course, and back to the main Kelvin Heights Road. A few hundred metres up the main road, turn right up Poplar Drive and ride to the end, where you will find Jardine Park. The Jacks Point Track starts here and has some steep hills!

The impressive rock outcrops of Jacks Point are your goal. After soaking up the views, head back the way you came, or drop down to Jacks Point Clubhouse for a bite to eat. Most of the downhill is on Lodge Road. Turn left at Homestead Bay Road, and left again a few hundred metres later to reach the clubhouse.

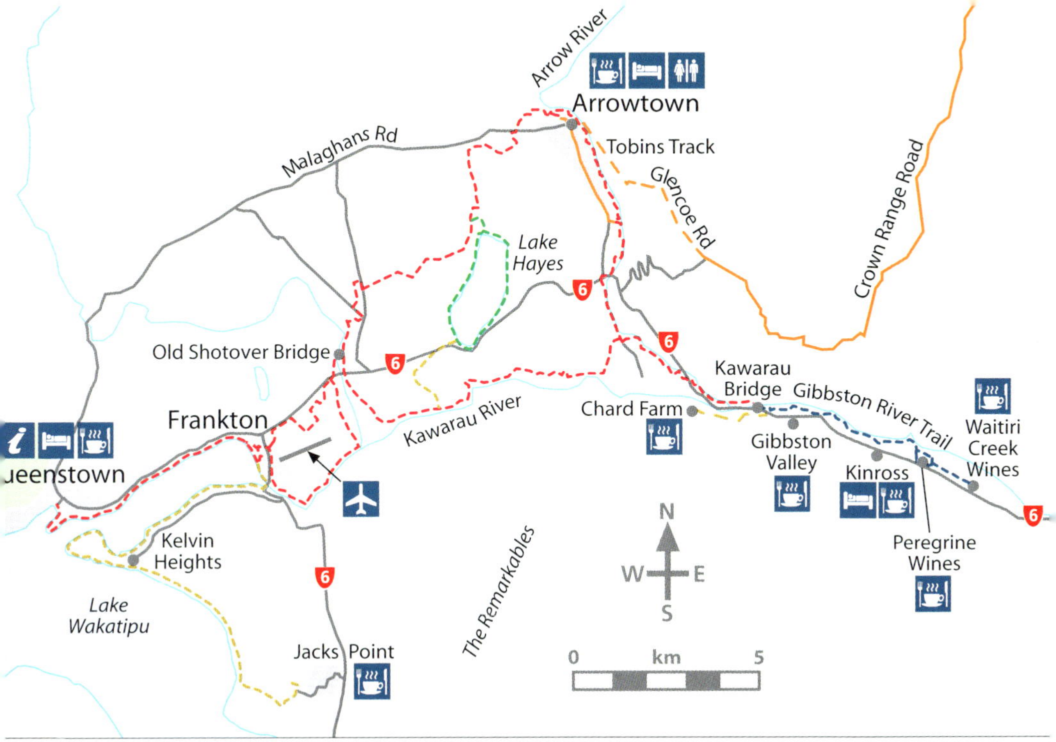

Optional Stage: Gibbston River Trail
7 km one way, 1 hour, Grade 1 (Very easy)

This is a nicely gravelled path that offers stunning scenery.

From the historic Kawarau River bridge car park, you will find a 'Gibbston River Trail' sign. From there, navigation to several wineries is easy. Ride to Chard Farm Vineyard (2 km), Gibbston Valley Winery (1 km side trip), Peregrine Winery (on the track) and, 7 km from the start, Waitiri Creek Winery. Turn around whenever you feel like it, or for more of a challenge ride back via the Gibbston Back Road. See Support Services (over page) for winery contact details.

We also did the 'dangerous' Wentworth Bridge Loop and, although DOC says this loop is not suitable for moutain bikes, we thought it was fine for Grade 5 (expert) riders.

FACT FILE

Overview The route includes seven bridges, with five crossing the spectacular Arrow and Kawarau rivers, which are recognised as places of outstanding natural beauty. The trail's terrain is varied and provides outstanding views of the famous Remarkables mountain range.

How to get there Riders will have the choice of accessing the trail from a range of locations along the trail, including Queenstown, Frankton (where the airport is) and Arrowtown. Queenstown is 15 minutes drive from the airport. There are regular airport shuttles, as well as rental cars available. Many accommodation providers also offer free shuttles to and from the town centre.

Bike hire and shuttles Around the Basin (Queenstown and Arrowtown): ☎ 0508 782 9253 or www.aroundthebasin.co.nz; Gibbston Valley Biking Centre (Gibbston Valley): ☎ 03 442 6910 or www.gibbstonvalley.com

Riding surface Mostly smooth gravel path but also a few short sections of gravel road.

Special considerations The trail is technically easy and suitable for most riding abilities. However, there are a few hill climbs and descents that may require walking.

Special features Other than this New Zealand Cycle Trail offering, Queenstown also caters well for mountain bikers, with the world-class Gondola Tracks that snake through the forested slopes above Queenstown. For more information, check out *Classic New Zealand Mountain Bike Rides*.

Maps Take a photo of the map boards along the route.

Trail website www.queenstowntrail.co.nz

SUPPORT SERVICES

Queenstown is the main tourist town in New Zealand. The place is buzzing and there are more support services than you could ever dream of: www.queenstownnz.co.nz and www.queenstowntrail.co.nz

Frankton Arm Cafe The Boatshed: ☎ 03 441 4146, www.boatshedqueenstown.com

Arrowtown is much smaller and more laid back. It still has a good range of shops and accommodation but nowhere near as many as Queenstown: www.arrowtown.com

Gibbston River Trail Gibbston Valley: ☎ 03 442 6910 www.gibbstonvalley.com; Chard Farm vineyard: ☎ 03 442 6110, www.chardfarm.co.nz, Peregrine Wines: ☎ 03 442 4000, www.peregrinewines.co.nz, Waitiri Creek: ☎ 03 441 3315, www.waitiricreek.co.nz; Kinross (store and cottages): ☎ 0800 131 101 or www.kinrosscottages.co.nz

Perfect riding between Arrowtown and the Kawarau bridge.

The Kawarau Bridge is where you can line up and take the plunge with a bungy jump, should you feel the urge; otherwise, just relax and have a coffee in the cafe: www.bungy.co.nz

GREAT RIDE

Around the Mountains
Queenstown to Kingston
Distance 196 km   Time 3–5 days   Grade 1-3 (mostly easy)

After taking a scenic boat trip across Lake Wakatipu from Queenstown, this new cycle trail circumnavigates the Eyre Mountains on a mix of easy cycle trail and quiet country roads.

From Walter Peak Station a gravel road leads through the mountains to Mavora Lakes where there is plenty of space for camping. From there the trail is mostly downhill, half on gravel road and half on cycle trail beside the Oreti River to the deer capital of New Zealand, Mossburn. The cycle trail is mostly off road from Mossburn, and hops from one town to the next before ending at Kingston, a holiday town at the southern tip of Lake Wakatipu.

Stage 1: Queenstown to Mavora Lakes
58 km, 4–6 hours, Grade 3 (Intermediate)

From Queenstown, catch a water taxi or the historic steamboat *TSS Earnslaw* across Lake Wakatipu to Walter Peak Station (phone 0800 65 65 01 to book in advance – $40 per person and $5 per bike). Over summer, the *Earnslaw* is scheduled to leave Queenstown daily every two hours from 10 am – 8 pm. We recommend not doing this trip in winter.

From the jetty at Walter Peak, cycle 12 km around to Mount Nicholas Station, then head south on the quiet Von Road, then Mount Nicholas Road for almost 40 km. There is one serious climb that sees you gain around 300 m elevation (a shelter may be built at the bottom of this hill in 2018).

Turn right at Mavora Lakes Road to visit the lakes. There is a camping area 7 km up this road at the southern end of North Mavora Lake. It is a beautiful area, but the sandflies will keep you moving (unless it's raining).

Stage 2: Mavora Lakes to Mossburn
50 km, 2–4 hours, Grade 3 (Intermediate)

Head back to the intersection and continue south on Mavora Lakes Road for 18.5 km before turning left onto Centre Hills Road. Ride down Centre Hills Road for just over 9 km before turning left and riding down towards the Oreti River for about 1 km. You're looking for the Around the Mountains Cycle Trail, which was built between here and Mossburn in 2015. Turn right at the cycle trail and ride roughly parallel to the Oreti River for 22 km to Cumberland Street at the back of Mossburn. There you will find two cafes, a hotel and a garage.

The Around the Mountains Cycle Trail heading towards Mossburn.

Stage 3: Mossburn to Lumsden
21.5 km, 1.5–3 hours, Grade 2 (Easy)

Ride east out of Mossburn on the main road and you'll find the cycle trail, just on the edge of town. It runs parallel to the highway most of the way, but ducks off down a couple of country roads. It's well signposted.

You'll pass the driveway to Brookhaven Country Garden at the halfway mark.

If you are aiming for Lumsden, then straight after crossing the Oreti Highway Bridge, turn left twice, to ride under the bridge and then south to Lumsden 3 km away. If you don't want to take the side trip to Lumsden, head north after the bridge.

Stage 4: Lumsden to Athol
35 km, 2–4 hours, Grade 1 (Very Easy)

It is 15 km from Lumsden to Five Rivers where there is a nice cafe and art gallery, just a few hundred metres off the main trail. It's all well signposted.

After refuelling, ride back to the main trail and continue north for another 20 km to Athol, a cute little town with cafes.

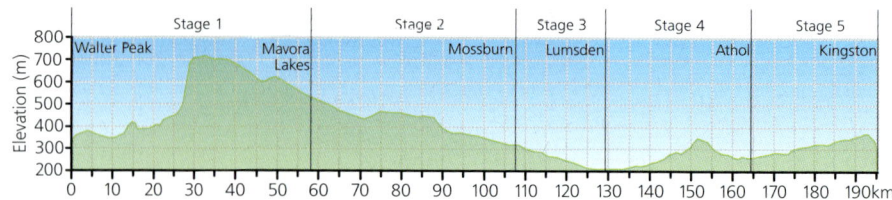

Stage 5: Athol to Kingston
32 km, 2–4 hours, Grade 2 (Easy)

From Athol, ride north and follow the trail to a pair of magnificent suspension bridges. From there the trail takes you right to the centre of Garston, a small village with a hotel, a playground, some interesting historical boards and a honey shop.

Leaving Garston, the trail is on country road most of the way to another suspension bridge which crosses the Mataura River at the boundary between Southland and Central Otago. On the far side is Fairlight, a small railway station building, which has seen better days.

Continue north and you'll soon be enjoying a gentle downhill to Kingston, a lakeside village with food and accommodation.

FACT FILE

Overview Riding this trail in the anti-clockwise direction (ending at Kingston) takes advantage of the predominant northwesterly wind.

How to get there Queenstown's town centre is 15 minutes drive from the international airport. There are regular airport shuttles, taxis, rental cars and a local bus service. Many activity and accommodation providers also offer free shuttles to/from the town centre.

Riding surface 50% smooth cycle trail, 40% gravel road, 10% sealed road

Special considerations Mavora Lakes is too darn popular over the summer holidays, but if you like a party, it's the place to be.

Special features The Eyre Mountains are the dominant feature of this ride. They are managed by the Department of Conservation and have several tramping tracks through them.

Maps Kiwimap *Southern Lakes Rural Road Map*

Trail website www.aroundthemountains.co.nz

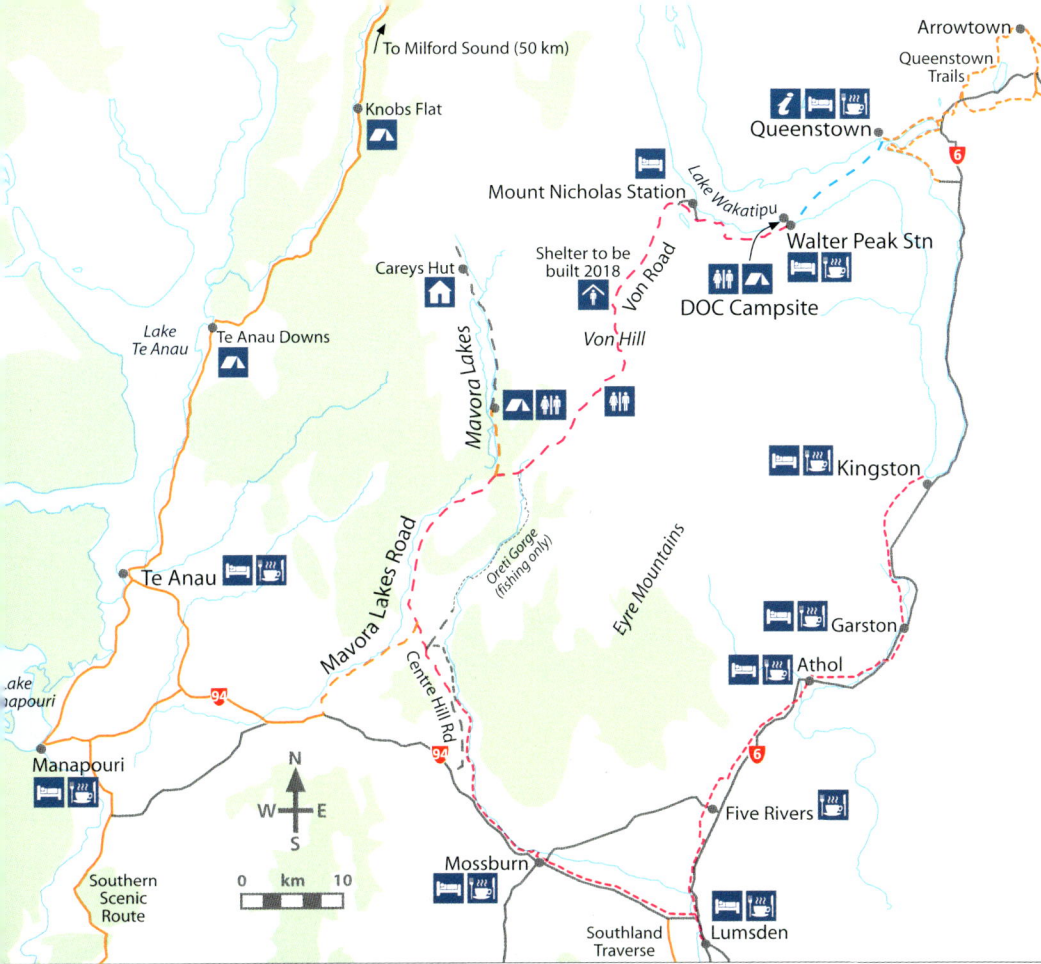

SUPPORT SERVICES

Booking You can book your whole trip thorugh www.aroundthemountains.co.nz and by doing so will automatically contribute to the maintenance of the trail.

Queenstown Accommodation, food, shops: www.queenstownnz.co.nz

TSS Earnslaw (historic steamship), book in advance: ☎ 0800 65 65 01, www.realjourneys.co.nz

Queenstown Water Taxis (these offer more flexible times): ☎ 03 441 1124, www.queenstownwatertaxis.co.nz

Walter Peak Station High Country Farm, food and luxury accommodation, ☎ 0800 766 854 or www.thelodge.net.nz. There's also a new free DOC campsite 900 metres from the wharf, on your right. Includes gas BBQs.

Mount Nicholas Lodge and meals, ☎ 03 409 0712 or www.mtnicholaslodge.co.nz (you must book for meals)

Classic New Zealand Cycle Trails   **265**

Mavora Lakes Campsite with toilets: www.doc.govt.nz

Mossburn A general store and the Mossburn Hotel, ☎ 03 248 6399, www.mossburnhotel.co.nz

Lumsden Wide range of places to eat and stay. There is an information centre in the middle of town.

Five Rivers Great little cafe, ☎ 03 248 7755

Athol Two stores with takeaways. Accommodation at Athol Lodge and Holiday Park, ☎ 021 184 5444. Also check www.aroundthemountains.co.nz ☎ 0800 668 682 46

Garston Garston Hotel and Cafe, ☎ 03 248 8820; Bed and breakfast at Naylor House, ☎ 03 248 8809 or 027 653 6110, www.naylorhouse.co.nz

Kingston Food, accommodation, picnic area. Kingston Holiday Park has a range of well-priced accommodation and camping, ☎ 0800 807 836 or 03 248 8501, www.kingstonholidaypark.co.nz

Centre Hills Road between Mavora Lakes and Mossburn – cold but clear.

CONNECTOR RIDE

SOUTHLAND TRAVERSE
Mossburn to Bluff
Distance 140 km Time 2 days Grade 4 (Advanced)

This is the direct route used by Tour Aotearoa riders heading for Stirling Point at Bluff. It avoids most of the traffic and uses a couple of off-road paths.

Head south-east from Mossburn, deer capital of New Zealand, on the Around the Mountains cycle trail. After 13 km, turn right off the cycle trail, and cross the highway to ride south on Dipton-Castlerock Road.

When you are 34 km from Mossburn, turn right onto George St, then left onto South Hillend-Dipton Road. After another 20 km, turn right onto Hundred Line Road, then left onto Riverside Road. When you reach Highway 96, turn left and cross the Oreti River Bridge. Then turn right onto Winton Substation Road, and left onto Gerrard Road, which leads into the centre of Winton. The bakery is to your right, on the main road.

After refueling in Winton, head back out of town the way you came. Opposite Jane Street, turn left onto the Winton Walkway and follow it south around the edge of town. Turn right down Price Road, then left down Substation Road. You should now follow Substation Road, Calder Road, Nelson Road, Lochiel-Branxholme Road, Young Road and Ryal Bush-Wallacetown Road south into Wallacetown. There is a dairy/takeaways, public toilets at the garage and a pub in this small town.

From Wallacetown, head east on Highway 99 for 3.5 km before turning right down Steel Road, then left when you reach West Plains Road, right at Gloucester Street and south into Invercargill. Turn left along Bay Road and at the main road, right onto a signposted cycle path across the Waihopai Bridge. Turn right straight after the bridge onto a gravel path beside the river. this leads south around Invercargill to Kekeno Place.

The trail ended at Kekeno Place in 2018, but will be continued to Bluff eventually. For now, ride carefully beside the highway. There may be a short section of new path built to avoid a narrow road-rail overbridge. Then you'll have to ride more highway down to Bluff and through town to Stirling Point, at the end of the road, which is your destination.

Note This is the final leg of the 3000 km Tour Aotearoa journey from Cape Reinga to Bluff. You may meet some extremely fit, or fatigued, riders.

Mossburn Mossburn Railway Hotel, ☎ 03 248 6399 or 021 224 0088, www.mossburnhotel.co.nz also Mossburn has two cafes, the hotel and a couple of small garages.

Camp Taringatura Cabins and tent site, 809 South Hillend-Dipton Rd, ☎ 0800 827 464, www.camptaringatura.com

Winton Winton Commercial Hotel: ☎ 03 236 7769. Central Southland Lodge (cycle friendly): ☎ 03 236 8413. Winton has lots of places to buy food including a great bakery and a supermarket.

Wallacetown Dairy and takeaways

Invercargill Lots of services. Top 10 Holiday Park, Waikiwi (north Invercargill): ☎ 03 215 9032. Tuatara Backpackers in centre of town: ☎ 0800 4882 8272

Invercargill is the country's southern most city and has all amenities you need, but they are all off the route by several hundred metres. The most convenient way to get to them is down Victoria Ave to the main road. Turn right at the McDonalds and cruise the main drag for 1.4 km, past loads of shops, to Tweed Street. Follow Tweed Street west to Bond Street, where a link track takes you back to the cycle path beside the Waihopai River.

Bluff For accommodation options, see www.bluff.co.nz/accommodation

Lands End boutique hotel is 40 metres from the Stirling Point signs, ☎ 03 212 7575. Bluff Camping ground, Gregory St, ☎ 027 626 2018. Oyster Cove cafe is only 30 metres from Stirling Point.

CONNECTOR RIDE

MILFORD SOUND

Te Anau to Milford return
Distance 240 km return   Time 3–4 days
Grade 5 (Expert) because it's a big hill

Undeniably the most spectacular scenery accessible from any road in New Zealand surrounds the Te Anau to Milford Sound road. But there are three reasons we haven't provided a lot of detail about this ride: first, at certain times of day it is overrun with tourist traffic; second, it's a dead-end road, miles from nowhere; and third, there's a 900-metre high hill in the way!

However, these challenges can be overcome in the following ways. Do some hill training before your ride, go late in summer and ride early in the morning before the tourist traffic arrives. Give yourself extra time to fully enjoy completing a there-and-back trip to one of the most beautiful places on the planet.

From the beautiful small town of Te Anau (30 km west of the Mavora Lakes ride), start pedalling early. The tourist traffic from Queenstown leaves at 7 am and will arrive at Milford in a wave between 10 am and 11 am. If you left Te Anau at 6 am and rode at 20 kph, you could reach the Hollyford Valley turn-off before the traffic (that's 87 km under your belt). Then veer off the highway to head down the Hollyford Valley for 8 km to Gunns Camp, which offers accommodation as well as camping options. You'll have all afternoon to explore or rest up for the next day's adventure.

Leave Gunns Camp by 8 am, and you will beat all the traffic to Milford Sound. Ride back to the Milford Highway, turn right and climb up to Homer Tunnel, at 900 m elevation (20 km from Gunns Camp, which sits at 100 m elevation). The tunnel is 1 km long, steeply sloping down to the west and has traffic lights. From the far end, you'll have a blistering 17 km downhill to Milford Sound.

Most visitors take a scenic boat trip, then hop in their buses and head back to Queenstown. It's madness really, but there is only enough accommodation for a fraction of the day trippers. You, on the other hand, could book ahead and spend a night in paradise but take some super strength insect repellent as the sandflies work in squadrons.

The view from the western side of the Homer Tunnel..

Some cyclists pay to take a bus back up to and through the Homer Tunnel. We can't really blame them, but it's not our style. If you're up for the challenge, start early in the morning and give yourself a few hours to complete this 18-km slog. When you meet the daily pulse of Queenstown day trippers, just pull off the road for an hour and kick back with some lunch while you enjoy the scenery.

By now, you'll have a good idea whether you want to ride back to Gunns Camp for another night in the Hollyford or ride the mostly downhill 100 km back to Te Anau.

Notes Gunns Camp has no phone or cell phone coverage. Contact: www.gunnscamp.org.nz, email gunnscamp@ruralinzone.net for information.

Milford Sound: accommodation and minimal food supplies, see www.milfordlodge.com

Take front and rear lights for the tunnel. And take extra food as there is no supermarket or dairy in Milford Sound.

There are loads of options for accommodation in Te Anau.

CONNECTOR RIDE

SOUTHERN SCENIC ROUTE
Te Anau to Invercargill
Distance 196 km   Time 2–3 days   Grade 3 (Intermediate)

This is a beautiful corner of New Zealand, and the quiet and scenic roads run beside New Zealand's largest wilderness, Fiordland National Park.

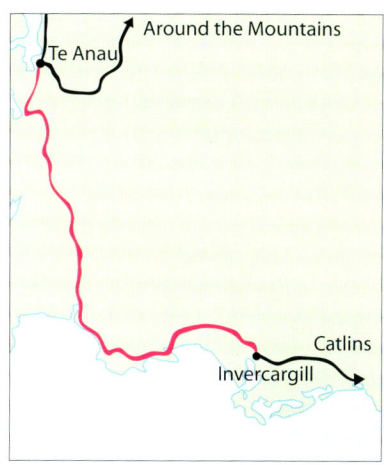

From behind the National Park Visitor Centre on Lakefront Drive in Te Anau, follow the Lake 2 Lake Trail south. This leads most of the way to Manapouri, – an ideal place for your first stop. Possum Lodge Backpackers is a really nice place to stay at Manapouri (☎ 03 249 6623, www.possumlodge.co.nz).

Leave Manapouri on Hillside-Manapouri Road, and after 5 km, turn right on Weir Road. There is water and toilets available at the community centre/school between Manapouri and Clifden. Stay on Weir Road, which becomes Clifden-Blackmount all the way down past Clifden (historic bridge, golf club, a great freedom camping ground and caves) to Tuatapere (Sausage Capital of New Zealand). That's 100 km.

From Tuatapere, follow Highway 99 down to the coast and around to Riverton, a popular holiday town tucked at the base of Jacobs River Estuary. That's almost 50 km from sausage land.

From Riverton, the traffic builds up as you approach Invercargill, so from Wallacetown, we have devised an elaborate back route into town. Head east from Wallacetown on Highway 99, crossing the very narrow bridge with care (stop and wait for a gap in the traffic). Turn right down Steel Road, left down West Plains Road, right down Gloucester Street and left down Durham Street. This leads to Highway 1, just next to a big supermarket. Use the pedestrian crossing 50 metres away to get across to Bainfield Road, which has cycle lanes.

A few hundred metres down Bainfield Road, you can turn left and ride through Donovan Park to get to a good holiday park, owned by a couple of cyclists. Otherwise, ride down to the next big roundabout and turn right down Queens Drive to pedal 4 km to Gala Street. Turn right to ride to the I-Site and the centre of town.

Trail website   www.southernscenicroute.co.nz

HEARTLAND RIDE

Catlins Coastal Route
Balclutha to Invercargill
Distance 186 km   Time 3–5 days   Grade 3 (Intermediate)

The Catlins is an intricate landscape with hidden scenic treasures around every corner. The wild coast, vast tracts of native forest, native birds and animals, and engaging local hospitality make for an unforgettable holiday.

After riding from Balclutha out to Kaka Point, slow down and take it all in. There are dozens of short side trips, both biking and walking, that take you to spectacular natural features such as Nugget Point, where the southern seas do their best to erode the land. Further on at Owaka and Papatowai, you will get a feel for the quirky and creative side of Catlins culture by visiting Teapot Land and the Lost Gypsy.

At Curio Bay, there is a petrified forest, Hector's dolphins and at certain times of the year seals and penguins. And don't miss out on New Zealand's very own Niagara Falls! There are also several stunning short forest walks and a few good cafes to sidetrack your journey to Invercargill via the southern tip of the South Island.

ITINERARY

Stage 1: Balclutha to Owaka
37 km, 3–4 hours

From Balclutha, take the main street as far as High Street. Follow the Southern Scenic Route signs out of town for 6 km, then turn left down Kaka Point Road. Kaka Point, 20 km into the ride, is a great little coastal town to have a break at. Check out the cafe right on the coastline. It also has a camping ground and backpackers, and a 6-km side trip to the Nugget Point lighthouse is well worth the effort.

From Kaka Point, continue south along the coast for 2 km before turning right onto Karoro Creek Road. Turn right at Ahuriri Flat Road to travel back to the Southern Scenic Route. Turn left to roll into Owaka, 16 km from Kaka Point. Owaka has a museum, camping ground, motels, a general store, a cafe and … Teapot Land! You'll be away with the fairies in no time.

Nugget Point Lighthouse, and in the distance, the Great Southern Ocean and terra incognita.

Stage 2: Owaka to Papatowai
26 km, 2 hours

From Owaka, you can continue following the main Southern Scenic Route south or take the following, more adventurous, deviation (it's a bit shorter but is mostly a gravel road). Turn off the main road at Owaka and head south on Royal Terrace. After 1 km, turn right onto Hina Hina Road and follow this across Catlins Lake. Turn right across the bridge and follow Lakeside Road. At the head of the lake, turn left and follow Purakaunui Falls Road. (The 10-minute walk to the falls should not be missed.) Then follow Puaho Road to a wonderful downhill leading to the Tahakopa River. Turn left and ride 2 km to Papatowai. There is a DOC campground and a few places with accommodation. Make sure you check out The Lost Gypsy interactive gallery – it's amazing!

Stage 3: Papatowai to Waikawa
38 km, 3–4 hours

This is a fairly hilly section. Head south and after 11 km you'll pass McLeans Falls Holiday Park, which also has the highly recommended Whistling Frog Cafe. This is a good base for side trips to the Cathedral Caves and the McLean Falls walk.

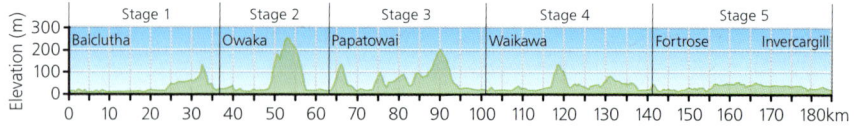

Continue west along what is now called the Chaslands Highway. After about 31 km, at the big 'Curio Bay Coastal Route' sign, turn left and head 6 km to Waikawa. A few kilometres down the way, you'll pass the Niagara Falls Cafe.

Stage 4: Waikawa to Fortrose
40 km, 3–4 hours

From Waikawa, ride 5 km around to Porpoise Bay/Curio Bay, where you can visit the amazing fossilised forest and swim with the Hector's dolphins if you are lucky, and don't mind freezing half to death – it's well worth a mild case of hypothermia.

Curio Bay is 1 km off the route to Fortrose. Back track and follow the obvious signs west. Up to 13 km of this road is gravel, and it can be tough going. But there is good scenery to take your mind off the toil. Fortrose has a big cafe and is right on the coast.

Stage 5: Fortrose to Invercargill
45 km, 3–4 hours

Generally flat and uninspiring, this is the only stage worth missing if you felt like calling up a shuttle from Invercargill. There are some rolling hills in the middle and often a westerly headwind.

FACT FILE

Overview To get the most out of a holiday in the Catlins, be prepared to take your time. Many of the highlights are off the main road.

How to get there There is plenty of public transport to both Invercargill and Balclutha. If riding from the Clutha Gold Trail to Balclutha, it is best to avoid Highway 1 as it is busy and narrow in places. Instead go via Remote Road and Lakeside Road to Kaitangata and then cross the 'banana bridge' to take Riverside Road most of the way in to Balclutha. You will cross the Clutha Mata-au River again about 5 km before Balclutha.

Riding surface 83% sealed road, 17% gravel road

History Although much of the forest was logged, there is still more virgin forest in the Catlins than any other part of the east coast of the South Island.

Special considerations This can be a chilly part of the country. Take extra warm clothes.

Special features Seals, rugged coastline, fossilised forest, native forest.

Maps Kiwimap *Otago-Southland Rural Road Map*

Trail websites www.catlins.org.nz and www.southernscenicroute.co.nz

SUPPORT SERVICES

Pick up the *Catlins Coastal Highway* pamphlet from an information centre in Balclutha or Invercargill. It gives an excellent description of the services on and around the Catlins Coastal Route.

Balclutha Plenty of accommodation, food, shops: www.cluthacountry.co.nz, info centre: ☎ 03 418 0388, www.catlins.org.nz (a great website)

Papatowai A cafe, general store, petrol station, DOC campsite, and accommodation: the Hilltop Catlins: ☎ 03 415 8028, Papatowai motels and store: ☎ 03 415 8147, Whistling Frog Resort for food and accommodation: ☎ 03 415 8338, www.whistlingfrogresort.com

Waikawa Picnic area, toilets, museum, accommodation and a takeaways caravan.

Curio Bay Accommodation options ☎ 03 246 8797 or www.curiobay.co.nz; Curio Bay Holiday Park, ☎ 03 246 8897

Fortrose Shops, accommodation, and there is a toilet 100 metres down Factory Road, which is 15 km from Fortrose.

Invercargill Accommodation, food and shopping: www.invercargill.org.nz

The following settlements along the route also offer accommodation and some services: Owaka, Kaka Point, Pounawea, Tahakopa, Tokanui.

Tour Aotearoa: Cape Reinga to Bluff

How best to ride the length of the country is something we've been asked a lot. So eventually we decided to design a course for a brevet-style event called Tour Aotearoa. The route for Tour Aotearoa is 3000 km long and connects several of the Great Rides with the safest, most enjoyable and logical back-country roads available. The route is also fully open to the public and can be ridden by anyone at any time. However, weather wise, the best time of year to do this ride is mid-January to mid-April.

The Tour Aotearoa route is perfect for a bikepacking adventure. In order to get away from traffic, and into the most scenic parts of the country, it often follows the path less travelled. We recommend a tyre width of 50 mm (2.0 inches), as over half your riding time will be on gravel roads and cycle trails.

There are 30 photo control points (see page 285) along the Tour Aotearoa where riders stop and take a photo. They are listed in the tour guidebooks. Your control point photos will make a great album at the end of your trip!

Additional information The Tour Aotearoa Official Guides have cue sheets, maps, photo control points, and services such as; food, transport and accommodation/camping – all printed in two small water resistant booklets. See www.kennett.co.nz. You can also find information at www.touraotearoa.nz.

THE ROUTE
The route is broken up into six major sections:

1. Cape Reinga to Auckland (442 km)
Cape Reinga to Rawene via Far North Cycleway (see page 20). Almost 83 km of this 170 km section is beach riding, with the rest being sealed and gravel roads, finishing with a 2 km ferry trip. 170 km

Rawene to Dargaville via Kauri Coast Cycleway (see page 28). This hilly 110 km section is on sealed and gravel roads and passes through magnificent kauri forest. 280 km

Dargaville to Auckland via the Kaipara Missing Link (see page 32). A 162 km section that includes a 44 km, 3-hour boat trip across Kaipara Harbour, which must be pre-booked. This ride finishes along a cycle path leading right into the centre of Auckland. 442 km

2. Auckland to Taumarunui (482 km)
Auckland to Hauraki (see page 46). A 112 km ride on a mix of cycle paths and lanes, streets, roads and highways. This a great route, but the navigation demands careful attention. There is an alternate route, which is the slightly longer coastal option via Clevedon (however, don't ride it during weekends due to high traffic volumes). 554 km

Tour Aotearoa: Cape Reinga to Bluff

Hauraki Rail Trail Pukorokoro/Miranda to Te Aroha (see page 52). 82 km of rail trail where you can just roll along and relax. Eventually, it is likely to be extended to Matamata.   636 km

Te Aroha to Waikato River Trail (see page 56). After leaving Te Aroha, this 67 km section is almost all on quiet country roads, but does include a section of highway.   703 km

Waikato River Trail as far as the town of Mangakino (see page 62). This 75 km section of the Waikato River Trail involves some stretches of mountain biking. Fattish tyres are needed.   768 km

Mangakino to The Timber Trail (see page 94). An interesting but very remote 50-km link via the centre of the North Island. The official Tour Aotearoa route takes a short cut past a historic tractor (well signposted off Link Road). There is a 6 km longer 'alternate' route, to the very start of The Timber Trail, where there are cabins and a large camping area.   818 km

The Timber Trail (see page 90). A fabulous 80 km 'tramping on wheels' trip through magnificent forests and across massive swing bridges. This is a highlight of the North Island.   899 km

The Timber Trail Link (see page 95). A 24 km back-country road to Taumarunui – the largest town you've seen since Matamata, almost 300 km behind you!   924 km

3. Taumarunui to Wellington (681 km)

Taumarunui to Whakahoro on the Owhango Connection (see page 97). Another 68 km of very quiet back-country roads to a holiday lodge and cafe beside the Whanganui River.   992 km

Whakahoro to Whanganui City via the Mountains to Sea (see page 102 and 107). This 151 km section includes 20 km of mountain biking and a 28 km boat trip down the Whanganui River, which must be pre-booked. Cycle as far as the i-SITE on the outskirts of town, then turn off the trail onto The Three Rivers ride.   1143 km

Whanganui to Hunterville via the first 61 km of The Three Rivers (see page 108). This starts with a trip up the Drury Hill Elevator. If you arrive after hours, then you'll have to plod up the steps beside the elevator entrance to get to the Drury Hill lookout. There are three significant hills in this section.   1204 km

Hunterville to Rangiwahia via Gorges to Sea Cycleway (see page 114). A 42 km mix of highway, sealed road and gravel road.   1246 km

Rangiwahia to Palmerston North via the Manawatu Cycleway (see page 120). This is a 100 km section in which Tour Aotearoa riders travel to Apiti and on to Ashhurst via the gravel roads on the west side of Pohangina Valley. This provides a shorter yet more remote ride than the route on the east side of the valley.   1346 km

Classic New Zealand Cycle Trails

Palmerston North to Masterton (see page 124). This 109 km ride hops from one town to the next, providing plenty of places to refuel. 1455 km

Masterton to Cross Creek via Wairarapa Back Roads (see page 140). A 77 km ride via the town of Martinborough to the Remutaka Cycle Trail. 1532 km

Remutaka Cycle Trail to Wellington (see page 142). Follow the cycle trail over the Remutaka Ranges, down the Hutt Valley and around Wellington Harbour to the capital. The last 10 km of this 73 km section, from the Petone wharf, is not part of the Remutaka Cycle Trail. Navigation for this last section is tricky, so we'll lay it out for you here.

From the Petone wharf, continue along the foreshore by riding through the car park, along a path, through another car park, and then when you are 1.1 km from the wharf, take the cycle path on your right, to zigzag up to and over an overbridge, and down to the shoulder of Highway 2. Stay on the highway shoulder for 4.6 km (note: there is a separate cycle path beside the road shoulder, but it is so bad that only 3% of commuters use it).

As soon as you ride underneath a motorway overbridge, turn left onto a cycle path, and follow it beside Hutt Road for 3 km (passing La Cloche bakery at 134 Hutt Road), to another overbridge, where the cycle path forks. To go to the Interislander ferry terminal, turn left over the overbridge, then at the far end spiral right underneath it and enter the terminal car park – distance 350 metres.

Otherwise, carry straight ahead for 2 km to reach central Wellington, for bike shops, the Bluebridge ferry terminal, accommodation, etc. The Bluebridge ferry terminal is opposite Wellington Railway Station. 1605 km

Notes There is an iRIDE bike shop 800 metres from the Interislander ferry terminal at 242 Thorndon Quay, ☎ 04 471 1299.

You now have roughly 1600 km of the journey under your belt, so you're over halfway!

The ferry trip from Wellington to Picton is 92 km long and takes 3–3.5 hours, plus 40 minutes to check in. As the Cook Strait is a narrow gap between the two islands, there is a funnelling effect on wind and tide, which can create rough sailing conditions. During big storms, especially southerlies, the ferries may be cancelled.

4. Picton to Greymouth (500km)

Picton to Nelson (see page 150). 94 km from the ferry to the Nelson i-SITE. Tour riders will go via the infamous Maungatapu Saddle – a historic route that climbs high into the mountains before diving steeply to Nelson's Maitai Valley. 1699 km

Nelson to Wakefield via the Great Taste Trail (see page 158). A cruisy 33 km with plenty of places to fuel up. 1732 km

Wakefield to Kawatiri Junction via Tadmor Valley (see page 165). A great 89 km cycle touring link via Tapawera. 1821 km

Kawatiri Junction to Greymouth via The Pioneer Heritage Trail (see page 194). This 284 km route has plenty of towns for stocking up on supplies, but it also includes a tough section of single track – Big River to Waiuta Ghost Town (see page 198). 2105 km

5. Greymouth to Queenstown (639 km)

Greymouth to Ross via the West Coast Wilderness Trail (see page 202). This 136 km trail is one of New Zealand's Great Rides and is a real treat. 2241 km

Ross to Wanaka (see page 208) via Fox Glacier (see page 214). This 417 km ride is mostly on the West Coast Highway but includes a great cycle trail up to Fox Glacier and some excellent tracks leading into Wanaka. 2658 km

Wanaka to Queenstown via the Crown Range (page 215). On this 86 km ride, make sure you peel off the main road and down Glencoe Road to take Tobins Track into Arrowtown. Then follow the Queenstown Trails to Queenstown. 2744 km

6. Queenstown to Bluff (256 km)

This section begins with a 13 km ferry trip across Lake Wakatipu to Walter Peak Station.

Queenstown to Mossburn via the Around the Mountains Cycle Trail (see page 262) 117 km of remote gravel road and new cycle path.   2861 km

Mossburn to Bluff via the Southland Traverse (see page 267). The last 139 km leg down to Stirling Point at Bluff. Time to rest easy.   3000 km

Total Distance Travelled _____ **3000 km**

Add a few kilometres for side trips, navigational errors and weaving around when you're tired.

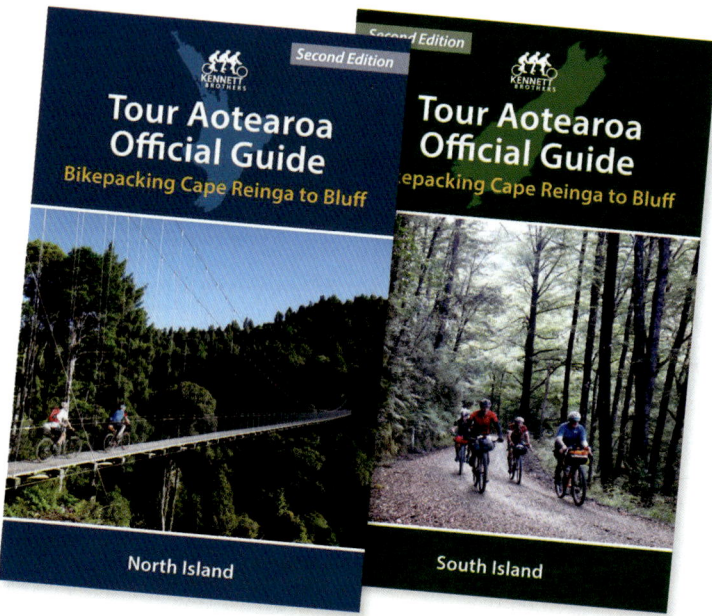

This two volume set provides riders with step-by-step instructions, route maps, elevation charts, and insider tips on how to cycle from Cape Reinga to Bluff. It also lists all the of the important and out of the way services such as shops, accommodation, camping and transport.

Available from your favourite bike shop, book store or **www.kennett.co.nz**

Significant climbs

New Zealand is a hillier country than most people realise, so it's best to travel light. Here is a table of the significant climbs you will encounter on the Tour. But there are, of course, many more climbs under 100 metres high.

	North Island climbs	South Island climbs
100m	38	28
200m	10	12
300m	6	3
400m	2	0
500m	2 (Centre of NI, Mangapurua)	2 (Big River, Haast Pass)
600m	0	0
700m	0	1 (Mangatapu)
800m	0	1 (Crown Range)

Trail surfaces

The 3000 km Tour takes in a variety of trail surfaces, and the percentage of time spent on each trail type is shown in the following pie chart. For this chart we have estimated that people will travel between 5 kph (on rough single track) and 20 kph (sealed road average). Total riding time is around 220 hours.

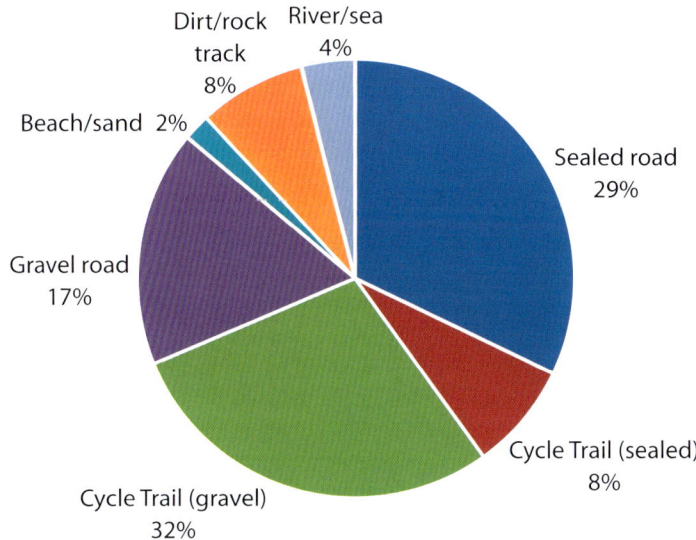

Time you'll spend on different trail surfaces

Note: The 'river/sea' portion comprises five separate boat trips.

Tracking

Any time you want to do the Tour, you can hire a SPOT tracker and sign up to the Tour Aotearoa tracking website www.touraotearoa.maprogress.com. That way, friends and family can follow you on your ride, and in case of an emergency, the tracker also functions as a personal locater beacon (PLB). To connect to this service, email shane@maprogress.com. MAProgress also hires and sells SPOT trackers.

Celebrating at Bluff with new found friends.

The 30 Tour Aotearoa photo control points.

Photo credits

Adam Perry   287
Ashley Peters   17
Barna Bán   203
Brian Farrant (CTONZ)   228, 228, 232, 233
Bronwen Wall (editor on wheels)   23, 38, 42, 115, 136, 219, 222, 247
Dana Kirkpatrick (Rere Falls)   79
Dave Mitchell   172
Greg Lever-Minzeye (Twin Coast)   25
James Burgess   188
Jim Polland   257
John Dunn   173
John Randal (Lake Waikaremoana)   82, 83
Jonathan Jarman   270
Jude Ellis   125
Karyn Burgess   121
Lance Webster (the lone cycle tourer)   241, 262, 273
Motu Trails, Bay of Plenty   72
Murray Drake   11, 53, 155, 157, 177, 187
Simon Kennett   60, 194
Troy Baker   73
Jonathan Kennett   all other photos

Paul and Simon Kennett line up to try out the new track on Mountains to the Sea.

No one knows more about exploring New Zealand by bike than the Kennett Brothers. If you can get there by bike, the Kennetts have done it. I can't think of better guides for your next cycling holiday.

Patrick Morgan, Cycling Advocates' Network

About the authors

Like most Kiwi kids, Paul, Simon and Jonathan Kennett grew up with bikes, mucking about and cycling to school in Christchurch and Invercargill. It didn't take them long to latch on to the idea of using their bikes to explore tracks and backroads all over New Zealand.

In 1989, Paul and Simon toured and raced in North America. In 1990, Jonathan and friends became the first people to cycle across Nepal to Everest Base Camp. In 1991, the Kennetts wrote *Classic New Zealand Mountain Bike Rides*. Seventy thousand copies and nine editions later, it is known as the mountain bike bible. The brothers have written a guide to road cycling, a series of biographies about famous New Zealand cyclists and a history of cycling in New Zealand. They also design and build cycling tracks.

When the New Zealand Cycle Trail project was launched in 2009, Simon and Jonathan came onboard as advisers, and Paul provided mapping.

Simon now works at NZ Transport Agency as a cycling policy adviser. When he is not riding his bike he builds cycling tracks around Wellington. Jonathan is a project manager developing the New Zealand Cycle Trail network. Paul designs the Kennett Brothers' books and mucks about on bikes with his son.

Thanks from Simon, Jonathan and Paul Kennett.

Also from the Kennett Brothers

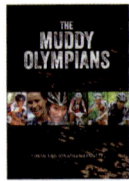
The Muddy Olympians
By Simon Kennett and Jonathan Kennett
Tracing the stories of our six cross-country mountain bike Olympians; Kathy Lynch (1996), Susy Pride (2000), Kashi Leuchs (2000, 2004, 2008), Robyn Wong (2004), Rosara Joseph (2008), and Karen Hanlen (2012).

Louise Sutherland: Spinning the Globe
By Bronwen Wall
Louise was a small woman with a big heart. She knew virtually nothing about bicycles yet cycled right around the world and became the first person to cycle across the Amazon Jungle.

Tino Tabak: Dreams and Demons
By Jonathan Kennett
Tino Tabak was loved and hated in equal measure. He won every major tour in New Zealand. In Europe, he turned pro to race the Tour de France, and his dreams turned to nightmares.

Warwick Dalton: The Lone Eagle
By John Rhodes and Jonathan Kennett
Warwick Dalton was a champion all-round cyclist. He won major races on road and track in New Zealand, Australia and Europe, including the British Milk Race green jersey.

Bill Pratney: Never Say Die
By Jim Robinson
Bill 'The Ironman' Pratney was our greatest Maori cyclist, with a career that spanned seven decades. After defying death in a horrific crash, he recovered to win national titles from 1–120 miles.

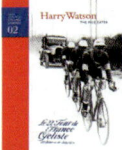
Harry Watson: The Mile Eater
By Jonathan Kennett, Bronwen Wall and Ian Gray
Harry Watson was New Zealand's greatest endurance rider. In 1928, he was the first Kiwi to race the Tour de France when many stages were over 300 km long on gravel roads. [Watch Phil Keoghan retrace Harry's Tour de France route at www.philkeoghanleride.com]

Phil O'Shea: Wizard on Wheels
By Jonathan Kennett and Bronwen Wall
The champion of champions, Phil O'Shea's consistent victories, from quarter-mile sprints to 265-km road races, made him New Zealand's greatest all-round cyclist.

See kennett.nz for more info

Also from the Kennett Brothers

Classic New Zealand Mountain Bike Rides
North and South Island 9th edition
All the mountain bike rides you want to know about.
- 144 North Island rides, 179 South Island rides
- 88 mountain bike parks
- 14 lifetime adventure rides
- All rated so you know which are the best rides for your maximum riding pleasure.

Short Easy Bike Rides
52 of New Zealand's best
Enjoy the simple pleasure of a leisurely bike ride to a cafe, playground or picnic spot. These safe and easy cycle paths enable you to enjoy the outdoors at your own pace.

- traffic free and safe
- 1–3 hours riding time
- cafes, playgrounds and much more.

Classic New Zealand Road Rides
100 recreational road rides
By Jonathan Kennett and Kieran Turner
The best road rides New Zealand has to offer, complete with:
 • Comprehensive route guide details
 • European climb categories
 • New Zealand's most popular cycling events.
Kieran Turner was CEO of BikeNZ and is a competitive road cyclist.

See kennett.nz for more info

Your trail tales

Helmets off to...

To John Key and Kevin Hague for launching the New Zealand Cycle Trail project, and guiding it through the fractious halls of Parliament and the fastidious bureaus of the public service, out into the real world, out and across heartland New Zealand. The journeys are now enjoyed by thousands of cyclists, pedalling their way through healthy holidays, growing communities and stunning countryside.

We would also like to thank our colleagues at the New Zealand Cycle Trail team: Richard Leggat, Evan Freshwater, Gerry Dance, Mark Walter, and Trudy Hadley, who have worked with passion and dedication on the cycle trail.

Then there are the trail teams around the country, working on the ground to construct new trails. Some of these teams have faced extraordinary challenges and overcome them in ways that ensure a truly unique and fantastic trail for you to ride. Those who have had specific involvement with this book are acknowledged below.

We also want to give special thanks to those who have built or are building trails that did not receive New Zealand Cycle Trail funding. Your results are especially impressive. These include: Te Awa River Ride; the New Plymouth Coastal Pathway; Rimutaka Cycle Trail; Queen Charlotte Track; Heaphy Track; and Little River Rail Trail.

And a heartfelt thanks goes to those who helped specifically with this book, mostly by joining us on research rides and checking the write ups.

Northland Jonathan and Ruth Jarman, Chris O'Donohue, Alan Smith, Ray Clarke
Auckland Peter Brooking, Barbara Cuthbert, Jackson Foster, John Gregory, Julian Hulls, John McKillop, Chris Tennent-Brown
Raglan Dirk De Ruysscher
Hamilton Jennifer Palmer, Glyn Wooller
Opotiki Jim Robinson, Fred and Salena Wingate
Gisborne Hans van Kregten
Rotorua Chris Heywood, Erik Westra
Taupo Ted Webb, Erin Lempiere, Richard Balm, Pete Masters, Rowan Sapsford
Pureora Hoz Barclay, John Stock
Tauranga Lyn Manning, Jo Pentreath
Whakahoro Blue Duck Lodge, Dan Steele
Whanganui River Joe from Bridge to Nowhere
Hawke's Bay Paul, Meg, Sam and Bella McArdle
Purangi Ian and Laurel Aitken
New Plymouth Carl Whittleston
Rangitikei Tam Hiscotte
Palmerston North Bill Russell
Masterton Karyn Burgess, Willie Wichman
Wellington Dave Bamford, Ashley Peters, Richard Davies, Sarah Drake, Henry Fisher, John Hitchcock, Kaya McCammon, Ron McGann, Andrew McLellan, Sonja Mitchell, Maryann Nesbit, Geoff Plimmer, John Randal, Hannah Proctor, Marjolein Ros, Lance Webster, Kathy Ombler

Picton Roy Grose
Nelson David Bonnet, Murray Drake, Stuart Hughes, Dugald Ley, Ginny Wood, Mike Brien, Andrew Scott
Takaka Martin and Marie Langley
St James Jeff Dalley
Hanmer Springs Mark Inglis
Westport Phil Rossiter
Hokitika Liam Anderson, Peter Anderson, John Strange, Ric Keen, Chris Steel
Christchurch Scott and Jo Emmens, Brian Farrant, Craig Mason, David Owen
Dunedin Hamish Seaton
Twizel Jason Menard
Roxburgh Tim Dennis, Barry Willis, Dave Crawford
Clutha Graham Dillon, Rod Peirce, Kath Kelly, Peter Cummings, Phil Oliver
Queenstown Kaye Parker, Paul Wilson
Southland Rex Capil, Mike Barnett, Mckayla Holloway, Catherine Robinson
United Kingdom Jon Spark
No fixed abode Mary Molphy

Thanks for the good times.
Paul, Simon and Jonathan Kennett

Index

A

Accommodation 16
(See also Support Services *at the end of each trail description*)
Ahipara 20–21
Alexandra 242, 246
Alfredton 124–125, 137
Alps 2 Ocean Cycle Trail 231, 234–239, 240
Anikawa 148
Aoraki/Mt Cook 231, 234, 235
Apiti 120
Arapuni 57, 62–63
Around The Mountains 262–266
Arrowtown 215, 256–257
Arthur's Pass to West Coast 201
Ashhurst 120–121, 124
Atiamuri 64, 67
Auckland Airport to City 36–37
Auckland City 33, 36–37, 42, 46
Auckland's Great Escape 42–45
Auckland to Hauraki Rail Trail 46

B

Balclutha 270
Bay of Plenty 72–79
Beaumont 251–253
Big River 198
Bike Waiheke 38–41
Bikes, Types of 16
Blackball 195–196
Blenheim 171
Bluff, Cape Reinga to 15, 270–276
Bridge to Nowhere 103–104, 107
Bryant Mountains 150
Buller Gorge 184–186

C

Cambridge 56, 57, 58, 59, 62
Cambridge to Waikato River Trail 57
Canterbury Plains 228
Cape Reinga 20
Cape Reinga to Bluff 15, 276–284

Catlins Coastal Route 272–275
Centre of the North Island 94
Christchurch 218, 220, 221, 228, 231
Christchurch to the Alps 228–233
Clutha Gold Trail 250–254, 255
Clyde 242
Coppermine Saddle 154–155
Coromandel 46
Crown Range 215

D

Dargaville 28, 29–30, 32, 34
Doctors Point 246–249
Dun Mountain Trail 154–157
Dunedin 255
Dunes Trail, Opotiki 72
Duntroon 238

E

Eastwoodhill 76, 77
East Cape 80
Eketahuna 124

F

Fairlie 224
Far North Cycleway 20–23
Featherston 140
Fernhill, Hawkes Bay 128
Fisher Road & Kaiwhakauka Track 107
Forgotten World Highway 96, 98–101
Fortrose 272
Fox Glacier 209, 214
Fox Township 208–209
Franz Josef Glacier 209, 214
Frasertown 81

G

Gentle Annie 126–129
Geraldine 230
Ghost Road Roundabout 189, 190–193
Gibbston 259
Gisborne 76, 80, 81, 82
Glacier Tracks, The 214

Classic New Zealand Cycle Trails **293**

Golden Downs Trail	164–165
Gorges to Sea Cycleway	114–118
Grades, trail	12–13
Granity	190–191
Great Lake Trail, Taupo	86–89
Great Taste Trail, Tasman	158–163
Greymouth	194, 196, 202

H

Haast	210
Hamilton	58–59
Hanmer Springs	166–168, 171, 172
Hastings	130, 134
Hauraki Rail Trail	46, 52–55, 56
Hauraki Rail Trail to Cambridge	56
Havelock, Malborough Sounds	150
Havelock North	130, 132, 136
Hawke's Bay	126, 130–135, 136
Hawke's Bay Trails	130–135
Headland Loop, Taupo	86
Heaphy to Old Ghost Road	183
Heaphy Track	178–182, 183
Hokianga Harbour	20–31
Hokitika	203–205
Horeke	25
Horopito	102
Hororata	228–231
Hunterville	108–109, 114–116
Hurunui Heartland Ride	218–223
Hyde	243–244

I

Invercargill	267, 268, 272

J

Jacks Point	258

K

Kahurangi National Park	178–182
Kaikohe	24–25
Kaipara Missing Link	32–35
Kaiteriteri	159–160
Kaiwhakauka Track	107
Karamea	183
Kauri Coast Cycleway	28–31
Kawakawa	24, 26
Kawakawa Bay	86–87
Kawarau River	257–258
Kawhia to Waitomo Caves	48–51, 94
Kinloch	86
Kumara	200, 202–203
Kuripapango	127
Kurow	232

L

Lake Guyon	172–173
Lake Hayes	258
Lake Karapiro	59, 62
Lake Ohakuri	70, 71
Lake Ohau	235–236
Lake Paringa	210
Lake Pukaki	231, 234–235
Lake Tekapo	230–231
Lake Waikaremoana	81, 82–85
Lake Wairarapa	144
Lawrence	250, 251–252, 255
Lawrence to Dunedin	255
Little River Rail Trail	224–227
Lumsden	262–263, 267
Lyell	184, 190–192

M

Makaroa	210–212
Malborough Sounds	146–153
Maling Pass	172
Manawatu Cycleway	120–123, 124
Manawatu Cycleway to Route 52	124
Mangakino	64, 94
Mangaweka	114–115, 120
Mapua	160
Maraetai	64
Martinborough	140
Marton	116
Masterton	137–138, 139, 140
Matamata	56
Matawai	76, 77, 78, 79
Matiatia Bay, Waiheke	38, 39, 40, 41
Mavora Lakes	262
Maymorn	142–143
Middlemarch	242, 244
Milford Sound	269–270

Millers Flat	250–251
Miranda Hot Springs	46, 52
Molesworth Muster Trail	169, 171
Mossburn	262, 267
Mount Somers	229–230
Mount Cook	231, 234, 235
Mount Cook village	234–235
Mountains to Sea	97, 102–106, 107
Motu Trails	72–75
Motueka	158, 159–160, 161
Motukarara	224–225
Murchison	194
Murupara	82–83

N

Napier	128, 130–131
National Park	107
Nelson	150–163
Nelson Lakes	164–165, 166–170, 194
New Plymouth	98, 99–100
Ngaruawahia	58
Ninety Mile Beach	20
Northland	20–35

O

Oamaru	234, 237–238
Ocean Beach, Wairarapa	144
Ohakune	102, 108, 109, 112–113
Ohakune to Taihape Trail	112–113
Ohura	96
Okaihau	25
Old Ghost Road	183, 184–188, 189, 190
Omakau	216, 242–243
Omarama	236, 240
Omarama Saddle	240
Onetangi Bay, Waiheke	38–40
Ongarue	90, 91–92, 95, 96
Opotiki	72, 73, 78, 79
Opua	26
Orongorongo	144
Otago Central Rail Trail	216, 242–245
Otematata	236, 238
Oturehua	243
Owaka	270–271
Owhango Connection	97

P

Pacific Coast Highway, East Cape	80
Pahiatua	124
Pakihi	72–73
Palmerston North	120, 121, 124
Papatowai	271
Pelorus Bridge	150–151
Petone	142
Picton	146, 148, 150
Picton to Nelson	150–153
Pine Grove	209–210
Pioneer Heritage Trail	194–197
Pipiriki	104
Piropiro Flats	90–91
Pokaiwhenua Bridge	62–63
Pouto Point	32-33,
Prison Break, The	96
Public Transport	17–18
Pukekohe	42, 44
Purangi	98–99
Pureora	90, 94

Q

Queen Charlotte Track	146–149
Queenstown	215, 256–260
Queenstown Trails	256–260

R

Raglan	42, 43, 48
Rainbow, The	166–169
Rainbow Mountain	83
Ranfurly	243
Rangitikei River	126–127
Rawene	20–21, 28
Reefton	195
Rere Falls	77, 81
Rere Falls Trail	76–79
Rere Falls to Lake Waikaremoana	81
Resolution Bay	146
Remutaka Cycle Trail	140, 142–145
Ross	202, 204, 208
Rotorua	68–71
Route 52	124–125, 136–139
Roxburgh	250

Roxburgh Dam	246, 247, 250
Roxburgh Gorge Trail	246–249

S

Seddonville	183, 184, 186, 190
Ship Cove	146
Southern Alps	208, 214, 228, 231, 234
Southern Scenic Route	271
Southland Traverse	267
Springs Junction	194–195
St Arnaud	166, 194
St James Cycle Trail	169, 172–176

T

Tadmor Valley	165
Tahora Saddle	98
Taihape	112–113, 114, 126
Tai Tapu	228–229
Tane Mahuta	28
Tasman	158, 160
Tasman Sea	114, 116
Taumarunui	92, 95, 97, 98
Taupo	62, 86–89
Te Anau	266, 267, 268
Te Ara Ahi	67, 68–71, 83
Te Aroha	52, 56
Te Awa River Ride	58–61
Te Kuiti	50, 90, 94
Te Urewera	82–85
Thames	46, 52
Thermal By Bike	67, 68–71, 83
Three Rivers, The	105, 106, 108, 111
Timber Trail, The	90–93, 94, 95, 96, 97
Timber Trail Link	95
Tirohanga	78
Tophouse	166
Tour Aotearoa	276–285
Touring the Wild West	208–213
Tours, bike	14
Trounson Kauri Park	28–29
Twin Coast Cycle Trail	24–27
Twizel	235

U

Urewera Rainforest	82

W

W2K track	86
Waihaha, Taupo	87
Waiheke Island	38–41, 46
Waihi	52–53
Waihora Bay	87
Waikato	57–67
Waikato River Trail	57, 62–66, 67
Waikato River Trail to Te Ara Ahi	67
Waikato River Trail to Timber Trail	94
Waikawa	271–272
Waikite Valley	69–70
Waimangaroa	189
Waimangu Volcanic Valley	68–69
Waingaro Hot Springs	42–43
Waipapa Dam	63–64
Waipukurau	136
Wairarapa	136, 140, 142–145
Wairarapa Back Roads	140
Wairoa	81, 82
Waitomo Caves	48, 49–50, 94
Waiuta Track	198
Wakefield	158, 164
Wanaka	208, 212, 215, 216
Wanaka to Otago Central Rail Trail	216
Wellington	142–145
West Coast Wilderness Trail	201, 202–207
West Coast Tour	208–213
Westport to Ghost Rd Roundabout	189
Whakahoro	97, 107
Whakaipo Bay	86
Whakamaru	64
Whanganui	102, 104, 108
Whanganui National Park	102–103
Whataroa	208
Wimbledon	136–137
Winton	267
Woodstock	158–159